PRIVILEGING AUSTRALIAN INDIGENOUS KNOWLEDGE

Sweet Potatoes, Spiders, Waterlilys & Brick Walls

Nerida Blair

PRIVILEGING AUSTRALIAN INDIGENOUS KNOWLEDGE

Sweet Potatoes, Spiders, Waterlilys & Brick Walls

Nerida Blair

COMMON GROUND PUBLISHING 2015

First published in 2015 in Champaign, Illinois, USA
by Common Ground Publishing LLC
as part of Diversity in Organizations, Communities, and Nations books

Library of Congress Cataloging-in-Publication Data

Names: Blair, Nerida, 1957-
Title: Privileging Australian indigenous knowledge : sweet potatoes, spiders,
   waterlilys & brick walls / Nerida Blair.
Description: Champaign, Illinois : Common Ground Publishing, 2015. | Based on
   the author's thesis (doctoral). | Includes bibliographical references. |
   Description based on print version record and CIP data provided by
   publisher; resource not viewed.
Identifiers: LCCN 2015045731 (print) | LCCN 2015034172 (ebook) | ISBN
   9781612298184 (pbk) | ISBN 9781612298191 (pdf) | ISBN 9781612298184 (pbk.
   : alk. paper)
Subjects: LCSH: Aboriginal Australians--Social conditions. | Aboriginal
   Australians--Intellectual life. | Aboriginal Australians--Research. |
   Knowledge, Sociology of--Australia. | Knowledge, Theory of--Australia. |
   Eurocentrism--Australia. | Decolonization--Australia. | Aboriginal
   Australians--Civil rights. | Australia--Race relations.
Classification: LCC DU124.S63 (print) | LCC DU124.S63 B55 2015 (ebook) | DDC
   305.899/15--dc23
LC record available at http://lccn.loc.gov/2015045731

Cover Photo Credit:
Arafura Swamp, 1990 by Lin Onus. Permission by Tiriki and Jo Onus; Lin's estate. I respectfully acknowledge and celebrate Lin and his extraordinary body of work.

This book is dedicated to Jaambe; my soul mate.

Table of Contents

ACKNOWLEDGEMENTS

This journey has been fraught with peaks and troughs, calm and stormy seas. There are many people to acknowledge and thank.

To Dorothy, my mother for her unconditional love, her sustained nurturing and sacrifice and extraordinary patience. I love you. Dr Brooke Collins-Gearing, for your energy, passion and friendship which drove me and this project from a PhD dissertation to a book. Dr Robyn Cox, for you faith in the text and my ability to turn this into something useful for others to read: a book. Pilawuk White: you inspire not only your students but all around you with your energy, creativity and dogged pursuit of tangible outcomes. You and Nuwili, and Shadow opened your hearts and your home to me. I am eternally grateful and have grown from the richness of the experience you facilitated. Ann Thomas (I use your name respectfully, in your passing) for your wisdom and generosity of spirit. For your Knowing and willingness to share this with me in countless ways.

ARTISTS AND TECHNICAL HELP

Janet Long Nakamarra and Jinta art for the artwork and Iconography used. Jo and Tiriki Onus for permission to use the painting 'Arafura Swamp' by Lin Onus. Warren Blair: Didjeridoo playing used on 'Tellin' Me and Showin Me' the webpage, and for being my brother. Hugh Ryvers-Ellicott for his artistic skills with some of my mind maps. Leigh Collins for sound transference from tape cassette to computer friendly files for the webpage and Colin Rosewell for computer imaging of some photographs and images for the webpage. Mark O'Bryan: for his facilitation of and assistance with the original Webpage development and for friendship and belief in my abilities to do! Stewart McMinn: Didjeridoo playing used on home page in the webpage. Paul Kneipp for his dedication beyond and above, patience and creative focus for the revised website that accompanies this book.

COLLEAGUES FROM DESERT AND COAST

My teachers, Knowers, guides, facilitators and family without any of you this journey would not have been possible. Your generosity of spirit and Knowing has nourished and nurtured my soul and spirit, my intellect and heart. My inner and outer being. I thank each and every one of you and give back your words in a different form, in the form of this book as this is my cultural responsibility.

Thank you all for your contributions to this book, to my personal, spiritual and intellectual journey and to the discourse on the place of Indigenous Knowings in the academy.

Symbols Used:

Community

Jinta Art
Janet Long Nakamarra

Mind Mapping

Jinta Art
Janet Long Nakamarra

Indigenous Knowing

Colliding Trajectories

Vacuum; suck in, nothing returns

Qualitative Research : Quantitative Research Methods & Practices : Paradigms & Philosophies		
Post colonialism	Critical race theory	Feminism
Archival	Ethnomethodology	Grounded theory
Anthropology	Cultural Studies	Marxism
Clinical	Psychoanalysis	Decolonisation
Hermeneutics	Ethnography	Narrative
Survey	Action Research	Rhizomatics
P.C.T.	Participants Observation	Oral History
Focus Groups	Questionnaire	Interviews
Positivism	Foundationalism	Post structuralism

Eurocentric/Western Knowledge

Indigenous Research Methodology

List of Figures

To Indigenous peoples reading and engaging with this book, there are names and images of people who have passed from this world. Please engage accordingly.

Prologue

Centring Indigenous Knowings[1] when conducting research is more than placing the word 'Indigenous' in front of the word 'research'. Indigenous Knowings represented and embodied here as a Waterlily[2] is fundamentally different to Western Knowledge (represented by a Brick Wall). This book explores some epistemological consequences of Knowledge production in Australia; it is a Story[3] I Know, told by many voices, many different Storys – Storys that do not contradict each other, they simply co-exist.

This book documents my struggles and those of other Indigenous researchers operating and existing within a contested zone. A zone of colliding trajectories between The Academy (the Brick Wall) and Indigenous Knowings (Waterlily). Adventuring and exploring within this zone the book voices challenges, options and most importantly choices for us as Indigenous researchers; not Indigenous peoples who happen to be doing research about Aboriginal issues, Aboriginal peoples. This zone is also apparent for Indigenous and non-Indigenous educators working across all components of the system: from early childhood teaching, primary and secondary schools as well as vocational and higher education institutions.

A webpage designed to accompany this book creates and gives dimension and depth to the linear, Western framework that is a book. The webpage gives you the reader the opportunity to experience some of the learning experiences I have had throughout this journey; experience them visually through short movie clips, sound bites and images. I have journeyed with my Colleagues in Desert and Coast yarning with them, being told and shown experiences that form the essence of this book. An essence that unequivocally centres and privileges Indigenous voices, Indigenous Knowings.

This book contributes to a new and vibrant theorising space; one that Denzin and Lincoln identify as the Eighth Moment (Denzin, N. & Lincoln, Y.S. 2005.

---

[1] I have used the term Indigenous Knowings throughout this text to identify Indigenous knowledge as something different and distinct to Western Knowledge. The word Knowing is capitalised and pluralised to reflect and respect diversity across Indigenous Countrys

[2] Waterlily/waterlilies are spelt this way throughout the document to embody a re-imaged concept.

[3] I have chosen to use the term Story/Storys to reflect and show respect for Indigenous diversity and Knowing of the concept of Story. The word is capitalised throughout the book to embrace its significance in the Story that is this book. The spelling of the plural – Storys – reflects cultural distinctness of the concept.

p.20). It is an act of intellectual self-determination (Battiste M. , 2002, p. 4); an effort to develop new analyses and methodologies to decolonise myself, my communities and the institutions that impact on our daily lives. I reclaim and re-position Indigenous Knowings so that we can all find a path ahead making sustainable and good choices (Youngblood Henderson, 2000, p. 274). This reclamation takes us from a PhD dissertation exploring Indigenous Knowings to the concept evolved after some lived experience in the zone, of 'Lilyology'[4].

I, like Kovach (2009) have chosen to use a Prologue to 'structure space for introductions while serving a bridging function for non-Indigenous readers' (p.3). Understanding conceptual differences are fundamental if we are to journey this book, this Knowing together as reader, research Colleagues and author.

Cultural protocol dictates that we introduce ourselves, our connections and relatedness to Country[5], and to you the reader as a means of 'honouring the lessons I have learnt' and the 'relationships grounded in communities' (Wilson, p.123) and Country. I, like Wilson (2008), Kovach, Arbon and Martin share a personal story. We share such Storys because it is important for us to 'impart [our] own life experience into the telling' whilst giving the listeners to the story the space to 'filter the story being told through their own experience, adapting the information to make it relevant and specific to their life' (Wilson, 2008, p.32).

My story is not like these Storys in that it does not talk about Country, ancestral connections and geneology. It Storys like these Storys do, belongings and relatedness that have been scattered, and shattered. It Storys belonging and relatedness to Aboriginality through many periods of policy adjustments and through many guises. It Storys survival. I invite you the listener, the reader to hear this Story, the historical contexts it is embedded within so that you can filter with clarity the Story that this book ultimately presents.

This Story begins with my father; Harold Blair. He was born on Barambah mission in 1924, (renamed Cherbourg in 1932) Barambah mission was located 170 km north-west of Brisbane, Queensland). A 14 year old Aboriginal girl my grandmother had been raped by her step-father and was pregnant as a result. My

---

[4] The term 'Lilyology' evolved as the result of many conversations with Associate Professor Karen Martin. These conversations engaged reflections, questions, silences, images, shared experiences in Countrys. I valued these engagements and sharing of learnings. Associate Professor Karen Martin said during one of these conversations 'you should call this Lilyology' to which I laughed but incubated until some time later.

[5] Country/Country's is the term I have chosen to use to describe Aboriginal Countrys, spaces and places. It is capitalised and pluralised to give respect to our diversity. The term Country embodies ecological systems so much a part of Indigenous Knowings; it is not just limited to geographical space and place. I have chosen to spell the plural differently to embrace distinctness of concept.

grandmother Esther and her new son Harold were banished from Barambah to Purga mission, (14 km south of central Ipswich, Queensland). In tracing this story; (one that had been hidden from us until a film was made of my father's life), some of the women at Cherbourg who I am indebted to told me how my grandmother; a petite young girl, baby in her arms, and swaddle of blankets tied together was made to walk up the main street of the mission; a small dirt street – being paraded to show what was seen by the missionaries and managers as her 'shame'. As she neared people's homes on either side of the road they shut their doors and windows, acknowledging her 'shame'.

These storytellers, these women also shared what they had been told by the manager and administrators of the mission – my grandmother's baby would be a 'dark baby' because she had 'broken' the law and become pregnant. Esther becoming pregnant in the midst of the 'Protection' Period of our history was tantamount to committing the worst imaginable crime. My grandmother was sent out to be a domestic worker while my father grew up on the mission eventually working on local farms as a part of the servitude Aboriginal men and women endured until the 1960's. At the age of 21 my father was heard singing in the cane fields by a young communist man who was amazed by the depth of his voice.

Cutting a very long story short, my father at the age of 21 years was illiterate but taken to Melbourne to pursue a singing career at the only place that would accept a young Aboriginal man with his educational background – the Melba Conservatorium, after he had gained his matriculation at Tintern; a school I was to later go to for 13 years of my life. Here he met my mother Dorothy Eden, a non-Aboriginal woman from Gippsland in Victoria. For an Aboriginal to marry a non-Aboriginal person at this time in Australia was illegal and subject to in some places a hundred pound fine and twelve months imprisonment with hard labour, unless permission was sought from the Protector of Aborigines. No such permission was sought but in what was to become the label assigned to my father – he was the perfect assimilated Aboriginal man held up as a role-model to others. Of course my father did not see himself through this lens.

Within two years of arriving in Melbourne from the mission in Queensland my father went to Juliard School of music in New York; travelling overseas was a difficult proposition for an Aboriginal person in such times. A birth certificate was necessary but non-existent because Aboriginal people were considered part of the Flora and Fauna Act, not human and therefore having no need of a birth certificate. A birth certificate was needed for travel overseas so the government made up a birth date for him and stamped a passport and birth certificate with this date. It was not the date his mother remembers giving birth to him just a date plucked out of the air by a willing bureaucrat. This fabrication and disregard of my father, his mother, his father, their connection to Country was further fed by the idea that my grandfather was Italian – after all Harold was an opera singer and this is where opera singers came from – not from a mission in Australia. I grew up believing this Italian cultural heritage and connection and relatedness to Country.

My father returned home to Australia and to my mother after two years in the United States of America where he had performed at the New York Town Hall; the first Aboriginal man from Australia to do so. As I tell this story I pause to honour and marvel at him; his capacity within three years to go from a mission where he worked farms for no money, was illiterate because government policy presumed that Aboriginal children were not capable of being educated, to living in suburban Melbourne with a non-Aboriginal family, to New York studying and finding his voice in Harlem at a church where as a 'black man' he saw things he had never dreamed. He saw 'people of colour' in large numbers freely walking the streets, owning businesses, practising law – not on a mission.

It was Jubilee time in Australia as the 'nation celebrated' its sesquicentenary so my father returned to sing for the national broadcaster the ABC. He had not finished his studies and never returned to them. He and my mother raised two children very much under the microscope as it was said in hushed corners and circles and printed in newspaper articles that this 'role-model' would be sure to fail. My father was unable to pursue his singing career such as it was for an Aboriginal man in the operatic world at this time. He worked in a hardware store, a petrol station and eventually teaching music in technical schools in Melbourne. He worked for a period at Gerard mission in South Australia and at the North Adelaide Community College all the while being actively engaged in Aboriginal rights through his membership of the Federal Aboriginal Arts Board, the struggle for land rights at Lake Tyers in eastern Victoria, the struggle for access by Aboriginal children to the local swimming pool in Murgon just outside of Cherbourg, and his engagement with the FCAATSI (Federal Council for the Advancement of Aborigines and Torres Strait Islanders) to name a few of his roles and responsibilities. My father died at the age of 51 in 1976 with a despondent spirit and confused sense of place. He had spent his lifetime being subjected to the very public western gaze through the Government policies and associated practices of Assimilation, Segregation and Protection.

I am the eldest of two with my brother Warren a father of 3 children, a grandfather of 3, and working as a builder in Melbourne. I was born and raised in Melbourne in a family full of love but a family watched by the media. Every major stage of my life was covered in the press in Melbourne; my birth where it was asked "will she have the brains of the white side or go 'walkabout' like her black side", my first day at school where it was asked if the non-Aboriginal parents at the school would object to my presence in the school, such was the law at the time, to the perceived 'oddity' of my captaincy in grade 6, my graduation from university (where I was one of 2 identifying Aboriginal students at the largest university in Melbourne) to my engagement, and wedding. After I became involved in Aboriginal education and left my marriage moving to NSW I moved around but found a home through the NSW Aboriginal Education Consultative Group who welcomed a stranger with opinions and a voice; my voice not the voice of Harold Blair's daughter. This is not meant to sound narky – it was my reality, I was always being compared to my father who I idolised and adored as a father and as an Aboriginal man but I was being boxed and labelled as he was during his lifetime.

Much of our energy as Indigenous peoples has been trying to 'fit in' to the Western Eurocentric system or fight being 'fitted in' by Eurocentric scholarship (Kovach, 2009, p.31), (Wilson, 2008, p.127), Arbon (2008, p.27). I liken this to one of those boxes a lot of young children had in schools, at home to learn shapes, colours and numbers. The box was rectangular. The box has a number of different shapes cut in to it; triangle, circle, square. The child has a corresponding shaped block to fit in to the shape in the box. If we as Indigenous peoples are the diamond shape you can eventually fit us in to every other shape in the box.

Figure 1. 'Fitting In'

At what cost? How much of our exterior shape is rubbed raw in an effort to make us 'fit'; hammering, twisting, manipulating? Another word for this is assimilation.

Here I became involved in Aboriginal education; curriculum development and higher education specifically. From day one at school I went home and did homework, I knew I wanted to become a teacher. I shared my father's passion for and belief in education as a means to self-determination for us as Aboriginal peoples in Australia.

I have worked for over three decades in Aboriginal education establishing Aboriginal Support Units in universities, teaching and developing curriculum, supporting and supervising Aboriginal post-graduate students. I have had many advisory roles. After I had completed a Masters Degree which looked at Aborigines in Higher Education in NSW since Affirmative Action I tried my hand at the Public Service through the Commonwealth Department of Education as they were writing policy in Aboriginal and Torres Strait Islander education. Within six months of working in an environment that employed a few Aboriginal people as tokens to rubber stamp the policy that had already been written I moved to the Human Rights Section of the Department of Foreign Affairs and Trade. Here in the United Nations Forum, Geneva for the drafting of the Declaration on Indigenous People's Rights after witnessing a speech by Kenneth Deer, a Mohawk leader from Canada – a speech full of passion as people in his community had been shot in the early hours of the morning by Canadian Mounted Police I reassessed where I was and what I was doing 'representing' the Australian government. I chose to stand and applaud, acknowledge Kenneth and the Mohawk as other Indigenous people did. Totally 'inappropriate' behaviour in this Forum and one I could have been sacked for. I could not sacrifice my identity for 'towing' the government line on Indigenous Rights and left the Department to go to the Human Rights and Equal Opportunity Commission. As with other public service roles in government and semi-government institutions I felt my voice being silenced or being tokenised. I moved back to the higher education sector. This struggle to locate was family history repeating itself; a travesty of colonisation, dislocation.

I now live in Darkinjung Country, about ninety kilometres north of Sydney and work in Cammeraigal Country, North Sydney. My Country belonging could be Wakka Wakka where my father was conceived and born or it could be in the Kulin nation in Melbourne, where I was born. I have come to know my connection to Country in Darkinjung Country as in no other place. I have travelled extensively in Australia and been lucky enough to be engaged in different ways in many different Aboriginal and Torres Strait Islander communities. I am grateful to my teachers; of whom there are many.

My passion has always been education and I chose to work in universities for the bulk of my lifetime being told at one point to develop the curriculum for the unit to be delivered on Aboriginal Studies, only to be told once it had been passed through the processes that I didn't have the 'academic depth and rigour' to teach it. This is when I enrolled in my Masters, successfully graduating some eight years later. The taint of this statement drew me to complete my PhD; knowing as an Aboriginal women employed in a university that I would always be considered less rigorous and having less depth if I did not complete the PhD. My PhD journey took me to places unimaginable; places geographically, places in my head, my heart and my spirit. It took me to connections and relatedness in ways that such a scattered life, a seemingly culturally disconnected life that grounded me in my Knowing, my Indigenous Knowing. It afforded the opportunity to reflexively consider how the western gaze in my lifetime, in my mother and father's lifetime, my grandmother's lifetime – 3 generations spanning policies of Segregation, Assimilation, Protection and Self-Determination – has reported our lived experienced, tried to shape where we 'fit' through such legislation and showcased what I metaphorically explore in this book as – the Brickwall: The Academy, Western Knowledge.

The journey that was my PhD took me through confusion, chaos, and sense of place as I swam through the waters of academia often being dragged out to sea as the waves crashed in and over me. The journey that was my PhD helped me find my voice and this book is an articulation of that voice.

The journey to this book over a decade from when the PhD journey began has been to engage in scholarly discourse about the importance of centering Indigenous Knowings in all that we do so that we can all find our voice and place in this Country. Without the articulation and feeling for an Indigenous Knowing, different and diverse Indigenous Knowings this Country has shallow roots and lacks nutrition. Shallow roots do not grow our sense of place as a nation, our sense of place as Indigenous peoples in Australia. Our self-determination as Indigenous people in Australia, our sovereignty is dependent on us connecting to the voices of Country, spirits and entities of diversity. It is dependent on us being silent for a moment and listening to the Storys around us and getting to know our Indigenous Knowings; our ontologies and epistemologies no matter what our background. We have the right to claim our place and not be identified and 'fitted into' the box that western disciplines feel best serve them or us.

Remember I spoke about the importance of conceptual differences; of understanding such differences if we are to truly Know Story? To do this is not to compare but to understand the differences so that the lens applied, the gaze applied is done knowing that there are differences not from the vantage of trying to label and box these differences in values and concepts that speak a different language, but that they have different ontological and epistemological roots. The conceptual differences I choose to Story at this point ever so briefly include concepts of 'Country' 'Story' and 'Indigenous Knowings'. I do this so that the ride through this book is made easier for you to read, to hear and to understand.

Concept Of 'Country': An Introduction

You may hear Indigenous peoples in Australia refer to 'Country'. You may have heard of an Acknowledgement of 'Country' being done before meetings or events.

There has been and it continues a debate in Australia about such Acknowledgment being 'political correctness gone mad'.

Acknowledgement of Country is an important act of connection and connecting. It is an act of relatedness to Country. An act ensuring relatedness to each other. It is cultural protocol in many geographical parts and many systems including universities and schools within Australia. Acknowledgments connect us through Story for as Thomas King asserts 'story, story is all that we are' (King, T. 2003). This book is one connecting story that relates and celebrates past practices; hundreds of thousands of years of practice in Australia, with current practices and ideas. This book is designed to enrich and nourish and to be enriched and nourished by Country and the many voices, the many expressions of Australian Indigenous Ontologies. In so doing we have two different ontologies in conversation in this instance working towards renewed conversation, understanding and practice. I now engage some other Indigenous voices to story the concept of 'Country'.

Country, ruwe, is central to the theory, method and story of this book. It is as Watson evokes the source of all our growth, our being as Indigenous peoples. It is our 'Knowing'.

> Ruwe, is the land, 'the land is our mother'. She nurtures us and from her all things grow. Without ruwe there is no self. One can not be without her....The earth is known to us (Indigenous Peoples) as a feminine being, a mother. And while the feminine in the natural world is powerful, it is not a power that is hierarchical and dominating. For it to be that would be to become muldarbi, and demonising of the laws of creation. The love we hold for the –ruwe – mother – land is unlike Christianity's hierarchical reverence of the father. The dimension for loving ruwe is whole; it is circular, not linear. The love of ruwe, and its energy moves through all of the organs; it is more than a thought that is sublimated in to an ideology that is used to dominate. Love of ruwe does not change form. It remains the same. Love of ruwe is a way of life; it is practiced and it is sung; the songs of ruwe are sung across the land. The love of ruwe is a passionate and interdependent one, which moves throughout and unifies all things (Watson I. , 1998, p. 32).

Many Indigenous peoples liken Country to such a source and they embody this source with life, spirit, timeliness. Bird Rose (1996) likens 'Country' for Aboriginal peoples as a 'nourishing terrain'; a place that gives and receives life:

> Country is not something that is just imagined or represented it is lived
> in and lived with. Country is a living entity with a yesterday, today and
> tomorrow. Aboriginal peoples talk about Country the way they would
> talk about a person; they speak to Country, sing to Country, visit
> Country, worry about Country, feel sorry for Country and long for
> Country. People say Country knows, hears, smells, takes notice, takes
> care, is sorry or happy' (Bird Rose, 1996, p. 7).

In Australia pre-invasion, Country could not be bought and sold, it could not be
fought over. Country had/continues to have a spirit. People are guardians of this
spirit. People are the guardians of Country. Without Country we as human beings
have no space on this earth as Patten an Aboriginal Elder from New South Wales
and Trask from Hawaii so aptly say:

> We and the land are one. When you take it from us you kill the spirit that
> gives us life. We end up as shells of human beings, living in other
> people's Country (Watson I. , 1998).

> … land is inherent to the people; it is like our bodies and our parents.
> The people can not exist without the land, and the land can not exist
> without the people (Trask, 1993, p. 116).

> We never fought over ground, we never fought over territory. The land
> had created the boundaries, not us (McConchie, 2003, p. 58).

Country is a space where knowledge is learnt, lived, practiced, renewed,
regenerated through ceremony:

> Indigenous knowledge is inherently tied to the land, not to land in
> general but to particular landscapes, landforms, and biomes where
> ceremonies are properly held, Storys properly recited, medicines
> properly gathered, and transfers of knowledge properly authenticated.
> Ensuring the complete and accurate transmission of knowledge and
> authority from generation to generation depends not only on maintaining
> ceremonies, which Canadian law treat as art rather than science, but also
> on maintaining the land itself (Battiste, 2002, p. 13).

Indigenous Knowings and Western Knowledge have fundamentally different understandings of the concept of 'Country'. Ontological, epistemological differences that shape our relatedness and being in this world.

STORY: AN INTRODUCTION

> The truth about Storys is that that's all we are (King, 2003, p. 2).

Indigenous Knowings across the globe are as King states 'all we are'. Story explains, explores and projects our being, our connections and relationships. Fixico, Battiste, King, Hokari, Little Bear, Chamberlin and Youngblood Henderson identify that Indigenous Knowings are dependent on Story to transmit and grow, that the storytellers and the listeners are connected through Story and that Storys have many dimensions, many perspectives which all contribute to Indigenous Knowings:

Metaphor and story are expressions and forms of transmission of Indigenous Knowings:

> In fact, one aspect of the Indigenous worldview is that it takes a thousand voices to tell a story. (Wilshire, 2006, p. 160).

This book, this Story has involved many voices and its ongoing journey will involve many more. Story is often transmitted through the storyteller who is both the storyteller and the listener:

> Through my language I understand I am being spoken to, I'm not the one speaking. The words are coming from many tongues and mouths of Okanagan people and the land around them. I am a listener to the language's Storys, and when my words form I am merely retelling the same Storys in different patterns [Jeannette Armstrong in (King, 2003, p. 2)]

Storys do not merely describe or explain events. They are the vehicle for transmitting Indigenous Knowing in many different Indigenous nations around the globe. Storys do this involving patterning and repetition as they 'grow from the inside out' (Denzin, N. & Lincoln, Y.S. 2005, p.933).

> Story-telling is not just about content. It is, David Unaipon points out, more like a dramatic performance and it contains the truths of his people.

No wonder the story-tellers of today find the written record to be lacking. ... It fails to engage the reader in this interactive process of finding meaning (Bell D. , 1998, p. 394).

There may be many Storys as 'it is quite normal that the different Storys which contradict each other, do not conflict but simply co-exist (Hokari, 2000, p. 8). Remember it takes a thousand voices to tell a story (Wilshire, 2006, p. 160). Story has structure, a number of voices and movements. How do we listen to such Storys?

Story then, is a pivotal point of ontological and epistemological difference. To continue to layer Western lenses of interpretation being guided by their concept of story distorts, devalues and misinterprets Indigenous concepts of Storying. We must realise and appreciate the differences if we are to productively engage in transformative dialogue.

INDIGENOUS KNOWINGS: AN INTRODUCTION

Indigenous Knowings embody Country and Story. Indigenous Knowings are different to Western Knowledges because the ontological and epistemological bases are different. Until we can embrace these differences as equals we will remain disconnected to Country, peoples and Storys from and about each.

READING AND ENGAGING WITH THIS BOOK

This book has different parts, different mediums with which to explore the concept of Indigenous Knowings and the production of Knowledge. The text itself, in parts, is a speaking text. This is designed to give a sense of oration and harness voices throughout, wherever possible. Metaphor, imaging, sounds and text have been integrated through the use of the text in this book and the accompanying webpage. Because Indigenous Knowings ask us to engage with all of our senses this book is presented in a multi-dimensional form. You can understand some of the journey that this book takes us on by just reading and engaging with the text. We can however understand and engage more actively if we read the text and engage with the website.

The form of each chapter, and the book as a whole document, represent my argument, my vision. Indigenous Knowings are privileged in the design, layout, in the use of language, images, text boxes and a webpage. The accompanying webpage has been designed to give dimension and depth to the linear western framework that is a thesis, a book. Mind maps have been included at the beginning of Chapters 2,3,4 and 5 as well as the beginning of the book. The mind maps are my representation of the book and chapters; if you like a summary of each. Each map is organic and uses symbols I evolved to represent different moments in the research journey, in the research Story. They are not drawn by an artist and I ask that you take the essence of the maps and not judge the artistic abilities. Mind maps capture spirit and energy as well as key points in ways the 'author', the creator finds meaning. The maps are designed to demonstrate what I am talking about in this book; they are an alternate means of conceptualising, evolving and communicating knowledge, thoughts, feelings, Knowing ...

There is a poem at the beginning of the book and it is repeated at the end. The poem was the original abstract for the thesis and summarises the concepts of this book. The poem is the heart of the book. Verses are repeated at the beginning of a couple of the chapters with the intent of engaging and re-engaging you the reader with the whole of the story as you are taken through the bits of it.

The book serves two main purposes. One involves Storying my thought processes and experiences as an Indigenous PhD candidate engaging in an Academic institution; in the Brick Wall. Four Arrows states that such engagement can be a 'series of hoop-jumping machinations' (2008). In this scenario we are floundering in a Zone of Colliding Trajectories where Indigenous Knowings until recently have been denigrated and we ask where is our place? It is important that our Storys are shared so that other Indigenous students engaging in doctoral studies can more easily find their place. This book takes us as reader and storyteller from the challenges of engaging in such study to those challenges associated with publishing through the production of this book. For non-Indigenous readers working in the Academy this offers insights into Indigenous students you may be supervising. For readers outside of the Academy you engage in a Story about cultural differences; a space where differences mingle with each other and play out in many different ways.

The second purpose of this book is to showcase a multitude of Indigenous voices. Voices that have been silenced for too long. I have chosen to share their voices through what would be seen by some as too many quotes and not enough of the storyteller's voice. Wilson (2008) has said he stands of the shoulders of other Indigenous scholars (p.13) which I do here as well. I also want you the reader to hear their voices, through their voices their words rather than through me as the filter, the translator. As the storyteller I privilege their words, the diversity, passion and power of these words.

The webpage is a visual and sensory experience of this research involving photos shown on power point, video, photos shown through the medium of movie and sound; language spoken, didgeridoo playing, and singing. The webpage demonstrates epistemological and pedagogical consequences of knowledge production across and deep within the contested zone between the Brick Wall (The Academy) and the Waterlily (Indigenous Knowings). This book packages these consequences through the different mediums used. You may well be asking what are the images, the metaphors and you will be taken to them as the time is right. You will be taken to them the way they evolved for me as the researcher.

USING THE WEBSITE

Page Title	Imaging	Imaging	Imaging	Imaging	Imaging
1. Home Spiders, Sweet Potatoes & Waterlilys	i. Acknowledgement of Country	ii. Abstract	Stewart McMinn: Didjeridoo playing throughout page		
2. Country	Bill Neidjie's poem	A beginning	Photos of Coast and Desert		
3.Indigenous Knowing	Images of Lilys	Images of Lilys by Pilawuk White with accompanying Storys			
4.Tellin' Me & Showin' Me Didjeridoo played by Warren Blair	Land, Law and Song :Desert Video Clip & Song	Experiencing Country: Desert	Coolamon making : Desert	Body painting : Desert	Colleagues : Desert singing a special song Colleague : April from Desert speaking in Amatyere language
5.Contested Space	'Brains of the White Side …'	Images representing Research journey; specifically Indigenous Knowings, Western Knowledges & Contested Space			
6.Mind Mapping	Storying the Mind Mapping Journey				
7.Acknowledgements					
8.Related Links					

Figure 2. Using the Webpage

Figure 2 above entitled 'Using the Webpage' provides a summary of each page in the website. Each page is titled; read across each column to see what sounds and visuals are presented; what images are used.. This site will give people the opportunity to blog, to respond to the imagings.

THE WEBPAGE:

Page 1 Home Page: Spiders, Sweet Potatoes and Waterlilys

This page opens with the sound of the didgeridoo; a piece of music specially crafted for the thesis that has evolved into this book. It is played by Stewart McMinn a young Aboriginal man, who at the time was a pre-service teacher. The sound of the didgeridoo asks us to engage with our hearing sense and to be able to feel rhythm, vibrations and patterns. The didgeridoo is the heart beat of some Indigenous Countrys within Australia.

Page 1 A Reading of My Alternate Abstract.

Again we engage with the sense of hearing in this reading of the Abstract. You can hear my voice as the author and watch the text and as you go. You will notice though that the text is slightly different to the oral reading; it is different because the poem has grown since the abstract was recorded.

Page 1 A Verbal Acknowledgement of Country.

I can write an Acknowledgement which you can read but here you can engage with the Acknowledgement through my voice; the tones, rhythms and intonations – the silences and pauses.

Page 2 Country

A verbal reading of a story' Feelin' im Country', by Uncle Bill Neidjie, an Aboriginal Elder and Kakadu Man, (recently passed so his name is used respectfully), explores the concept of 'Country' through Aboriginal English words. The sound bite gives a sense of rhythm, intonation and feeling the written text cannot give.

'A beginning' illustrates through photos and narration the starting point of the field research; perhaps the 'false start', perhaps the moment to springboard the research experience into a completely different space. The use of the slides gives you the chance to see the physical characteristics of Country where this research journey began.

Images from Coast and Desert show the different Country.

Page 3 Indigenous Knowings

Pictorial images of Indigenous Knowings are represented on this page through the photo of the waterlily; there are no hyperlinks on this page. The image is there for us to see all of the different elements of the waterlily. Art by Pilawuk Whits is used with Story to showcase some of the elements of Waterlilys; especially the fruit pod and seeds in it.

Page 4 Tellin' Me and Showin' Me

This page opens with the sound of the didgeridoo played by Warren Blair. Sound is used to introduce images and text in different languages from different Countrys visited. Experiential insight into some of the teachings, some of my learnings in Desert Country is presented here.

'Land, Law and Song'

This shows senior class students from Ti Tree school in a video and song entitled 'Land, Law and Song'; developed during my stay in Desert. The words and experience of the making of the video embody Indigenous Knowing. This video also illustrates Desert Country; relationships, connections.

Experiencing Country: Desert

Goanna hunting and being taken out to Country to see rock holes, where people used to grind seeds with Colleagues from Desert. This scape indulges the sense of sight and it helps us to be in the space in real time and experience a trip to hunt for goanna. This is an illustration of Country, practice of Indigenous Knowing in Country; it is tellin' me and showin' me.

Coolamon Making

Illustrates Desert Colleagues Tellin' me and Showin' me how to make and design a coolamon in Country.

April's Song and Amatjyere Language

We are taken by Colleagues from Desert singing a song they developed for me as part of my research journey in Desert. This song is unedited and may appear to be repetitive to someone unfamiliar with the repetition involved in Indigenous

Knowing; song, dance, art...It is presented as presented to me by my female Colleagues from Desert. This soundscape gives us a different rendition of the importance of cycles/circles and repetition in Indigenous Knowings. We can hear, feel the language of Amatjyere people as well as hear and feel the working of this song; the pauses and questions as the song is developed and sung for the tape.

Desert Colleagues allow us to hear their voices speaking Amatjere/Amatyere language during the interview/Yarn process. This is poor quality and has been included because Desert Colleagues and I discussed the importance of hearing the rhythm, sound, spaces between the notes, silences of the voices. It is less than two minutes sound and shows speaking language is different to singing language in other material presented.

Body Painting: Desert

Desert Colleagues Tellin' me and Showin' Me body painting in Country and dancing. This is a particularly personal experience. Desert Colleagues advised I could show the photos as an illustration of what we Yarned about.

Page 5 Contested Space/Contesting Space: Indigenous Research Methodology

The Research Journey Narrated

These images illustrate with my narration the evolution and connection of the concepts used in this book.

'Brains of the White Side or Go Walkabout Like the Black Side'

The background song is 'You'll Never Walk Alone' sung by Harold Blair, the first Aboriginal tenor to be recognised in a Western context and to study at Julliard School of Music in New York and my father. This affords an opportunity to hear my father's voice now; Knowing his story with images from the print press documenting the major periods of my life as identified by them. This is an illustration of how the western lens, the western gaze has reported my lived experiences; remember this is part of the Brick Wall I story later in this book (Chapter 3).

Page 6 Mind Mapping

This research journey began with the concept of mind mapping and this illustrates through photos and narration the significance of mind mapping in this Story.

Page 7 Acknowledgements

Page 8 Links

Web addresses are provided for Kanyini; an Indigenous model of Knowing illustrated by Bob Randall an Indigenous Elder from Pitjatjantjarra Country, Garma a model of Indigenous Knowing from Arnhem Land in Northern Australia, the Buzan Centre Australia which provides more information about mind mapping and is the centre I have my Licensed Instructor accreditation through. These links and this webpage will grow as more people engage with it. Thanks.

http://spiderssweetpotatoesandwaterlilys.com/home/contested-space/

> **All of the photos and images used on the website have approval from people photographed or involved.**

The bridge has been built through the previous discussion to move into the essence of this book; exploring some epistemological consequences of Knowledge production in Australia. Let's begin this part of the Story with a poem that has become the representation of my premise.

THERE IS A STORY I KNOW… LILYOLOGY STORYD

There is a story I Know …
Waterlily flowers visibly float listlessly, serenely atop fresh water
Emerging out of a subterranean world
A subterranean world busy with rhizomes
Rhizomes patterning, weaving, threading and connecting
Rhizomes reaching out to others, creating relationships, webs of connections
Storing starches, proteins, nutrients
To propogate, to reproduce
To grow and strike newness that reaches from below
Grounded in Country
Grounded in water
Grounded in the dynamics of air, water and soil,
Dynamics that are Country
Dynamics and space that are Indigenous Knowings
Rhizomes reaching from subterranean worlds to worlds above
Worlds where sunlight and air take over
Re-cast from rhizomes to a stem, slender and strong
A stem reaching upward transplanting the food, the nourishment from below
To leaves which offer breath and oxygen, down
Cyclically reinvigorating the rhizomatic world below
A stem reaching upward transplanting the food, the nourishment from below
To flowers with petals, delicate, elegant, vibrant and colourful
Varying sizes, shapes and shades
Curving and reaching up to the sun, the light, the warmth
Layering
Overlapping petals, not homogenous
Joined by a stamen centred and strong
Petals held together
Blooming daily at times, only for a few days at a time
Several every day when the conditions are right
A cyclic, holistic patterning of life
Patterning of Indigenous Knowings; of connectedness
Cast in the story that is the waterlily

Spiders weave webs, woven webs
Weaving fine, strong, transparent
Gossamer

Sticky
Vibrations felt from one end to the other
Sensory, connecting, patterning
Connecting across colliding trajectories
Trajectories from Brick Walls, from waterlilys

Sweet potatoes
Rhizomes radiating out from a nourishing, rich core
A core of starch, of carbohydrate
Sustaining, energising, foundation for growing, for life, for living
Rhizomes radiating above and below the earth
Inwards and outwards from the centre,
The periphery.
Sweet potatoes grounded
Grounded in Country
Grounded in Indigenous Knowings
Sweet Potatoes
Patterning, connecting, radiating
Like
Spiders and
Waterlilys.

The colonisers came
Constructed walls, fences, boundaries
Walls of bricks
Bricks made from earths substances; clay, sandstone and more
Walls that stand strong, on top of the earth
Or that stand manually constructed and placed within the earth that is cast out
Walls that cry for their own sense of identity?
Walls that dominate the more organic
Cutting off the source of water, earth and air; of life
Containing the flow of water, earth and air; the nourishment, the stimulus
Some waterlilys lay dormant
Revitalised with each new rain
Each new flow of water and ray of sunshine
Replenishing
Nourishing
Waiting for the walls to come down?

Searching for,...finding mutual space to co-exist? Perhaps?

Mutual space that embeds waterlily within the crafted beautiful mosaic of co-existence

Searching for, space that has no fear to privilege Indigenous Knowings in the mosaic

The mosaic where waterlily is embedded not marginalized

The mosaic where waterlily radiates energy, beauty, connectedness, relatedness

Nourishing identity and Knowings

Nourishing identity and Knowledge

1. INTRODUCTION
2. WESTERN RESEARCH
SPACE
3. CONTESTED SPACE
4. TELLIN' ME AND SHOWIN' ME
5. REFLECTING: LITERATURE, TEXTUAL
SOURCES AND LITERARY GENRES
STORY
ELDERS
KNOWING
COUNTRY
SOVEREIGNTY
ACADEMIA
RIGHTS
SELF DETERMINATION
6. WATER LILYS AND BRICK WALL
7. CONCLUSION?

CHAPTER 1

Introduction

This book is a Story, one Story rolling into another Story, which rolls into another Story like waves along the shore in a constant sea. Each wave is a Story that rolls forward and mingles with others. That retreats into others. That feeds the rivers, the lakes and in turn is fed. It is constant, always returning. This story, this book, was fed and nourished by extraordinary people. Generous people with wisdom in abundance. It was fed by Country, diverse Countrys. It was fed by literature. This story is organic. This book is organic. There can be no end point when reflecting and writing about Indigenous Knowings.

It began when a friend, tired of seeing me rolling the electronic white board from meeting to meeting, up and down corridors, in and out of lifts, over rough office terrain, suggested I read a book she had just finished reading. The book had many wonderful images of trees, lightning, microscopic images of plants, lichen, elements of Country. I thought it looked interesting and began to read it on the hour and a half train trip home. If I read, I read because I had to, having lost the pleasure of reading many years before. I devoured this book, nearly missing my stop. I devoured the images, the words, the design, the concepts.

As I read, a part of me that lay dormant, or that I felt never existed, was awakened. I often said that I didn't have a creative bone in my body. After reading the book, I thought 'why didn't I know about this before, this is the way I think'. A phrase I have since heard often in Indigenous communities throughout Australia; communities I have worked with. The book was *The Mind Map Book* by Tony Buzan (Buzan T. , 1997). The concept was mind mapping and, more importantly, thinking and communicating in non-linear ways.

This was an entry point. Catching the train to work on another occasion I happened to glimpse the end of the billboard and caught the words 'Tony Buzan' and 'Sydney'. After a great deal of what can only be described as effective detective work, I found out where and when. When booking the session I was told that Tony Buzan would love to meet me because he was interested in the way I was conceptualising the use of mind mapping with Indigenous peoples. In my then work, which was developing a national education package for Indigenous peoples on human rights, I needed a way to share and communicate information other than through a linear framework.

After the days session I talked with Tony Buzan about my vision, my thinking. He understood! No one else, other than my friend who introduced me to his book, understood.

Here the next phase and entry point presents itself. I admit I had no concept of a PhD thesis at this point, I just wanted to communicate information to my mob[1] in a way that would deliver results, in a tangible way. I boarded a plane to the UK and travelled to the colonisers shores; something I had vowed never to do. I arrived in Lilliput and spent one of the most memorable periods of my life there. I connected to something that had meaning, something that radiated a new spirit from within me.

After returning to Australia and being retrenched from my public service job, I set up a small training company. I worked with many Indigenous peoples from all over the Country drawing on the concepts associated with mind mapping. I asked participants to draw their concept of human rights using colour, a landscaped page, words if they felt like it, images or symbols of some kind; all good mind mapping rules. Tony would be proud. In one such session a participant, Alison, a high profile leader from her community, used her page to capture her feelings. I have, with her permission, reproduced her images here.

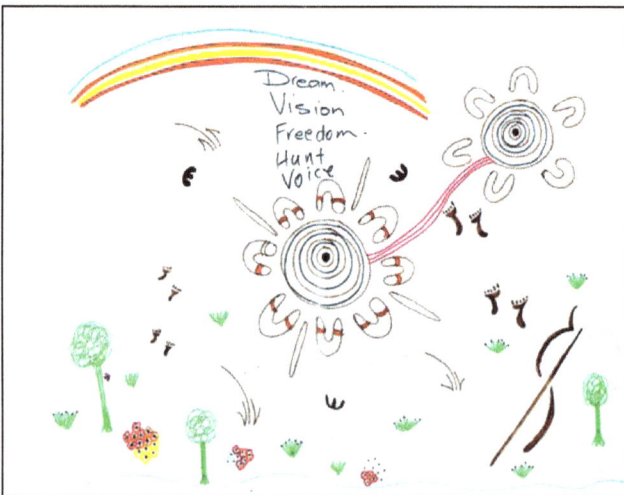

Figure 1.1. Mind Map of Human Rights 1 by Alison Anderson

---

[1] Mob/s: an expression used by Indigenous peoples to denote groups; either large or small.

Alison entered into a dialogue with me during the presentation about decolonising our language and the whole "human rights stuff". A heated, intense and real discussion. After our discussion Alison went away and returned the next day with two new images (Figures 1.2 and 1.3). The second image of a spider's web was seen to represent patterning, connecting the way mind maps do. Spiders then, become part of the relatedness so significant in Indigenous Knowings. This is further developed in chapter five.

Figure 1.2. Mind Map of Human Rights 2: Alison Anderson

Figure 1.3. Mind Map by Alison Anderson

Alison, a traditional artist, found mind mapping to be the bridge between cultures for her expression. Not the be all and end all but a bridge. She employed these new realities in the days that followed by means of a briefing presented to the new Federal Minister of Aboriginal and Torres Strait Islander Affairs. There was still something to come in the workshop though. A later discussion, after watching a video on mind mapping, revealed yet another layer of what I was thinking but had never had a way of communicating before. Alison said "that mind mapping, that stuff is sweet potatoes"' I asked her to help me decolonise my mind because for me, someone living in suburbia sweet potatoes were bulbous red looking things I bought in the local fruit market. After declaring me 'wamba' (a little bit silly and simple) the participant told me about sweet potatoes growing in the ground in her Country; how they grew, what they looked like and what they were used for. Other people in the training session joined in, in very animated ways, yarning about sweet potatoes and yams and bush potatoes in their own Country. She explained that sweet potatoes have roots in and on top of the ground and have a nourishing centre. A mind map looks like a sweet potato growing in the ground. Simple and yes, it does.

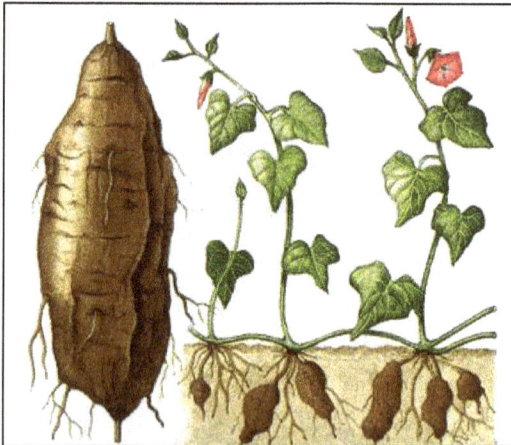

Figure 1.4. "Sweet Potato" 29 October 2008. HowStuffWorks.com.
<http://science.howstuffworks.com/life/botany/sweet-potato-info.htm> 15 October 2015.

Interestingly, in presenting this to other Indigenous people at a conference in Aotearoa, I found Maori and other Indigenous peoples had a form of sweet potato that was highly significant in peoples' lives. Maori and other people from Alaska to Aotearoa participating in the conference became very excited about the concept and shared their own Storys. Indigenous peoples from different parts of the world strongly connected to the link between Indigenous Knowings and its expression through the concept of sweet potatoes. Mind maps at this point are seen as a potential bridge between two cultural worlds helping me to decolonise my own thinking, reflection and presentation. Mind maps became connected and imaged as sweet potatoes.

So, now we have been introduced to spiders and sweet potatoes! What of it?

We have a clear visual way of conveying differences between Indigenous Knowings and those of the coloniser. At this stage I was employed at the University of Newcastle and enrolled in a PhD. My research focus went from pure mind mapping and Indigenous peoples to a point backwards in the Story (remembering waves go backwards too!). I realised I needed to explore Indigenous Knowings before embarking on research into the effectiveness of mind mapping with Indigenous peoples. As I framed my research I also realised I needed something else and was not entirely sure what. Where did I sit in all of this? This last question is one Watson, an Indigenous scholar and barrister asked (Watson I. , 1998). I take up this question later using Watson's words as a springboard for my own thought and writing processes. I realise now that Indigenous peoples the world over have asked and continue to ask this question as part of an emerging discourse on Indigenous Research Methodology.

Smith privileges her 'vantage point as a colonized' (Smith L. , 1999, p. 1). In some ways I am doing more than privileging it. I am as an Indigenous thinker unapologetically in the centre of this research with other Indigenous peoples. I privilege Indigenous Knowing rather than Western Knowledge. The book will develop this thought as it gathers voices and their energies. I get emotional about this research and the writing of it. This journey is full of the most memorable experiences of my life, the sharing by peoples of their passion and wisdom, their trust in me, the immersion in Country, diverse Countrys. This research centres what is tangible.

The waves continue to lap against the shore. The shore that is this research journey. The shore that this book represents. The fusion of Storys, experiences, reflections, challenges and most of all, relationships.

How do I research this? Should I research this at all? Some waves are less formed than others. Some as they roll in to shore have white water, where the torrid mixing of sediment and chemicals combine to announce their entry and arrival onshore. This research process embodied waves where a torrid mixing of ideas, concepts, reflections, doubts and challenges presented themselves. Interestingly, even these waves contribute to the land formations, the shoreline, the living entities within the ocean. These waves announce the formation of an even bigger wave. This metaphoric ideal is the discourse about and the concept of an Indigenous Research Methodology.

The linear text that was presented in the form of my thesis and now has been re-organised as a book offers seven chapters, with 'book ends' through a Prologue and Epilogue; this being the First Chapter. The Second Chapter explores Western research and the space that exists for Indigenous research and Indigenous researchers. It tells a story contextualised in colonialism, imperialism and eurocentrism and identifies a zone where the space is contested. Chapter Three delves further into the contested space; space between Waterlilys and the Brick Wall. Chapter Four would traditionally be known as the fieldwork chapter. Titled 'Tellin' Me and Showin' Me' it represents the essence that is this Story. It is the voices of my Colleagues from Desert and Coast in many cases verbatim. This chapter should be read as if you are reading a script for a play or film. Chapter Five would traditionally be known as a Literature Review. Given that the notion of a literature review in the context of Indigenous Knowing is very much an oxymoron (Battiste M. , 2002, p. 2), this chapter reflects on literature, textual sources and different literary genres in the contexts of Indigenous literacies, the concepts of 'Country', 'Knowing', the notion of Story and Indigenous Elders as scholars. Across a contested zone the chapter rolls in to discussion and reflection about The Academy, how The Academy has used Indigenous Knowings and 'gone about' Indigenous research, and intellectual cultural and property rights and ethics. It then explores new terrain and alternate tools such as mind mapping and potential relationships to the decolonisation of Indigenous research. The texts and sources chosen privilege Indigenous Knowings; they are predominantly Indigenous authors. Chapter Six, (would traditionally be described as an analysis chapter) harnesses the energies and the Storys from Chapters Two to Five and reflects and converses connections, linkages and relationships between the Brick Wall and Waterlilys when the Waterlily is centred not the Brick Wall. Decolonisation, the importance of language; performance, imaging, words and text, the notion of bricoleur, institutionalism and managing, dealing with, and 'doing' Indigenous Knowing and research are played out in this chapter. 'Finally', Chapter Seven explores Indigenous intellectual self-determination; it is not the end so therefore not a conclusion – it is a point at which we take breath, reflect listen to what is around us and then embark further on a journey to enrich the one just taken, just experienced. It is the point I ask and respond to three questions:

1. Why did I do this research?
2. What did I learn from this journey?
3. How can what I learnt from the many voices Storyd be shared, taken away and become a part of other peoples lived experiences?

This book is a Story. A Story shaped by many different Storys rolling in and out at different times and places, in different ways, with different emotions. I hope you enjoy it. I hope you find value in it, in its simplicity, its honesty and its presentation of Indigenous voices as the essence of it rather than Western Eurocentric Knowledge bases and philosophies about how we should think and represent ourselves. I reclaim through this Story our right to define and re-present ourselves as Indigenous peoples through in this case 'Lilyology'. I hope that you can engage with and translate this Story into something useful for yourself.

ENRICHED

PLAY IS IMPORTANT

TIME TRAVEL

CHILDPLAY

COMPLICATION

ENGLISH

WESTERN RESEARCH

HISTORY

STORY

ROLES

CONTESTED

ZONE

ADMINISTRATION

CATHOLICISM

DIFFERENCE

CHAPTER 2

Western Research Theory: The Space for Indigenous Research?

> All in all it's just another brick in the wall (Floyd, 1979)

I grapple as the researcher at this point of the Story with the correct, the appropriate approach to conduct my research journey within. The waves are high and churning powerfully with paradigms, research strategies, epistemologies, methodologies and analyses all embedded within what I describe as the Brick Wall. Western research has a rich tradition of scholarship, of research. I wonder however, if Indigenous research and Indigenous Knowing is 'all in all it's just another brick in the wall'. This book explores this quandary as an undercurrent throughout.

Smith from the vantage point of the colonized so eloquently asserts:

> [The] term research is inextricably linked to European imperialism and colonialism. The word itself, 'research' is probably one of the dirtiest words in the indigenous world's vocabulary. When mentioned in many Indigenous contexts, it stirs up silence, it conjures up bad memories, it raises a smile that is knowing and distrustful. It is so powerful that indigenous people even write poetry about research. The ways in which scientific research is implicated in the worst excesses of colonialism remains a powerful remembered history for many of the world's colonized peoples. It is a history that still offends the deepest sense of our humanity. Just knowing that someone measured our 'faculties' by filling the skulls of our ancestors with millet seeds and compared the amount of millet seed to the capacity for mental thought offends our sense of who and what we are. It galls us that Western researchers and intellectuals can assume to know all that it is possible to know of us, on the basis of their brief encounters with some of our ways of knowing, our imagery, the things we create and produce, and then simultaneously reject the people who created and developed these ideas and seek to deny them further opportunities to be creators of their own cultures and own nations (Smith L. , 1999, p. 1).

I and others have so many different reactions to this statement. Students in some of the tutorials I have facilitated have been appalled at what they perceive as Smith's racism. Others have been confused. All have felt something. I recall being shown comments in newspapers at my birth that asked 'would she have the brains of the white side or go walkabout like her father's side'; my father was Aboriginal, my mother is Anglo Australian. Major periods of my life were documented in the press to map 'my progress'. The implications of such research and belief in the findings and establishment of these findings as 'truth' profoundly impacted on me, on us as peoples. I cannot and I choose not to disengage from my research. I choose not to be objective as defined by Eurocentric science as this would be dishonest, this would negate my own Indigenous Knowings. It is in this context I engage in this research as do other Indigenous scholars through: self-location (Kovach, 2009, p.110), (Arbon, 2008, p.22), self-aware subjectivity (Martin, 2008) and the role of the story-teller (Wilson, 2008, p.32).

My own research (discussed in more detail in Chapter 4) has identified community people who have when asked, on many different occasions and in many different locations, if they would like to be involved in research have simply said in unison "tell them to fuck off, we have been researched to death, just leave us alone". Smith is correct in her assertion that the word 'research conjures extreme emotion'. The practice has even more profound effects. It is this that any Indigenous scholar undertaking postgraduate work within the halls of The Academy must first deconstruct. This is a journey that like the waves in the sea is constantly changing yet remaining the same; a space where there are many obstacles, many features, many factors being tussled around and impacting on the outcomes.

In this chapter I engage in a Story that presents the background against which my journey as an Indigenous scholar evolves. The embeddedness that is Colonialism, Imperialism, Eurocentrism is contextualised. A reference to a history of Western research, as told so astutely by Denzin and Lincoln (Denzin, N. & Lincoln, Y.S. 2005), teases out issues that have impacted on the roles Indigenous peoples have played in this larger story. The role of anthropology as a 'founding' discipline for the study of Indigenous peoples features significantly in this story. A conversation is begun on the need to find our space as Indigenous researchers if we are to change the impact of the word research and the process in our communities and on ourselves. This conversation leads into the following chapter which engages the essence that is Indigenous research; Indigenous voices and Indigenous models of research.

COLONIALISM, IMPERIALISM & EUROCENTRICISM

Colonialism became imperialism's outpost, the fort and the port of imperial outreach. Colonialism was, in part, an image of imperialism. It was also, in part, an image of the future nation it would become (Smith L. , 1999, p. 23). Smith asserts that 'the reach of imperialism in to 'our heads' leads us to a need to decolonize our minds and claim a space to develop a sense of authentic humanity' (Smith L. , 1999, p. 23). This book is an endeavour to decolonise my mind. It is an endeavour to illustrate ways we, as Indigenous peoples, have and must continue to do this.

Imperialism was a way to systematically categorise and classify peoples through hierarchies of race and typologies. The combination of imperialistic power and science shaped the relations between the colonizers and Indigenous powers globally (Smith, 1999, p.25). This classification and analysis by Eurocentric anthropologists led to the homogenising of Indigenous peoples, Indigenous cultures (Battiste & Henderson, 2000, pp.30-31). This shaped the way we viewed ourselves.

Eurocentrism conceived static traditional Indigenous knowledge and heritage. These 'conceptions served as a self-congratulatory reference point against which Eurocentric society could measure its own progressive evolution and served to limit the future… forcing Indigenous cultures to accept the inevitability of imitating Eurocentric modes of thought and dress' (Battiste & Henderson, 2000, p.31).

Battiste and Henderson assert "most existing research on Indigenous peoples is contaminated by Eurocentric prejudice" (Battiste M. &., 2000, pp. 132-133). In exploring further they identify the theory of Eurocentrism as "the imaginative and institutional context that informs contemporary scholarship, opinion and law". This theory, they argue, postulates the superiority of Europeans over non-Europeans; Indigenous knowledge and heritage appeared to need progress and economic and moral uplifting. What Europeans produced on the other hand was/is seen as 'fact'/'truth' (Battiste M. &., 2000, p. 23).

Nakata, a Torres Strait Islander scholar from Australia critiques the *Reports of the Cambridge Anthropological Expedition to the Torres Strait Islands*, 1898 and the seminal text *Among the Cannibals of New Guinea*, London Missionary Society, 1888, which both inscribe characteristics of the Islander in to Western disciplines so that they could be understood in the West not as animals but as a people in a lower stage of development, as savages (Nakata M. , 2007, p. 11). Nakata himself found conflict in the life he knew and lived and that inscribed to him, his family, his Country.

"Trading the Other" is a vast industry based on the positional superiority and advantages gained under imperialism. Trading the Other defines Western thinking and identity as superior, entwining with the notion of a need to 'bring progress' to Indigenous peoples, these principles then becoming embedded in institutional practice. Trading the Other involves theft, theft of other's knowledges and the use of it to benefit the thieves. (Smith L. , 1999, p. 89)

Diffusionism, is a central concept of this theory of Eurocentrism. This is a concept that saw 'product benefitting uncivilised peoples as a result of the flow of Western, more advanced Knowledge, product, ideas, etc. "The theory argues that because Europeans are superior, Indigenous peoples need the diffusion of creativity, imagination, invention, innovation, rationality, and sense of honour or ethics from Europe in order to progress" (Battiste M. &., 2000, p. 21). At the core of Eurocentric thought is the claim to be universal. The quest for knowledge from sheer wonder and the curiosity of what existed beyond inspired diffusion. "This quest for truth and value informed the concept of universal purpose and explains why Europeans went to such efforts to 'discover' the world" (Battiste M. &., 2000, p. 22). Smith refers to the significance of travellers' stories and adventurers' adventures on what was represented of the 'Other' to a general audience back in Europe which became the fixed milieu of cultural ideas' (Smith L. , 1999, p. 8). Messianic prophecy contained in monotheistic religions was according to Battiste and Henderson a second inspiration for Europeans to go outside of their worlds. This aspect is where the morality component, the need to save the souls of the 'savages' pervaded.

A further contaminate of Eurocentric research is the establishment and contestation of a notion of difference. Difference was assigned by race; a category that was linked to 'human reason and morality, to science, to colonialism, and to the rights of citizenship' (Smith, L. 1999, p.45). This racialized discourse has, and continues to have, enormous impact on how we as Indigenous researchers assert our position in the research domain today.

The intersections of race and gender in the notion of difference are important in this racialized discourse because these differences, our fundamental ontological and epistemological differences become apparent. Differences in the conceptualisation of the individual and society, as well as conceptions of space and conceptions of time (Smith L. , 1999, pp. 45-56). Research has been conceived and practised with the individual being perceived and portrayed as central in both psychological and sociological traditions of research where it is considered the basic unit of society. Social Darwinism heavily influenced and guided such ideas and practice (Smith L. , 1999, pp. 49-50).

Eurocentric theory made assumptions about the natural world which conflicted with Indigenous Knowings, specifically, that the natural world is usually thought of as a "single, wholly determinable realm". In this way of thinking "the world is a background against which the mind operates, and knowledge is regarded as information that originates outside humanity" (Battiste M. &., 2000, p. 23). Here is the most fundamental ontological and epistemological difference between Indigenous peoples and non-Indigenous peoples. We are led to a 'spectre of domination, propaganda, and false realities'. We are led to a space where Eurocentric models are imposed on Indigenous peoples and we are forced to assimilate to an artificial reality (Battiste M. &., 2000, p. 29)? A reality not of our own thinking. A reality so disparate to our world views. This research hopes to contribute some reflections which engage Indigenous Knowing; a Knowing that is encompassed in the natural world and one that showcases our realities.

This Eurocentric gaze on research practice is carried out through the Disciplines within The Academy. Disciplines which categorise bits of information according to their bias.

Indigenous researchers in Australia have gravitated toward disciplines and theories that have traditionally been used to conduct research about Indigenous peoples: these are discussed in more detail in Chapter 6.

WESTERN RESEARCH: AN OVERVIEW

An overview of Western research is appropriate at this point in this Story. Denzin and Lincoln (Denzin, N. & Lincoln, Y.S. 2005, pp.1-32), provide an excellent overview of the tensions between quantitative and qualitative research as well the tensions within qualitative research. They assert and I believe contextualise:

> Sadly, qualitative research, in many, if not all of its forms (observation, participation, interviewing, ethnography), serves as a metaphor for colonial knowledge, for power and for truth....In the colonial context, research becomes an objective way of representing the dark-skinned Other to the white world (Denzin, N. & Lincoln, Y.S. 2005, p.1).

This latter point echoes one being described by Nakata earlier in this chapter. Wilson (2008, pp.35-39) provides an overview of the dominant research paradigms while Martin (2008, pp.25-32) Storys the 'dispossession of our stories' through research practice in Australia taking us through changing patterns and different ways of doing research as well as our invisibility and dispossession through research practice (pp.25-32). Arbon (2008, pp.93-100) Storys how knowledge is constructed in the Western tradition. Kovach (2009) reviews the qualitative research as a backdrop to her research identifying how early qualitative studies were responsible for 'extractive research leaving those researched as disenfranchised from the knowledge they shared' and how 'tribal epistemologies' reflect the differences in traditions (pp.25-36).

Denzin and Lincoln engage in an enlightened and succinct history of qualitative research identifying eight moments of qualitative research from the traditional period in the early 1900s, the modernist phase (post war years to the 1970s), a moment of blurred genres (1970-1986), a crisis of representation in the mid 1980s, a triple crisis, the postmodern period of experimental ethnographic writing, post-experimental inquiry (1995-2000), the methodologically contested present (2000-2004) and finally the eighth moment; the future (2005 -). They emphasise that this history is not static with each moment still operating in the present. The qualitative research process is defined by three interconnected, generic activities.

They identify interpretive paradigms, specifically the paradigm or theory and associated criteria; the form of the theory; and, the type of narration (Denzin, N. & Lincoln, Y.S. 2005, pp.23-25). They note that objectivity in research and the notion of the use of single methods can no longer form part of research process because any gaze is always filtered through the lenses of language, gender, social class, race and ethnicity. They argue that consequently, qualitative researchers deploy a wide range of interconnected interpretive methods (Denzin, N. & Lincoln, Y.S. 2005, p.21).

I support the notion but, as a side bar, find the use of militaristic language interesting. Words like 'armed' and 'deploy' are very apt for any Indigenous peoples who have been subjected to what could be considered a war zone. A zone that has destroyed, stolen peoples' cultural Knowing, existence and being:'traded the other'. A zone in which the weapon 'research' has been deployed.

Within the context of the historical moments, Denzin and Lincoln provide research processes, specifically: the researcher as a multicultural subject; theoretical paradigms and perspectives; research strategies; methods of collection and analysis; and, the art, practices and politics of interpretation and evaluation (Denzin, N. & Lincoln, Y.S. 2005, pp.22-23). Sandoval (2000) like Denzin and Lincoln identifies the emergence of new modes as a result of oppression and in the context of a new world order, namely, globalisation (pp.6-9). Sandoval argues that there is 'a juncture where the thinking of western philosophers aligns, and from where a decolonizing theory and method accelerates (Sandoval C. , 2000, pp. 6-7).

ZONE OF COLLIDING TRAJECTORIES: DECOLONISATION

At the juncture of what I describe (in Chapter 3) a zone of colliding trajectories, decolonisation theory has accelerated. Decolonisation is discussed in the context of process in Chapter 5. Why do we as Indigenous researchers gravitate toward this theory more than any others? The following components of decolonisation speak to its meaning: the deconstructing of Western scholarship; addressing social issues within the wider framework of self-determination; decolonisation teamed with social justice; and, the ability to talk more widely about Indigenous research, Indigenous research protocols and Indigenous methodologies (Smith L. , 1999, p. 4).

Mutua and Swadener ask, Why "decolonizing research" and not "post-colonial research" "post (-) colonialism (with or without the hyphen) (Mutua, 2004, p. 255). They describe decolonisation as a concept that recognises the following:

i)   neo-colonialism, recognised as existing within decolonisation that supports a geo-economic hegemony, acknowledging a regeneration of other forms/means of coloniality, as articulated by Fanon (Fanon F. , 2001);

ii) the support for a geo-economic hegemony, where there is an uneasy relationship between the postcolonial scholar and the Western Academy to which many are beholden and dependent and where Western metropoles sustain and continue their oppression;

iii) Hybridity of 'Indigenous/Western' research methodologies that draw from and speak to both indigenous and Western ways of knowing and being. Authors have drawn on Bhabha (Bhabha, 1994), McCarthy (McCarthy, 1998) and Spivak (Spivak, 2003) in their discussion of hybridity;

iv) Border thinking as articulated by Mignolo (Mignolo W. , 2000) where decolonisation is embedded in border thinking. Border thinking is seen to be complementary to the 'double séance' within the experience and sensibilities of the coloniality of power; and

v)   Deconstruction as discussed by Mignolo (Mignolo W. , 2000) as complementary to decolonisation here a reforming of the field involves researchers actively decentring the Western Academy, the exclusive locus of authorising power defining research agendas. (Mutua, 2004, pp. 256-259).

How Do We Engage In Research?

The question remains how do we as Indigenous scholars engage in Eurocentric research, in research, if we so choose? Smith identifies 25 research projects being pursued by Indigenous communities which use approaches that have arisen from social science methodologies, others invited multi-disciplinary approaches yet others arose directly out of Indigenous practices (Smith L. , 1999, p. 142).

Denzin and Lincoln reflect on scholarship that will still be presented and judged from a positivist paradigm while there will be 'other scholarship travelling the margins and borders, searching for new and innovative forms through which to express non-Western modes of knowing and being in the world' (Lincoln, 2005, p. 1122). They refer to "The Rise of Indigenous Social Sciences" as an optional track and ask why "this generative spirit arise in social science at this particular moment in history?" (Lincoln, 2005, p. 1118). I find this labelling difficult. By adding the word 'Indigenous' in front of the words 'social sciences' does the essence of Indigenousness exist in the core of this concept or does a sense of Indigenousness, flavour the field of social science; a field evolved and structured within Western Knowledge, within the Brick Wall?

Butler-McIlwraith asks, "Is the centre willing to become more inclusive, or are Indigenous knowledges to remain the appendices to White thought?" (Butler-McIlwraith, 2006, p. 378). The question for me is will Indigenous Knowings continue to be subsumed within Eurocentrism, pulled under in that high tide of strong churning paradigms, research strategies, epistemologies, methodologies and analyses? This book with the conceptualisation and articulation of Lilyology is an attempt to move out of this framework in the smallest possible way.

Nakata suggests "a useful way to consider our [Aboriginal and Torres Strait Islanders] relationship to the corpus of knowledge circumscribed by Western systems of thought is that we need to know these systems so that we can position ourselves and engage with it in my own interests or on my own terms' (Nakata M. , 2004, p. 12). There is no doubt that 'we are in a new age where messy, uncertain, multivoiced texts, cultural criticism, and new experimental works will become more common, as will reflexive forms of fieldwork, analysis, and intertextual representation (Denzin, N. & Lincoln, Y.S. 2005, p.26).

Is this enough of a response, enough of an approach for us as Indigenous peoples? For some it will be. For others we will need to engage from a different perspective. We will need to operate from a point of difference; one that centres Indigenous Knowings and not Eurocentric Knowledges in the challenge that is research. I caution, this acknowledgement of difference is not a call for apartheid.

It involves Indigenous Knowings becoming the centre of our reflections, our research process; drawing on components of Western Knowledges as we see fit.

What I offer here is an array of perspectives and truths. These are not so much evaluated as recorded, as voiced, as placed in the centre to be heard and contemplated. I cannot signal a conclusion "but rather a punctuation in time that marks a stop merely to take a breath… (Lincoln, 2005, p. 1115). I cannot signal a conclusion as this is only one series of voices in the story told so far. There are many more voices yet to engage in this Story.

The following chapter extends the conversation about Indigenous peoples' place within research domains by further exploring the concept of 'Research', Indigenous peoples experience of research, Indigenous peoples models of research, the centring of Indigenous knowledge in research, Indigenous space and the Cultural Interface/Contested Space. It explores the tensions, contradictions and hesitations within the "messy new age". It explores my research process for the thesis and the conceptualisation of Lilyology.

The next chapter explores, it Storys the research journey for many Indigenous scholars. The challenges of working as an Indigenous scholar in a contested space that has defined, categorized, castigated and severely impacted on the daily lives of Indigenous peoples. This space created, evolved, harnessed by the bastion of colonization; The Academy, and its function of growing knowledge through the act of research. The next chapter is also the Story of colliding trajectories where two very different domains exist; the space in between.

3

CONNECTEDNESS

CONNECTEDNESS

TRAJECTORIES

TRAJECTORIES

ECHOES

COLLIDING

COUNTRY

TRADE CORAL

COLLIDING

COMMERCE

E FLOWS

COLLIDING

COLONISERS

DECOLONISATION

DECOLONISATION

COLLIDING

CHAPTER 3

Contested Space/Contesting Space: Indigenous Research Methodology

> Linguistic competence is a requisite for research in Indigenous issues. Indigenous researchers cannot rely on colonial languages and thought to define our reality. If we continue to define our reality in the terms and constructs drawn from Eurocentric diffusionism, we continue the pillages of our own selves (Battiste M. , 1996)

In this Story I endeavour not to continue the "pillages of our own selves" as identified by Battiste and Youngblood Henderson above. The very concept and construct 'research' is born from the colonisers' language. How do I conduct research as a 'researcher' in one of the bastions of colonisation; a university? What 'methodology" and 'philosophy' do I employ? With what voice do I speak?

Like Watson, who I referred to earlier as positing a challenge, I struggle with the correct voice to facilitate the voices of my Colleagues, I struggled with the correct space knowing I was doing a PhD dissertation for the Western Academy. Watson writes of her challenge within The Academy:

> Lately I have reflected on why and how I speak, and write and that is because I feel a pressure to perform. Why do I feel a pressure to perform, and in what context do I feel it? In this one. The pressure to locate myself within a space where the muldarbi[1] has been working for centuries in dismantling my Nunga[2] being. The risk of entering this space is to become assimilated by the muldarbi, the challenge is to survive and remain a Nunga. In writing this article I see myself as being engaged in a process of translation, rather than one of co-option in to the academic narrative...

---

[1] Meaning demon spirit (Watson I. , 1998, p. 28)
[2] Meaning a member of the Tanganekald People custodians of the Coorong (Watson I. , 1998, p. 28)

How much do I have to know or change about myself to make the communication happen? And once engaged in the process, how do I maintain the harmony and balance of still being me, as I engage in the process of communicating ideas, ideas that may or may not be received or even understood? So why do I even bother to speak (write) to this audience here now? Because the voice quite obviously needs to be heard. Because the voice of the grandmothers has been – being killed for so long. To speak in that voice is an act of survival and resistance to a long and continuing struggle, against the rape and murder of the mother [the land, earth, country] (Watson I. , 1998, p. 28).

I, like Watson will write in a voice that is mine. A voice which 'may be construed by others as being a bit preachy, a bit angry, a bit sad, a bit desperate, entirely soulfully spiritual, dogmatically creationist'. It is all of this and more, as I work towards a more 'perfect' place, a place that is still for me a long way off; that is the place where the grandmothers sit (Watson I. , 1998, p. 28).

I present this journey, my journey as an Indigenous academic attempting to "define our reality in the terms and constructs drawn from European diffusionism" (Battiste M. , 1996, p. 232). In this way, my voice, like Watson, is that of a translator, operating from within a different worldview and translating elements of this for the Western Academy. It is also that of a facilitator, a facilitator of my Colleagues' voices, Colleagues who engaged in this research process. As translator and facilitator I privilege my Indigenous worldview. My voice throughout this dissertation is personal, it engages with the issues I and others raise in ways that illustrate the tension between "the academic world and the everyday world of my participants" (Adler, 2004, p. 108).

I, like many Indigenous academics, cannot escape the ambiguity of my role as a researcher, colonised/coloniser (Fine, 1994, Villenas, 1996) (Mutua, 2004, p. 101). I acknowledge the kinship connections amongst each other as well as with this earth. I acknowledge where the 'grandmothers' and 'grandfathers' sit. I work towards finding a space and presenting an alternative model for Indigenous research methodology. I do this with great apprehension. I do this acknowledging that what I say in the space that is this text and what I did in the original 'field' research were not completely compatible. I am working towards a space where Indigenous worldviews sit comfortably, where they are centred and strong, as do other Indigenous researchers identified by Mutua & Swadener (2004, p.11).

The research methodology and the research philosophy for the research that has evolved this book are evolving. They are an attempt to 'inscribe a new language of research' (Mutua & Swadener, 2004, p.11). The research philosophy and methodology are based on important constructs of Indigenous Knowing, Indigenous knowledge. It is based on being experiential, on the 'doing' and on 'tellin' me and showin' me'. This chapter was conceived and is presented without a centralised western framework. It exists within a centralised Indigenous framework. It is my attempt to struggle to "dis-encrypt discourses underpinned by investigatory research that has sustained colonial oppression" Mutua & Swadener (2004, p.11).

If, as this Story asserts, Indigenous peoples' sense of Knowing is different to non-Indigenous peoples then our knowledge, our thinking, the very concept of research is problematic. Indigenous research methodology is a major component of international Indigenous discourse and indeed the qualitative research agenda (Denzin, N. & Lincoln, Y.S. 2005). It is my intent to present an exploration of Indigenous research methodology not as the major content of this book but as an inter-related and critical part of my research process and intent.

Indigenous peoples' experiences of research are fundamental to any understanding of the concept and process of research as well as to any development and use of research methodology. This chapter presents findings from a research project entitled 'Researched to Death'. As Nakata (Nakata M. , 2007, p. 197) states "if the assumptions underpinning a new theoretical framework were to take more account of Islander experience then more useful theories of the Islander position can be generated ... rather than an analysis of the Islander position entangled in the Western order of things". This research listens to Indigenous voices and their feelings and experiences about research. These voices are like the waves constantly rolling in to shore. They inform and shape the perceptions.

I do not believe that we can separate research process from research philosophy. Hence the format of this chapter, and indeed the book, that is, an integration and interplay of a series of voices: community people' voices, Indigenous and non-Indigenous academic voices. In redefining what research is for Indigenous peoples some Indigenous researchers speak of an Indigenous Research Methodology, they speak of an Indigenous research agenda.

The Indigenous research agenda, as articulated by Indigenous researchers, (refer to Figure 3.1) is: overtly political (Brady, 1992), (Battiste M. , 1996), (Rigney, 1997), (Smith L. , 1999); highly emotive; about changing and improving conditions; and, concerned with the survival of Indigenous peoples, languages, lands and cultures. People articulating the purpose and activities of research must be strategic. The approach is critical of non-Indigenous world views of

Indigenous peoples and cultures. It is informed by an analysis of imperialism and colonialism; of what it has meant and what it means to be colonised (Battiste M. , 1996), (Smith L. , 1999), (Moreton-Robinson A. , 1998). It is concerned with social change and emancipatory outcomes for Indigenous peoples (Rigney, 1997), (Smith L. , 1999) . It is concerned with self-determination and liberation. It is concerned with a new linguistic competence, a new language. On their own these features may not be unique. Collectively they may not be unique. These features represent an Indigenous Research agenda, one which is evolving moment by moment.

This chapter asserts that by centring Indigenous voices and Indigenous worldviews a distinct Indigenous Philosophy is clearly seen to exist; one that demands different processes. Embedding and centring Indigenous worldviews allows us to frame our research to enable our voices and to deliver tangible outcomes to our communities. Knowing is dependent upon ontology and epistemology. My assertion is that where the epistemology and ontology are different, that is at its core, the very concept and its constructs are different and the production (using a very Western concept) of knowledge is different.

This chapter explores the following themes:

- Concept of 'Research'
- Indigenous peoples' experience of research
- My model of research: a philosophical foundation - Lilyology
- Centring Indigenous Knowledge in research
- Cultural Interface: contested spaces

CONCEPT OF 'RESEARCH'

The Eurocentric concept of research (Denzin, N. & Lincoln, Y.S. 2005). I could argue has no basis in Indigenous Knowing, Indigenous languages. However, when asking my Colleagues in Desert community if such a concept exists they identified 'Nyindirrum Inkyjuk'. They identified this as people sitting down, sitting around, telling and sharing Storys. Drawing on Battiste "Indigenous researchers cannot rely on colonial languages and thought to define our reality", I choose to position this notion and the concept Nyindirrum Inkyjuk in the evolution of my framework.

INDIGENOUS PEOPLES' EXPERIENCES OF RESEARCH: AUSTRALIA

> Every time research is done a piece of my culture is …erased (transcript
> from a yarn with an Indigenous woman in community #3).

Indigenous peoples in Australia are actively engaging in research in ways never before seen. Indigenous voices are centring themselves in the research process and in the Storys told. This position is the result of over two centuries of research that has defined, categorised and castigated us as peoples. Storytellers such as Darwin (Smith L. , 1999, p. 62) , (Arbon, 2008, pp.94-96), Haddon (Nakata M. , 2007, p. 228) , social philosophers like Spencer (Spencer, 1896) , eugenicists such as Galton (Arbon, 2008, p.95), Spearman (Spearman, 1923), and (Spearman, 1927) , Pearson (Pearson, 1991) , Binet (Binet, 1980), Connell , Elkin (Elkin, 1977) , Tindale (Tindale, 1974) and Threlkeld (Threlkeld, 1974) , to mention a few, have laid the foundations for the stories told about us as Indigenous peoples. Darwin's stories, told of 'the survival of the fittest' used to explain the evolution of the species in the natural world and translated into the human world, where it became a powerful belief that Indigenous peoples were inherently weak and therefore at some point would die out (Smith L. , 1999, p. 62); Haddon & Spencer's stories reported scientific findings on the daily lives of the Torres Strait Islanders 'embedding the Islanders in an evolutionary history' inscribing a particular and already prescribed relation with European and characterising the 'savage mind of Islander peoples' (Nakata M. , 2007, p. 30); Connell's stories ignore the place of Indigenous peoples in sociology in Australia (Butler-McIlwraith, 2006); Elkin's stories prescribe Aboriginal customs, rituals and religious practices (Elkin, 1977) and Threlkeld's stories fabricate cultural practice, cultural being by linking languages to customs adding words to the Awabakal language for servant, landlord – concepts that did not exist in Awabakal practice (Threlkeld, 1974). Spearman, Pearson and Binet all ascribe levels of intelligence in their stories; specifically a lack thereof in Indigenous peoples. The disciplines of anthropology, linguistics, sociology, phrenology, ethnography and biology are amongst many to have framed the stories which have and which continue to impact on the daily lives of Indigenous peoples in Australia today.

Many Indigenous peoples will no longer passively and politely comply with existing research methodology. Too much of ourselves has already been erased. Denzin and Lincoln identify that "Indigenous peoples were subjected to the indignities of both approaches (qualitative and quantitative research); each approach used in the name of colonizing powers". Further, they state that "qualitative research serves as a metaphor for colonial knowledge, for power and for truth" (Denzin, N. & Lincoln, Y.S. 2005. p.1).

'Researched to Death', research funded by the Australian Research Council identified an overwhelming degree of cynicism amongst Indigenous community peoples about the concept and experience of research. Sixty-five Indigenous people (25 male and 40 female) were interviewed in four communities: two communities in Western Australia (communities #2 and #3) and two communities in NSW (communities #1 and #4). The following table presents information about participant genders, locations and numbers.

		Number of Participants		Total Numbers
		Male	Female	
Community #1	NSW	3	10	13
Community #2	WA	5	9	14
Community #3	WA	10	11	21
Community #4	NSW	7	10	17
Totals		**25**	**40**	**65**

Figure 3.1. Participant Backgrounds in 'Researched to Death' Project

Participants in each of the identified communities were from the arts, performance, education, health, legal service, community development, women's groups, child care, employment, Aboriginal and Torres Strait Islander Commission, community welfare and included Elders and youth where possible.

Yarning and reflection were employed as the research process. A number of 'yarn times' (Hanlen, 2007) were conducted with Indigenous peoples in groups and individually. Using 'yarn times' the researcher sets the scene by providing information about background and the reasons for conducting the research. They then introduce a topic for discussion and allow participants to use narratives and storytelling to explore the topic. Yarning has become a research method grounded in Indigenous epistemologies (Bessarab & Ng'andu, 2010). It therefore requires connectedness and relatedness allowing then for deeper dialogue and deeper learning (Davis 2012 p.169-170). Yarning has no beginning and no end and is not a process in search of a right answer. It is a process engaging deep listening with thematic ideas engaging and prompting the yarn where necessary.

In this instance the topic for discussion was introduced in the form of an open-ended question:

When you hear the word 'research' what do you think about?

Various prompts were used when needed including:

1. In your own words what do you think research means?
2. What do you feel when you hear the word research?
3. If you had to tell other people about research and what it is what would you tell them?
4. When people come in to this community and say they are going to do research what do you think?
5. How do you feel when someone says they are going to do research in your community?
6. Have many people come in to this community saying they are going to do research?
7. When people have come in to this community to do research have you been involved with them and the research? If so, how?
8. What are your reflections of what happened?
9. What stories can you tell about that research?
10. What do you think is important when people do research with Aboriginal people? What should researchers remember when they do research in our communities?

Participants were shown a diagrammatic model of research; one that evolved from my analysis of the literature on Indigenous research methodology. Participants were then asked:

When you look at a model like this how do you react? How do you feel?

Do you have any other ideas?

Participants were asked if they would like to draw their own models. None of the participants took up this option. There was general interest in the idea of drawing models but people's scepticism and cynicism as well as the limited timeframe imposed by the funding authorities contributed to the lack of follow-through; here, I acknowledge is one of the flaws I experienced in conducting this research in the most appropriate way. I have grown my practice and my theory.

Overall Indigenous peoples voiced a number of concerns including:

i)   feedback from researchers, specifically the lack thereof;
ii)   researchers' personal agendas;
iii)   researchers' interpretation of participants voices and views;
iv)   lack of tangible outcomes for Indigenous communities;
v)   questions researchers pose;
vi)   researchers' time-frames versus Indigenous participants and their community time-frames;
vii)   exploitation of Indigenous peoples through research;
viii) theft of Indigenous knowledge and the need for the protection of intellectual property;
ix)   need for ethics in the research process that go beyond the rhetoric of ethics applications and are enforced in and by communities;
x)   need for greater collaboration;
xi)   need to explain the process to participants; and,
xii)   the need for a re-conceptualisation of 'research' as people currently understand it.

In essence Indigenous peoples in the communities involved in the above mentioned research expressed irritation, anger, and frustration as researchers; Indigenous and non-Indigenous, conducted research in their communities but rarely provided any feedback about the project at any stage of the research. It was extremely rare for people to receive a final product let alone any progress reports, update newsletters or workshops briefing people during the life of the research.

People identified the fact that researchers came to communities with a research question already developed and the way they conducted the research was dependent on the outcomes people already had in their mind. Researchers agendas were also perceived as being 'fixed' by funding constraints, times and desired outcomes. Peoples in the communities visited, identified that though researchers were doing research for the benefit of the community they were involved in, they already had outcomes in mind, agendas for conducting the research. The biggest comment here related to scholars conducting research in communities for PhD's; perceived as an immediate personal gratification that communities stated had no tangible benefits for them. Peoples also expressed the fact that many academics have made their names from 'black research'; publishing papers and books that the community never see or hear about.

As a result of such fixed agendas researchers posed insensitive and often rude and exploitative questions that have offended many people, for example; Does your man come home and bash you? When you fight do you bite, scratch, hit or pinch? (transcript from a yarn with an Indigenous woman in community #1). The comment 'shame' on that person 'how can they ask us such a question' was made by many participants.

People expressed the feeling that researchers having conducted the research return home and write the research up the way they want it written up. Rarely are transcripts returned for people to comment and if they are they are not in a form people can make any sense of. As a result the researcher interprets things through their own cultural lens, quite often missing a specific nuance of subtle but great importance. Researchers' interpretation of participants voices and views has in the eyes of those yarned with completely castigated them and disassociated them from the process and the findings. Quite often people said what is written up is just wrong and we don't know how they arrived at what they did...that is if people know what the outcome or report said.

Research is generally always conducted under tight time-frames and this rarely if ever meets community needs. Researchers push on regardless and say they have consulted, according to many participants. I remember conducting some research in a very remote location in Western Australia; this involved travelling 7,000 kilometres of very rough terrain in parts. Organising such travel through a bureaucratic structure was an extreme activity with the need to buy low cost airfares which could not be cancelled or changed, car hire etc. On three occasions the trip was cancelled; on one occasion the day before for Sorry business, on another occasion two days before because of a sports carnival and on another occasion 'just because'. When I finally arrived in the community I was warmly greeted and by the next morning I knew I had to leave straight away as ceremony business had begun. I did leave. Participants told me over and over again however that if researchers were told they could not come they generally still came and expected people to be there for them. Researchers, as we heard on every occasion also committed to one or two hours of direct research activity; fly in and fly out as quickly as possible, not spend time in the community, seeing it, hearing it, engaging with it.

People spoke about the theft of Indigenous cultural knowledge and the need for proper ethics. This is discussed later in the book in more detail (in Chapter 4). At this point I emphasise the intense feeling associated with such practice and lack of practice in the research process. People spoke about the need for greater collaboration in any research process and this is one area where this is possible. I have engaged my own local community and others I have worked in the development of an ethics process for the organisations in the community. In doing this the whole research process became known. People spoke about the lack of understanding about western research process, practice. They said they often just went along and 'gamon'/pretended they knew but no one really sat down and talked the process, talked it over time. If this were done more often Indigenous peoples would not need to feel as exploited as they have said they do. Ultimately, a re-conceptualisation of the research process would facilitate this as well; reconceptualising it by centring Indigenous Knowing as this book argues.

Some of the issues identified above are articulated in people's own words in an article in press with the International Review of Qualitative Research (Blair, 2015). They tell of poignant and gut-wrenching storys about research. The 'Researched to Death' project found that Indigenous peoples conceptualised the word and experience of 'research' in extremely negative, graphic and emotional terminology. In this article people's voices are presented as they were presented to me. The power of the experience is in the rawness of the voices not in my translation or interpretation. For example "If you want to make something dead ...research it (transcript from a yarn with an Indigenous male in community #4)!

TALKIN' UP RESEARCH

Indigenous scholars globally story how problematic research is for Indigenous peoples. From Australian shores Nakata (2007) with Indigenous Standpoint theory, Arbon (2008) with Arlathirnda Ngurkarnda Ityirnda (Being-Knowing-Doing) Martin (2008) Storys Quandamoopah, Moreton-Robinson (1998) acknowledges 'when the object speaks', and Irabinna Rigney 1997) enunciates Indigenist research. In Aoteoroa Smith (1999), and Bishop, R (2005) journey the Story through decolonization and Kaupapa Maori with Meyer (2001) and Trask (1993), engaging with Hawaiian Storying. In Canada and North America, Battiste (1996) Cajete (2000), Kovach (2010), Four Arrows (2008), Wilson (2008), Grande (2004) have amongst others opened the discourse that asserts Indigenous voices and frames of reference to research process offering alternatives to those articulated in the academy. These scholars have articulated how research involves an emotional rollercoaster journey, savours of humiliation, depression, anger, pain, outrage, guilt and anxiety. It is not simply an intellectual process. It conveys deep cynicism and suspicion. The concept of research elaborates histories of encounters between Indigenous peoples and researchers embedded in the story of imperialism and colonialism. Indigenous peoples until recently have always been 'the research'. We have been measured, judged and treated as the 'object', the 'subject' of research – the 'other'(Smith, 1999, p. 1).

Research involving Indigenous peoples and communities has been and continues to be 'methodologically flawed with multiple forms of cognitive imperialism' (Battiste, 1996). Racist practices and attitudes, ethnocentric assumptions and exploitative research have been integral to the conduct of traditional research involving Indigenous peoples and concerns; indeed to the research methodologies deployed (Tuhiwai Smith, 1999) resulting in a racialised research industry (Irabinna Rigney, 1997) which supports product-driven research (Battiste 1996).

Clearly many Indigenous scholars and community peoples have had and continue to have research experiences that leave us empty, void of spirit. We also note the benefits non-Indigenous scholars have gained from using us. The intensity of peoples' reactions cannot, and should not, be understated. Very little has been written about Indigenous peoples' experiences or feelings without it being labelled too emotional and subjective.

Indigenous people's experiences of research have overwhelmingly been negative whether this be personal or in the construction of our identity as peoples during and post colonisation: the 'noble savage', the 'ignoble savage', primitive, barbaric, and 'the other'. It is no longer appropriate for methodology deployed by Eurocentric researchers to be used to plant "real people and places in the imaginary gardens of anthropological texts (academic products)" (Behar, 1995, p. 10).

MY MODEL OF RESEARCH: A PHILOSOPHICAL FOUNDATION - LILYOLOGY

> In any consideration, we [Indigenous Australians] are not 'Other'. We are at the center of our own lives and our own history, and we need to give primacy to that position. We stand in relation to the mainstream but we do not have to view that relationship as secondary to it, as it has been inscribed in the corpus of Western Disciplines (Nakata M. , 2001, p. 115).

In an endeavour to picture Nakata's statement and conceptualise Indigenous research as inscribed in the corpus of western disciplines, I crafted the following images: Figures 3.2, 3.3 and 3.4. The web site page illustrates in a less linear way what these static images represent here. Figure 3.2 portrays research as a Brick

Wall comprising many different disciplines within The Academy. The clay that is fashioned into bricks comes from the earth and we often see a blend of different pigments in the bricks themselves. The bricks are laid in lines where they exist as separate entities, separate units, representing Disciplines of knowledge, theories and methodologies.

Qualitative Research : Quantitative Research Methods & Practices : Paradigms & Philosophies		
Post colonialism	Critical race theory	Feminism
Archival	Ethnomethodology	Grounded theory
Anthropology	Cultural Studies	Marxism
Clinical	Psychoanalysis	Decolonisation
Hermeneutics	Ethnography	Narrative
Survey	Action Research	Rhizomatics
P.C.T.	Participants Observation	Oral History
Focus Groups	Questionnaire	Interviews
Positivism	Foundationalism	Post structuralism

Figure 3.2. Brick Wall – Western Research Paradigms and Philosophies

The mortar holding the bricks of the wall together equates to Western knowledge. The brick makers are the scholars within The Academy. Each brick embodies a different research paradigm/philosophy and research strategy/method evolving from both qualitative and quantitative research. The notion of separate bricks embodies the concept of categorised knowledge disciplines where the concept of interdisciplinary and/or multidisciplinary thinking is much more rhetoric that reality in The Academy. The notion dates back to Aristotle as a founding father of western philosophy when knowledge became segmented and categorised in a linear fashion. Some of the 'paradigm bricks' are coloured differently as they embedded Indigenous perspectives in their research: 'Bricks' such as post colonialism, critical race theory, anthropology, feminism, grounded theory, action research, cultural studies, phenomenology. Some of the 'strategy bricks' are tinted as they find greater use in the research field; bricks such as participant observation, oral history, focus groups and interviews. In the construction of a Brick Wall the bricks are laid on top of the earth, forcibly dug into the earth. They are laid with hierarchy in mind; some disciplines have more validity than others.

A wall has the capacity to block things; to block ideas. It has the capacity to enforce boundaries. We can 'hit our heads against the Brick Wall' when we appear to be or to feel as if we are going nowhere, feeling frustrated as if we are stagnant. Walls equate with boundaries and in Australia through colonisation, Terra Nullius became law. The British invaders saw no fences, no Brick Walls and assumed that because Aboriginal people had no boundaries or territory, they assumed we did not exist.

Figure 3.3. Indigenous Knowings

Standing in relation to the Research Wall is Indigenous Knowings; represented as a circle with a bush potato centre (Figure 3.3). Here Knowings are holistic and circular. They have a nourishing core that feeds Storys and Knowings and which radiates both inwards and outwards from the centre and the periphery. A Story is told. It is told again by another custodian who has the authority to add new information. The process continues. Western research philosophies such as hermeneutics tell Story, Story that builds on Story but they do this from a different epistemological centre; a western centre or knowledge base.

Currently research can best be illustrated as a process whereby research centres western philosophy and knowledge, western paradigms and strategies. The researcher uses bricks from the wall as appropriate to build their centre, their research methodology/method, as illustrated in Figure 3.4. When doing research into Indigenous issues and/or with Indigenous peoples, researchers tend to look to the Indigenous knowledge circle and then suck excerpts, extracts of Knowings in to the Brick Wall like a vacuum. This Knowing never returns. For example if a researcher is investigating diabetes in Aboriginal communities they will look to the Brick Wall for the right bricks then some may think we should ask Aboriginal people what they think. Some may go as far as to think about Aboriginal Knowings of diabetes and look to this, extracting information from people to be later used in a different context without knowledge to those who have shared the information – Trading the Other. As Nakata states above, we are at the centre of our own lives and history. The image just presented does not centre Indigenous Knowings. One way to do this is pictured in Figure 3.4 below:

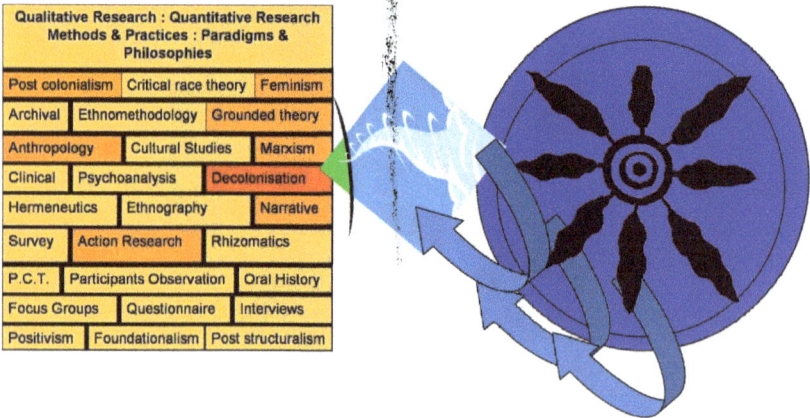

Figure 3.4. Current Western Research Process: Indigenous Knowings, Issues and Peoples

Figure 3.5 illustrates centring Indigenous Knowing. Where Indigenous researchers, look to the Research Wall and identify elements of the bricks that may apply to our research journey. In doing this we draw on the elements of the Knowledge contained within the Brick Wall as we choose. We do not centre Western Knowledge and philosophy. At the centre is Indigenous Knowing. For example if the researcher is investigating diabetes in Aboriginal communities they speak to Elders and those that Know about living in Country then use this information to identify the bricks from the Wall of most relevance to them.

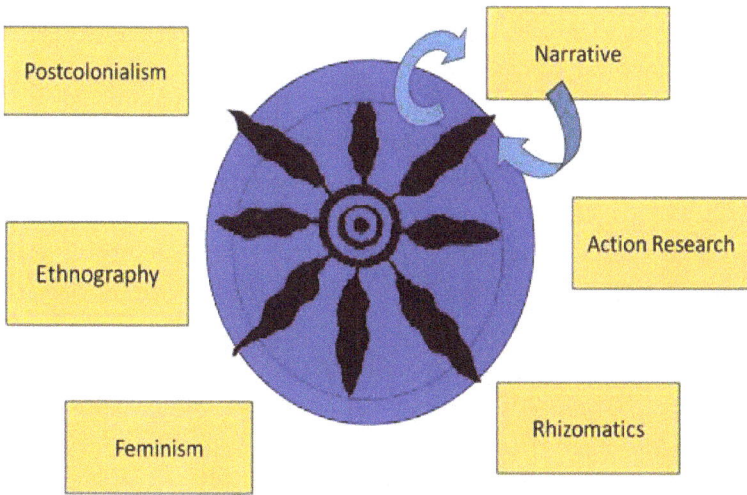

Figure 3.5. My Original Preferred Model of Indigenous Research Methodology

Currently we as Indigenous researchers sit uncomfortably in the domain that centers Western knowledge and philosophies. We feel that we must validate our research using western research bricks.

In the process of doing this research many conceptual images have evolved. I do not speak my Indigenous language. Up until this journey I have felt I only speak the language of the colonisers. I do not want to continue the "pillages of our own selves" in using the coloniser's language (Battiste M. , 1996). I discuss this further in Chapter 6 as depicting the linear part of my journey; its evolution of thought. How then do I construct meaning as an Indigenous researcher? Kelly (Kelly R. , 2006) speaking at a university graduation ceremony said we all have a language, it is English, and we bring our own selves to this language. This is a significant assertion. We not only speak English words, we come to the language from a conceptually different ontology and epistemology. For example, Aboriginal languages in Australia have different concepts of numbers with a sense of little bit, big bit – no sense of a hierarchy of numbers.

Hanlen (Hanlen, 2007) explores inspirational and environmental literacies as significant in our Knowings as Indigenous peoples. Inspirational literacies 'involve the transference of the meaning of thoughts regarding practices, ideas, records of events, messages, warnings, educational information and directions into tangible, decontextualised forms' (Hanlen, W. 2007, pp.233). Environmental literacies on the other hand are the 'knowledge and understandings that people use to read and interpret the natural world including reading the stars, sun and moon, seasons and the environment for food, water, shelter and weather. These are articulated through body language; landmarks; tracks or markings in the sand, dirt and bush and recognition of flora and fauna to use for specific needs (e.g. medicine, food, shelter, canoe and tool-making and so on)' (Hanlen, 2002b).

It is clear that colonial language and thought, as we currently express them, do not and can never do justice to Indigenous languages and thoughts. As contemporary Indigenous researchers, we must re-identify our centre, our languages. We must rename them. I do not believe we have effectively done this yet. This conversation is one that has evolved personally and critically for me throughout the research journey.

I speak English and do not know my own language which is being 're-vitalised.' For this research I drew on inspirational literacies specifically, images and symbols to help me think through, to reflect on and to re-present ideas. I drew on my experiences with mind maps in the first instance to assist me. I then evolved my own images and symbols namely the Brick Wall and the Lily, spiders and sweet potatoes. What evolved next was an individual symbol/image drawn from the environment to explain my research process (in Chapter Four) which emerged from a series of experiences with my Colleagues. Before presenting this I need to continue the story of my PhD research journey to highlight the tensions that arose.

As an Indigenous woman living a privileged life in an urban environment do I even have a dilemma? A woman who some would vehemently argue has 'no culture'. Quite simply, yes I have dilemma. Like many Indigenous peoples today I am 'attempting to decolonize my work and deconstruct my personal/professional experiences' (Mutua K. S., 2004, p. 1).

The reading and structure prescribed for my PhD were not working for me. Doing research method reading, determining method, doing a literature review and determining my research framework and research issues, before engaging with research, engaging with the people was and remains contradictory for me as an Indigenous researcher. Doing research this way was stifling, creating a pungent, stagnant body of water in which nothing bloomed, nothing grew, little could move or see. Western writers call this 'hitting the wall' or 'having a mental block'. It was much more than this as I struggled with the translation of process and the core and essence of the structure of the research and the thesis itself. It became a process of juggling, juxtaposing a multitude of pieces including thoughts, experiences, people's voices, Country relationships, relationships, the doings, and images seen and collected.

My PhD began with an attraction, a magnetic attraction to the concept of mind mapping (Buzan T. , 1997). Buzan created mind maps to connect, to reflect more of how the brain functions in a holistic, linear plus non-linear way. A way that uses all of the senses. I connected to mind mapping, to radiant thinking, to images, rhythm and sense of place. This was the first image, experience, doing, thought associated with the thesis. Next I drew parallels with the many forms of Indigenous art. A visit to the Papunya Tula exhibition in Sydney during the year 2000 strengthened by vision, my thinking. Art that in many situations has a story, has a meaning and has a series of connected nodes much like a bush or sweet potato as it grows in the ground. Much like a mind map. The mind map however is a construct of a western philosophical mind. My next step was to seek connections if in fact they existed.

To illustrate my point I present three early mind maps developed when I was conceptualising the meaning of human rights, as articulated by Indigenous peoples from over 100 communities throughout Australia, and a process for training people in human rights (Figure 3.6).

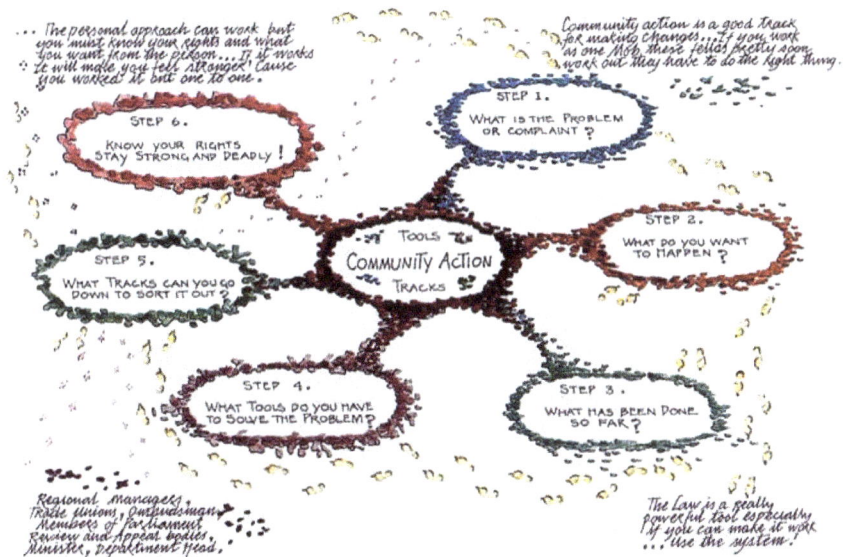

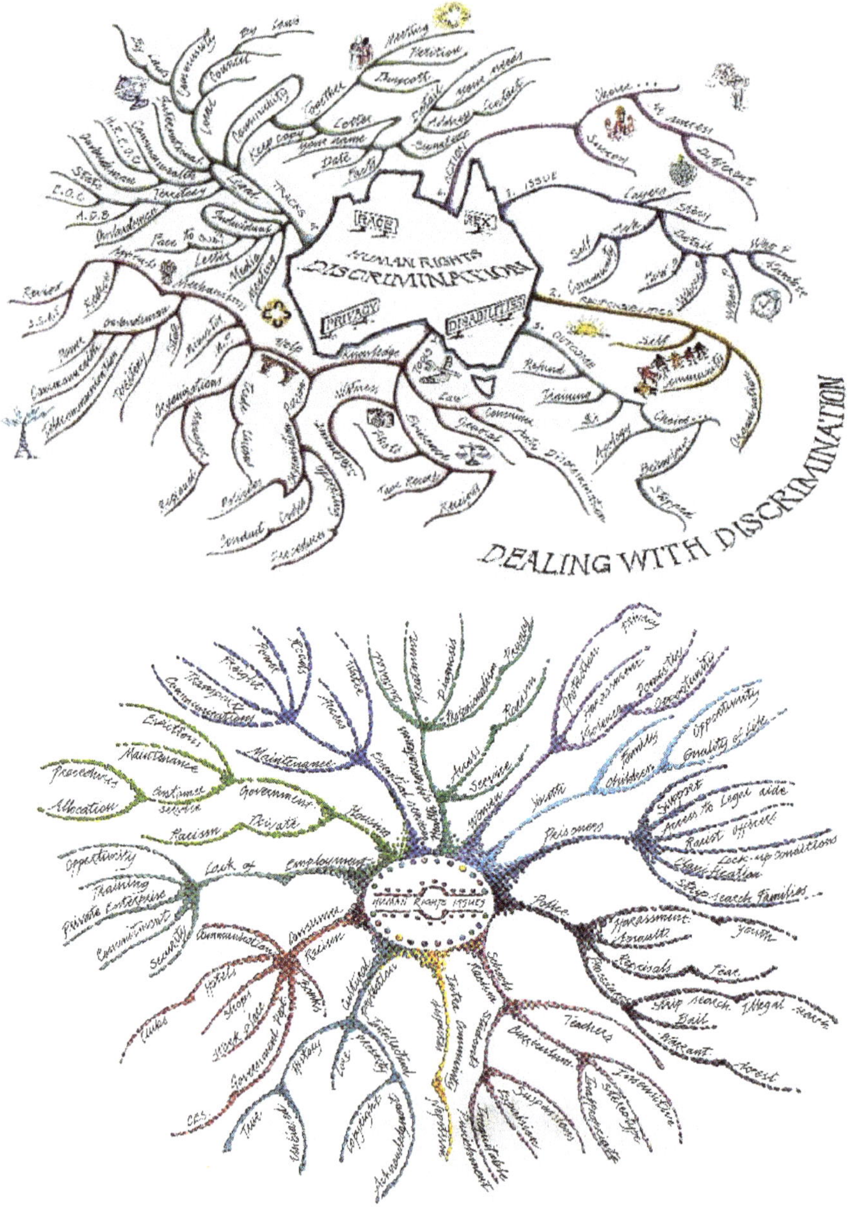

Figure 3.6. Mind Maps on Dealing with Discrimination and Human Rights. Acknowledge Hugh Ryvers Ellicot for his artistic translation of my drawings

It is not important to know or see the detail. View the map from above, see the series of connected nodes rooted in a central idea. Notice the flow, the movement, the capacity for growth of ideas, the interconnections and interrelationships between ideas and between movement – the space between the notes; the space where music can only exist if space does exist between the notes. These images are not directly related to this research; they serve as an illustration of my own thought processes and ways of dealing with information in what I clearly see is contested space. These images illustrate the use of mind maps in my thinking process.

A mind map has a nourishing core that expresses radiant thinking. It is organic, rooted in a central idea. Mind maps embody rhythm, dimension, pattern, colour, metaphor and story. Mind maps are non-linear and they focus on images, symbols as well as words if desired and/or appropriate. Whilst mind maps are a Eurocentric construct, they embody significant elements of Indigenous thought/thinking, allowing people who are victims of linear schooling the freedom to re-construct their own vision in their own ways. Mind maps become a bridge back to 'validation' and experience of Indigenous Knowings. Take your mind back to Alison's Story from Chapter 1; a classic illustration of the power of mind mapping as a tool to deconstruct. The notion of mind mapping and its relevance to my research journey is discussed further in Chapters Five and Six.

I found as a result of my journey, and as a part of the associated process, a series of images evolved. As Buzan himself states his first language is not English it is a language of images (personal communication, Melbourne, 2008). These images have given greater meaning to each individual piece than if it were to exist on its own. What are the bits, the pieces? The use of mind maps, the experiences with people discussing decolonisation and mind maps, as described in the story above, has helped me to decolonise my own thought processes and to understand my personal confusion and anxiety in communicating across two cultural ways of Knowing. This has made me look for new ways to position and express myself as an Indigenous person engaged in research. I am not alone in this process as described and illustrated below through the differing models presented.

LILYOLOGY

Lilyology emerged after playing with all of these Knowings, after my Storying with research colleagues, after reading and engaging with other scholars in the field, after producing a PhD dissertation and finally after practising and doing and reflecting. Lilyology showcases Waterlilys which are grounded in Country: water Country, connecting and relating through rhizomes, deep in a subterranean world. The Waterlilys and all of its components in this metaphor are our ontologies, our spiritualities. The rhizomes are both the storage and the carriers of nourishment and growth, much like the rich sources of carbohydrates they provide in biological terms. They skim the surface looking for light and where found new roots cascade from the rhizomes in web-like arrangements and complexities. Rhizomes metaphorically represent Spirit Knowings embedded in different 'Countrys'; the different waterways Waterlilys exist within. The rhizomes hold the Spirit Knowings, the nutrients. These are the Storys, the wisdom that guides our ontologies.

From the rhizomes emerge a Waterlily which has a strong slender stem representing in Lilyology, Indigenous Knowings. The wide, flat leaves attached to the stem and that float on top of the water, here represent the many voices that are Indigenous Knowings; human, animal and spirit. In this context these are the voices of those of us articulating Indigenous ontologies, Indigenous theories.

As we move up the stem and beyond the leaves we find a flower which represents the 'storying' through many different genres. The flower has petals which are not homogenous and which overlap each other like the many Storys our Knowing presents. The petals are what is visible, the different expressions of Indigenous Knowings; inspirational and environmental literacies (Hanlen, 2007). Inspirational literacies 'involve the transference of the meaning of thoughts regarding practices, ideas, records of events, messages, warnings, educational information and directions into tangible, decontextualised forms' (Hanlen, W. 2007, pp.233). Environmental literacies on the other hand are the 'knowledge and understandings that people use to read and interpret the natural world including reading the stars, sun and moon, seasons and the environment for food, water, shelter and weather. These are articulated through body language; landmarks; tracks or markings in the sand, dirt and bush and recognition of flora and fauna to use for specific needs (e.g. medicine, food, shelter, canoe and tool-making and so on)' (Hanlen, 2002b).

As we move further into the lily flower and we find a stamen that holds elements of the petals together. It holds what is visible together, the visible expressions of our Storys. The stamen regenerates life. There are many different Waterlilys, as there are many different Indigenous Knowings. 'Every element of the Waterlily is connected and dependent on each other for growth and sustenance, for generation. Every element is connected to Country in its broadest sense the ecological environment; water, land, soil, air, sun, light, dark, atmosphere' (Blair, in press). Goldsmith (1995) from the Indigenous environment network (USA) highlights this in his definition of LAWS as 'being keyed elementally and thus concerned with the basis of all life – LAWS – meaning Land, Air, Water, Sun'.

Spiders weave fine, strong transparent webs connecting across colliding trajectories where vibrations are felt from one end to the other. Webs that pattern and connect. A spider Knows when an insect, an intruder is hitting it and whether it is safe to approach. The spider also Knows, by the vibrations, if there is something out there that is caught which is dangerous. So it knows not to go near it, or to circle around it, and hope it breaks free. In this way the spider doesn't get himself killed by the rough actions of whatever it is that he has caught in his web. It is the same with us. We have to learn to feel the vibrations. And we can feel that with each other ... We should tune ourselves to that. (Randall, 2003, pp. 16-20).

Sweet Potatoes, are the rhizomes patterning and connecting Spirit Knowings which are grounded in Country; above and below the earth in water. Sweet potatoes radiate from a central nourishing core; one that sustains, energises and provides the nourishment necessary for growth.

Lilyology it is not just the Waterlily, it does not exist without a further context. In Lilyology rightly or wrongly it exists in relation to a Western context; that metaphored and Storyd as the Brick Wall, the Academy Figure 3.7 below.

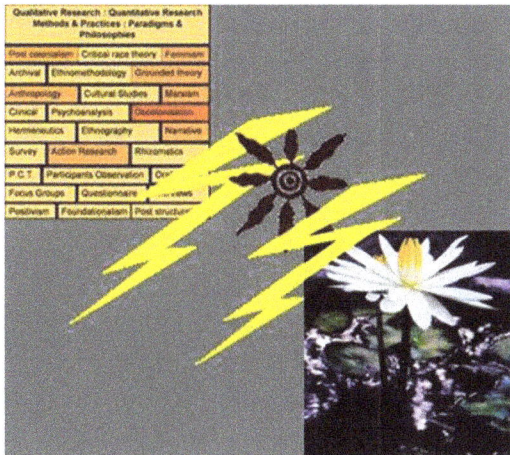

Fig. 3.7. Lilyology

CENTRING INDIGENOUS KNOWING IN RESEARCH

There is a new language of research evolving where we as Indigenous peoples are actively positioning our voices, our Knowing. There are commonalities. There are differences. Each stands grounded in its own Knowing and on its own right. I present and describe some of this new language in the next sequence of this chapter. I do this not to critique, as that would be inappropriate for me as an Indigenous woman to critique another Indigenous persons Knowing, someone from other Country.

I do this to illustrate the growing representations of Indigenous Knowings and Indigenous research methodologies. This is an emerging global discourse which cannot be overlooked, sidelined as 'primitive', insignificant or peripheral. I do this to project and privilege Indigenous Knowings. Clearly, "a quiet methodological revolution has been occurring; a blurring of disciplinary boundaries" (Denzin, N. & Lincoln, Y.S. 2005. p.ix). Privileging Indigenous Knowings goes beyond a blurring in the production of knowledge disciplines. Indigenous Knowings is holistic (this will be developed further in Chapter Five).

What is interesting across all of the models presented, is a form and sense that is localised, visual and organic. Some explore Indigenous Knowings, Indigenous knowledge. Others explore our position in Indigenous research. All are linked as we cannot evolve Indigenous research without Indigenous Knowings; we must know ourselves and our philosophies if we accept that in this contemporary world, western thinking views research as a concept and process that evolves knowledge.

The models presented evolved from Australia, Aotearoa, Canada, United States of America, Africa and Central and South America. From Australia I present Kanyini and Tjukurrpa, Garma[3], Indigenist research, Dadirri, Indigenous Standpoint Theory, the Japanangka Paradigm, Pattern and Triangle Thinking, Arlathirnda Ngurkarnda Ityirnda, Quandamoopah and The Knowledge Dreaming Model. From Aoteoroa the research paradigm, Kaupapa Maori, Rangihau's conceptual model of Maoritanga and Ka'ai's Maori worldview model. The Koru as an organising principle for thinking is identified as a model from the South Pacific. Pagtatanong-tanong identified as an Indigenous research method in Philippine social science is described. Hampton's 6 directional pattern which explores connectedness is drawn from Canada. The conceptualisation of research methodology as a rubber sheet for educational research conducted in Ghana is described. Mestizaje, from South American writing is presented. Navajo conceptual framework of self-determination from the United States of America. Research as Ceremony from Canada and Australia. Red Pedagogy, (Grande,S., 2008) and Tribal Crit (Brayboy, 2005) emerge from the United States of America. These representations are of course limited in number by the time available to

---

[3] Garma also spelt Ganma, Gaarma.

research and collate material for the original thesis. Clearly, however, there is an increasing, organic and stimulating discourse emerging amongst Indigenous thinkers and educators – a 'quiet methodological revolution'.

Chapter Five will further elaborate on some of the issues raised in the models as well as explore some models outside of the context of a discourse on research.

I believe that underpinning each of the models presented is what Mowaljarli (Stockton, 1995, pp. 42-43) describes as pattern thinking:

> Pattern thinking is Aboriginal thinking. There is no big boss. Patterns are about belonging. Nothing is separate from anything else. This land is not separate from nature, people, the heavens, and ancient stories. Everything belongs in the pattern. There is no 'ownership' in pattern-thinking. Only Belonging. Money cannot buy bits of a pattern. Power runs all through a pattern. It cannot be sold. It is not separate from the pattern.

AUSTRALIAN THINKING AND MODELLING

In terms of Indigenous Knowings, Indigenous Australians such as Randall (Randall, 2003), and Yunupingu (Yunupingu, 1994) have imaged some models of Indigenous Knowings. Randall talks about Kanyini which he describes as:

> Kanyini is the principle of connectedness through caring and responsibility that underpins Aboriginal life, linking four main areas of responsibility – tjukurrpa (philosophy, law and religion). Ngura (country), walytja (kinship and family) and kurunpa (spirit, soul and psyche)...that idea of connecting with all things was quite common throughout the different Aboriginal nations (Randall, 2003, p. 16).

The following image (Figure 3.8) represents Kanyini:

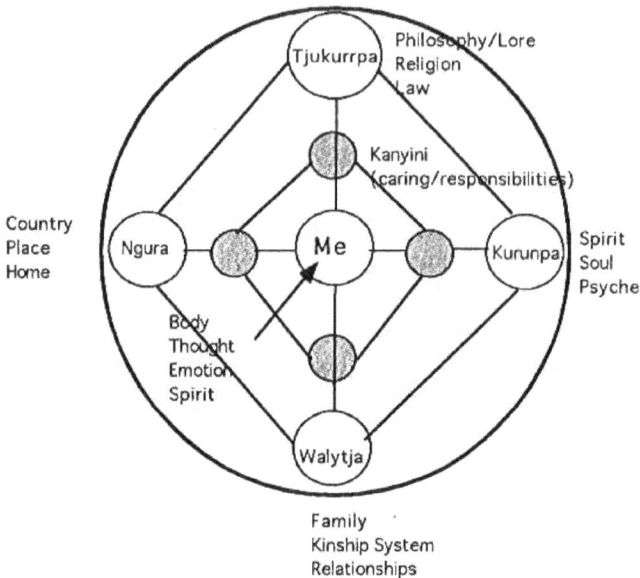

The Connectedness of Kanyini

Figure 3.8. Kanyini – Bob Randall

Tjukurrpa

Tjukurrpa is a Pintupi spelling of the word which means 'Dreaming', 'Story' or 'Law' in some Central Australian languages (also spelt Jukurrpa in Walpiri and Tjukurpa in Pitjantjatjara). All life and the laws by which people live were created in the Tjukurrpa by the ancestral beings who made the land and whose essence remains in the land. Tjukurrpa states the connections within the human world, physical world and sacred world – in its own right (Institute for Aboriginal Development, 2006) . The following image represents Tjukurrpa:

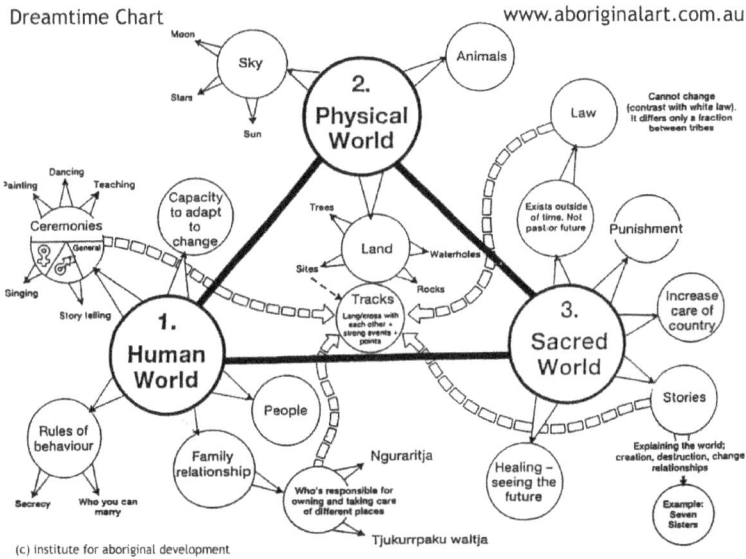

Figure 3.9. Tjukurrpa – Institute for Aboriginal Development
theaustralianproject.wordpress.com

Garma

Yolngu have created Garma. Garma is many things: a place, a festival, an open ceremonial area that everyone can participate in and enjoy (Marika R. , 1999), and a metaphor – a metaphor about natural processes but meaning at another level. Garma is social theory. It is "our traditional profound and detailed model of how what Europeans call 'society' works" (Yunupingu, 1994).

> Yolngu people see a powerful metaphor in the meeting and mixing of two streams which flow – one from the land, the other from the sea – in to a mangrove lagoon on Caledon Bay in NE Arnhem land. The theory of this confluence, called Garma, holds (in part) that the forces of the streams combine and lead to a deeper understanding and truth. It is an ancient metaphor ...in recent discussions among the Yolngu and those non-Aboriginal Australians they have chosen to work with them, Garma theory has been applied to the meeting of two cultures – Aboriginal and Western. Thus, we may use the term 'Garma' in English to refer to the situation where a river of water from the sea (Western knowledge) and a

river of water from the land (Yolngu knowledge) engulf each other on flowing in to a common lagoon and becoming one. In coming together, the streams of water mix at the interface of the two currents, creating foam at the surface, so that the process of Garma is marked by lines of foam (Watson H. C., 1989, p. 5).

Mason (Mason, 1995) sees the use of the Garma metaphor by Yolngu as an attempt to 'understand and grapple with the arrogance of western science. *Garma* is thus a framework for the development of a practice which aims for recognition of different knowledge systems, different ways of doing and thinking. Garma has been used by educators and health professionals to theorise, to explore and to provide explanation.

> *Ganma* is a place and a process and an aim. It is the meeting place of different knowledge systems, their own and that of the *balanda* [whitefella]. *Ganma* is a process of confluence of professional health care culture and others which meet and flow, sometimes mixing, often running side by side but separate. *Ganma* is like the balance where fresh water meets salt and its aim is to achieve a balance between different cultures and knowledge systems.
>
> Also, talk of Ganma brings another image to my mind. A deep pool of brackish water, fresh water and salt water mixed. The pool is a balance between two different natural patterns, the pattern of the tidal flow, salt water moving in through the mangrove channels, and the pattern of the fresh water streams varying in their flow across the wet and dry seasons. Often when I describe this vision to Balanda, non Aboriginal people, they wrinkle up their noses. For Balanda, brackish water is distasteful. But for us the sight and smell of brackish water expresses a profound foundation of useful knowledge — balance. For Yolngu Aboriginal people brackish water is a source of inspiration.
>
> In each of the sources of flowing water there is ebb and flow. The deep pool of brackish water is a complex dynamic balance. In the same ways, balance of Yolngu life is achieved through ebb and flow of competing interests, through our elaborate kinship system. And I feel that in the same ways balance between black and white in Australia can be achieved (Mason, 1995, p. 524).

Other academics have defined curriculum development as a metaphorical journey. Arbon (1998) for example draws on the metaphor of territory; Marika, Ngurruwutthun and White (1992) suggest that 'Garma' — which represents the point where the salt water and fresh water meet — may provide a useful metaphorical conception to describe the complex, cultural interactivity of Indigenous education. This notion moves away from the limitations of difference and the imposition of assimilationist models to encompass the interaction of cultures. Kemmis (Kemmis, 1997) refers to Garma in his discussion of social justice in universities and Greville (Greville, 2000) draws on the metaphor of Garma in her research about the ICMDP [Indigenous Community Management and Development]. As Greville notes with respect to the ICMDP this metaphor overcomes some of the problems and issues identified in the 'two-way learning' model with respect to the intersection between cultures; allowing both the turbulence and the 'mixing it up' of cultural Knowledges and practices to create new possibilities whilst simultaneously avoiding assimilationist and colonialist tendencies. This conception fits well with the ideas discussed throughout this research as I recount some of the key defining moments from the beginning through to the present.

> Some of the ideas for our practice come from theory related to the Garma Lagoon. Garma is a still lagoon. The water circulates silently underneath, and there are lines of foam circulating across the surface. The swelling and retreating of the tides and the wet season floods can be seen in the two bodies of the water. Water is often taken to represent knowledge in Yolngu philosophy. What we see happening in the school is a process of knowledge production where we have two different cultures, Balanda and Yolngu, working together. Both cultures need to be presented in a way where each one is preserved and respected. This theory is Yirritja (Greville, 2000, pp. 65-66).

Arlathirnda Ngurkarnda Ityirnda

Arbon (2008) an Arabana women from west Lake Eyre region of central South Australia has conceptualised Arlathirnda Ngurkarnda Ityirnda; Being-Knowing-Doing. In so doing she has 'gone deeply in to her own knowledge system to strengthen and centre herself while unravelling western theories and drawing on Hermeneutics and phenomenology (p.158). She uses metaphor through Yalka (a small onion) as metaphor, circles and tracks to conceptualise and strongly engage both the internal and external spheres of existence in the relatedness of an Aboriginal life world (p.27).

Quandamoopah Worldview

Martin (2008), from Stradbroke Island in Queensland has created an Indigenous paradigm 'Quandamoopah' which is embedded in Aboriginal ontology and epistemology. Martin uses storying through Storywork (Archibald, (2001) as a meta-process engaging us with layers of storys and images that draw you as the reader in to her Knowing.

The Knowledge Dreaming Model

Researchers such as Beckett and Proud (Beckett, 2004, p. 156) have considered the relation between theory and knowledge. In so doing they have developed a model entitled The Knowledge Dreaming Model. This model represents an idea of the flowing nature of knowledge that cannot be contained in written words. This model was used to help consolidate findings and to account for shared interests in theory issues. It required pictorial flowing symbols as illustrated below:

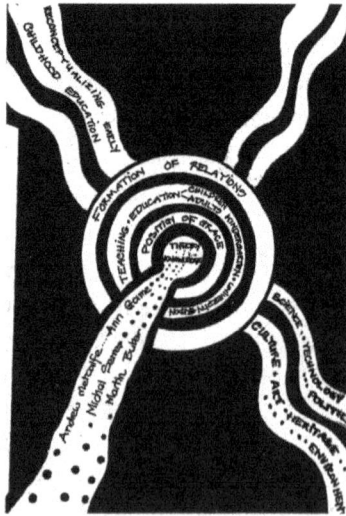

Figure 3.10. Knowledge Dreaming Model – Beckett and Proud

Beckett and Proud assert that 'the relation between research and theory may seem remote from daily practices and yet these are the very paths that can inspire whole new sets of practices that can in turn create new Knowledges' (Beckett, 2004, p. 156).

It was important for Beckett and Proud to capture the "creation of daily life connections, to transport the millions of messages and be able to explore the link between each message point with these links evolving the possibilities that might happen" (Beckett, 2004, p. 158).

The Knowledge Dreaming Model is an educational model and houses four key elements including: at the centre, theory and knowledge, emanating outwards the position of grace; teaching and education; and, finally the formation of relations. The authors advise their work draws on the theoretical positioning and writings of Game and Metcalfe (1996) and Buber (1958). They also draw on the theoretical positioning and visual images of Serres (1993). The model embodies their own "extension of feelings and ideas which in turn impacted on their ability to decolonize their work and their research spaces" (Beckett, 2004, p. 158).

> The rich interconnected networks of our lives and the extension of this through our shared positions of mutuality (Beckett, 2004, p. 158).

Indigenist Research

Indigenist Research as espoused by Rigney (Rigney, 1997) has three fundamental and interrelated principles that form a strategy to research rather than being a research process including:

- Resistance as the emancipatory imperative in Indigenist research
- Political integrity in Indigenist research, and
- Privileging Indigenous voices in Indigenist research.

Rigney draws on the similarities "found within Indigenous and feminist theorising, that of the lived experiences" specifically, the struggle against oppression:

> In constructing my research as Indigenist I have been indebted to some of the insights and principles of feminist research which involve emancipation and liberation strategies (see Lather 1987, 1991, 1992, Waldby 1995, Ebert 1991. Weiler 1988) (Rigney, 1997).

Rigney describes Indigenist research as:

> research undertaken as part of the struggle of Indigenous Australians for recognition for self-determination. It is research which engages with the issues in and which have arisen out of the long history of oppression of Indigenous Australians, which began in earnest with the invasion of Australia in 1788. It is research which deals with the history of physical, cultural and emotional genocide. It is also research which engages with the story of the survival and the resistances of Indigenous Australians to racist oppression. It is research which seeks to uncover and protest the continuing forms of oppression which confront Indigenous Australians. Moreover, it is research which attempts to support the personal, community, cultural and political struggles of Indigenous Australians to carve out a way of being for ourselves in Australia which there is healing from the past oppressions and cultural freedom in the future (Rigney, 1997).

Rigney (Rigney, 1997) identifies the need in the conduct of Indigenist research for political integrity. This must involve Indigenous Australians who set their own political agenda for liberation, where there must be a social link between research and the political struggle of our communities.

Rigney asserts that Indigenist research in which Indigenous Australians are the "primary subjects" gives "voice to Indigenous people" and its "goals are to serve and inform the Indigenous struggle for self-determination".

Rigney asserts that he wants Indigenist research to contribute to the liberation struggle "by unmasking some of the overt and brutal racist oppressions which have been and continue to be part of our reality, and by unmasking also some of its continuing and subtle forms". He does not claim that Indigenist research is characterised by any distinctive models or strategies and he has sought to adapt tools from critical theory and critical social sciences to inform his Indigenist research (Rigney, 1997).

Rigney (Rigney, 1997) provides an Indigenous justification/strategy where he draws on the work of West an Indigenous scholar (now past from this living world), who provides an Indigenous process through the many dimensions of The Japanangka Paradigm. The dimensions include the:

- Cultural dimension
- Spiritual dimension,
- Secular dimension,

- Intellectual dimension,
- Political dimension,
- Practical dimension,
- Personal dimension, and
- Public dimension.

Western epistemology differs from Indigenous in that we Koori peoples already know the origin, nature, methods and limits of our knowledge systems, what we unlike westerners seem to lack is the capacity to flaunt that knowledge as a badge of our intellect and cultural integrity, in a very public sense. The secret of our knowledge is the unbreakable connection between the spiritual realm and the physical Earth Mother (West, 1998).

Dadirri

Ungunmerr-Baumann an Indigenous woman from Daly River in the Northern Territory has developed the concept of Dadirri (Ungunmerr-Baumann) which Atkinson used as a model in her research (Atkinson, 2002). Ungunmerr-Baumann speaks of 'a special quality' and 'our most unique gift', perhaps the greatest gift we can give to our fellow Australians.

In our language this quality is called *dadirri*. It is inner, deep listening and quiet, still awareness. *Dadirri* recognises the deep spring that is inside us. We call on it and it calls to us. This is the gift that Australia is thirsting for. It is something like what you call "contemplation". When I experience *dadirri*, I am made whole again. I can sit on the riverbank or walk through the trees; even if someone close to me has passed away, I can find my peace in this silent awareness. There is no need of words. A big part of *dadirri* is listening. Through the years, we have listened to our stories. They are told and sung, over and over, as the seasons go by. Today we still gather around the campfires and together we hear the sacred stories.

As we grow older, we ourselves become the storytellers. We pass on to the young ones all they must know. The stories and songs sink quietly into our minds and we hold them deep inside. In the ceremonies we celebrate the awareness of our lives as sacred. The contemplative way of *dadirri* spreads over our whole life. It renews us and brings us peace. It makes us feel whole again... In our Aboriginal way, we learnt to listen from our earliest days. We could not live good and useful lives unless we listened. This was the normal way for us to learn - not by asking questions. We learnt by watching and listening, waiting and then acting. Our people have passed on this way of listening for over 40,000 years... There is no need to reflect too much and to do a lot of thinking. It is just being aware. My people are not threatened by silence. They are completely at home in it. They have lived for thousands of years with Nature's quietness. ...

And now I would like to talk about the other part of *dadirri* which is the quiet stillness and the waiting. Our Aboriginal culture has taught us to be still and to wait. We do not try to hurry things up. We let them follow their natural course - like the seasons. We watch the moon in each of its phases. We wait for the rain to fill our rivers and water the thirsty earth...

When twilight comes, we prepare for the night. At dawn we rise with the sun.

We watch the bush foods and wait for them to ripen before we gather them. We wait for our young people as they grow, stage by stage, through their initiation ceremonies. When a relation dies, we wait a long time with the sorrow. We own our grief and allow it to heal slowly. We wait for the right time for our ceremonies and our meetings. The right people must be present. Everything must be done in the proper way. Careful preparations must be made. We don't mind waiting, because we want things to be done with care. Sometimes many hours will be spent on painting the body before an important ceremony. We don't like to hurry. There is nothing more important than what we are attending to. There is nothing more urgent that we must hurry away for.

And I believe that the spirit of *dadirri* that we have to offer will blossom and grow, not just within ourselves, but in our whole nation (Ungunmerr-Baumann).

Dadirri is a way of coming to know through listening, waiting.

Indigenous Standpoint Theory

Indigenous Standpoint Theory has emerged as a theoretical framework and model in the last five years. Foley (Foley D. , 2002) and Nakata (Nakata M. , 2007) have described their sense of such a theory with the former referring more to a process than the latter who explores philosophical underpinnings, principles and elements.

Foley (Foley D. , 2002) has identified Indigenous Standpoint Theory as requiring the following:

> The practitioner must be Indigenous and must be well versed in theory. Not so that they may reproduce the mistakes made in western theory, rather so that they are aware of the mistakes made in western discourse. Knowledge is owned by the community, not the academy or the researcher. The traditional language should be the first form of recording, English interpretation is the second genre of recording. The research must be for the benefit of the Indigenous community. The emancipatory result is empowering and must be shared with the providers of the knowledge, not singularly to the researcher.

Nakata (Nakata M. , 2007) discusses Indigenous Standpoint Theory in terms of:

i) a method of inquiry
ii) a process for making more intelligible 'the corpus of objectified knowledge about us'
iii) it emerges and organises understanding of our lived realities
iv) it involves theorising knowledge from a particular and interested position ... not to produce the 'truth' ... but to better reveal the workings of knowledge (Nakata M. , 2007, p. 215).

Nakata describes three main principles of Indigenous Standpoint Theory including:

1. Indigenous people are entangled in a very contested knowledge space at the Cultural Interface
2. It would recognise Indigenous agency as framed within the limits and possibilities of what I can know from this constituted position – to recognise that at the interface we are constantly being asked to be both continuous with one position at the same time as being discontinuous with another

3. The constant tensions that this tug-of-war creates are physically
    experienced, and both inform as well as limit what can be said and what
    is left to be unsaid in the everyday (Nakata M. , 2007, pp. 215-216).

Nakata draws on the employment of an Indigenous Standpoint Theory to help to
"unravel and untangle ourselves from the conditions that delimit who, what or
how we can or can't be, to help ourselves with some charge of the everyday, and
to help understand our varied responses to the colonial world" (Nakata M. , 2007,
p. 217).

THINKING AND MODELLING FROM OUTSIDE OF AUSTRALIA

Six Directions

In his research on Indian education Hampton searched for and found "a model, a
metaphor or a pattern" to "organize the themes and serve as a mnemonic and a
matrix for new ideas" (Hampton, 1998, p. 16). In doing so he conceptualised the
Six Directions:

> My only remaining qualm is that I will be misunderstood as using the six
> directions as a model rather than allowing it to direct me. This way of
> thinking is sacred in the sense that it is bigger than anything I might say.
> It helps me to understand in that it stimulates my thoughts and feelings
> rather than being contained in my words. ... The six directions are not a
> model but a pattern or an organizing principle. Models connote a small,
> imperfect copy of something more real. The six directions are a way of
> thinking about existing in the universe. The pattern organizes and
> clarifies thoughts (Hampton, 1998, p. 16).

Hampton's pattern embodies direction, movement, history, connections and is
rooted in living experience and dialogical interaction. The Six Directions include
the earth, spirit, north, south, east and west. Spirit is the Great Spirit and
embodies identity, affiliation, freedom and spirituality. East, the direction of
spring acknowledges cultures 'reaching back to the time of beginnings'. East
presents the standards of diversity and identity. South is the direction of summer,
the time of fullest growth, a space for tradition. It embodies pre European
invasion and standards of tradition and respect. West, the direction of autumn
embodies the standards of history and relentlessness as well as being about
service. North, the home of winter teaches endurance and survival. North

demands knowledge and embodies the standards of vitality, struggle and conflict. The 'earth is our home'. It represents stability and reminds of the importance of a sense of place. Earth embodies standards of affiliation and transformation. Each direction presents 'a complex set of meanings, feelings, relationships and movements' (Hampton, 1998, pp. 16-33).

Hampton required this model as a means to thinking about his research process and his findings. Western models, patterns didn't quite work for him. He drew on something that at one point he felt was 'too deep', too private and 'too Indian' and in his presentation he followed his "impulse and interlaced narrative vernacular with academic discourse" (Hampton, 1998, p. 5).

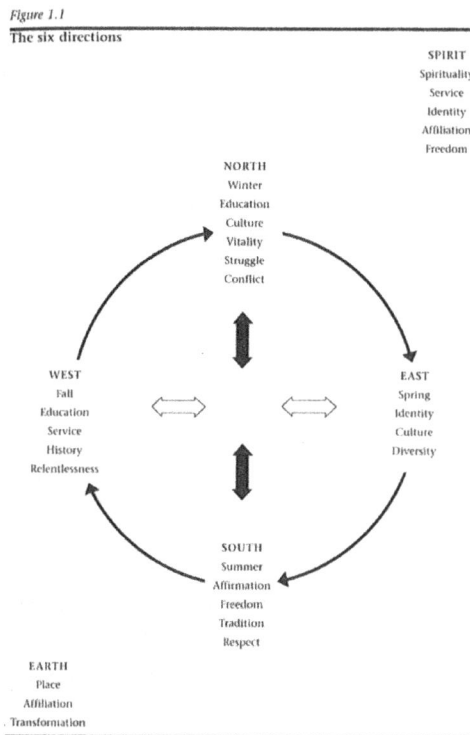

Figure 1.1

The six directions

SPIRIT
Spirituality
Service
Identity
Affiliation
Freedom

NORTH
Winter
Education
Culture
Vitality
Struggle
Conflict

WEST
Fall
Education
Service
History
Relentlessness

EAST
Spring
Identity
Culture
Diversity

SOUTH
Summer
Affirmation
Freedom
Tradition
Respect

EARTH
Place
Affiliation
Transformation

Figure 3.11. Six Directions - Eber Hampton (1988)

Research as Ceremony

Wilson (2008) an Opaskwayak Cree man from Canada has crafted an Indigenous research paradigm: Research as Ceremony, 'to maintain, transmit and clarify an Indigenous way of doing and being in the research process' (p.19). Research as Ceremony engages stories which evolve and articulate the ideas of relationality and relational accountability as well as all of the foundational elements associated with ceremonying, ceremonies.

Tribal Critical Race Theory

Brayboy (2005) in crafting Tribal Crit. values story and listening, engaging with issues of colonization, sovereignty, collectivity being rooted in a physical place – what I conceptualise as Country. Tribal Crit. emerges from Critical Race Theory.

Red Pedagogy

Red Pedagogy (Grande, 2008) whilst being informed by Critical Theories of education is rooted in Indigenous Knowledge and interrogates democracy and Indigenous sovereignty. It actively cultivates praxis of collective agency whilst being grounded in hope through community-based power (p.201). Red Pedagogy maintains the distinctiveness of tribal peoples as sovereign Nations aiming to 'construct a self-determined space for American Indian intellectualism' (p.200).

Self Determination

Manuelito (Manuelito, 2004, p. 250), identifies the process of dialogue where Indian people obstruct dialogue through their own internalized colonization....and has created a model that embodies self-determination:

The concepts from the Euro-Western world-view don't match the Navajo understanding of those concepts. In present day society, these Euro-Western definitions and criteria have become the evaluative guidelines for Indian people....As long as Indian people do not share or are not permitted to share their understanding of concepts...and as long as Indian people do not throw off their shackles of internalized colonization, they will continue to support the implementation of self-determination (research in the context of this paper) in the Euro-Western sense, which defies their own existence. Dialogue and the decolonization of our own minds as Indian people are vital for equality and survival...(Manuelito, 2004, p. 250). Figure 3.12 illustrates this model.

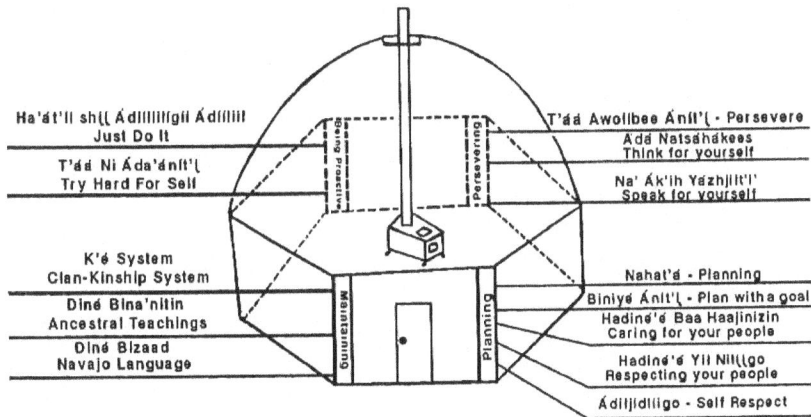

Figure 3.12. Self-Determination (with Navajo terms) (Manuelito, 2004, p. 248)

Reprinted by permission from *Decolonizing Research in Cross-Cultural Contexts: Critical Personal Narratives.* Edited by Kagendo Mutua and Beth Blue Swadener, the State University of New York. All rights reserved.

Pagtatanong-tanong

Canete (Canete, 2004, pp. 140-141) discusses pagtatanong-tanong, a research method he used with Philippine communities in Greece. In his quest to find the most appropriate research method he essays the tensions, contradictions and power imbalances he encountered:

> Pagtatanong-tanong is a Filipino word for asking questions. It has become identified as an Indigenous research method in Philippine social science research. The repetition of 'tanong' (question) to tanong-tanong indicates apparent casualness when the inquirer is truly determined to get answers to his or her questions. Pagtatanong-tanong includes a behavioral trait that Filipinas and Filipinos ordinarily exhibit. Pagtatanong-tanong as a research method is sometimes interpreted as an informal interview or at best an "improvisation", which approximates the interview method, but this is not correct. Although there are some similarities, pagtatanong-tanong is basically different from the interview in general.

Additionally, the use of the local term pagtatanong-tanong highlights the importance of tapping culturally appropriate indigenous research methods without claiming exclusivity to it for the particular culture. It has four major characteristics: it is participatory in nature, the researcher and informant are equal in status, it is appropriate and adaptive to conditions, and it is integrated with other Indigenous research methods (Canete, 2004, p. 140).

Rubber Sheet

Pryor and Ghartey Ampiah (Pryor, 2004), conceptualise research methodology for educational research they conducted in Ghana as a rubber sheet. This methodology involves intersecting sets where a rubber sheet is constantly being stretched and shaped by pulling from three directions macro (ethical and political), micro (practical and political), and epistemological/ontolological. It is a dynamic methodology, where the pulls come through similar sets of issues which may offer different strengths and come from different directions (Pryor, 2004, pp. 161-165).

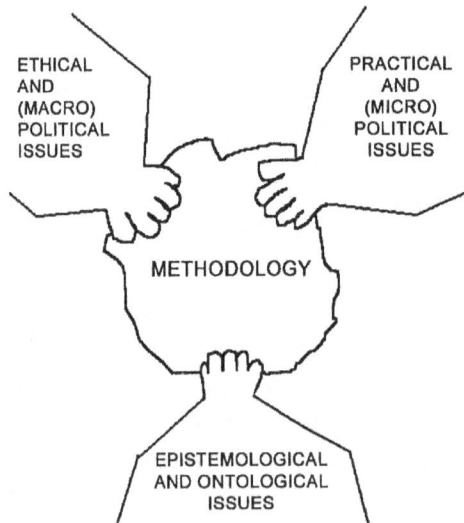

Figure 3.13. Rubber Sheet - Pryor and Ghartey Ampiah

Mestizaje

Mestizaje; Spanish, Indigenous, South American embodies as "intrinsic an analysis of power differentials, domination and social injustices...woven with anti-imperialist strategies and decolonizing lenses, ... illuminating pedagogical tools and challenging Euro-centric thought and notions of western objectivity, constructing new metaphors" (Demas, 2004, p. 218).

Demas and Saavedra employ "a critical postmodern/Chicana feminist lens" to their research analysis when (re)conceptualising language advocacy. Accordingly, mestizaje, that mode of Chicana feminism often referred to as "borderlands" feminism describes theorising and methodology that transverse boundaries, resist hierarchies, and transform social relations. Anzaldua encapulates this essence of La mestiza deconstructing oppressive colonizing traditions and constructing new metaphors; she unlearns patriarchal assumptions and engages in a transnational feminist struggle; she reinterprets history and writes new myths; she tears down categories and invites ambiguity (Demas, 2004, p. 218).

Anzaldua used the "borderlands" as a metaphor grounded in, but not limited to, geographic space to illustrate the positionality of Chicanas living in and crossing multiple cultures, multiple worlds (Demas, 2004, p. 218).

Within this discourse about mestizaje the writing of theory plays a central role:

> Necesitamos teorias that will rewrite history using race, class, gender and ethnicity as categories of analysis, theories that cross borders, that blur boundaries – new kinds of theories with new theorizing methods. We need theories that will point out ways to manoeuvre between our particular experiences and the necessity of forming our own categories and theoretical models for the patterns we uncover...[w]e need to de-academize theory and to connect to the community to The academy. 'High' theory does not translate well when one's intentions is to communicate to the masses of people made up of different audiences. We need to give up the notion that there is a 'correct' way to write theory. (Anzaldua 1990, pp.xxv-xxvi in (Mutua, 2004, p. 217).

Spiral or Koru

Professor Ngapare Hopa, formerly Head of Maori Studies at the University of Auckland spoke of Maori epistemology and takarangi; one embodiment of the spiral where the use of a spiral or koru can represent a world-view where opposites can converge and where knowledge is not a linear progression (Sullivan, 2005, p. 13). Sullivan has used the spiral as an organising principle using the multiple levels of the spiral to express the values he was interested in finding, helping him avoid Eurocentric notions of time; pre-historic, pre-contact and post-colonial, and the limits of western alienations of land and nature; the idea that guardianship is fixed time in space. In thinking spirally, Sullivan believes he "felt more closely aligned to an indigenous world view, despite recently switching neo-colonial societies" (Sullivan, 2005, p. 27).

Kaupapa Maori

Smith, L. asserts that "the development of new ways of thinking about indigenous Maori research, and approaches to the way this research should be framed, have emerged in the last decade under the rubric of Kaupapa Maori research" (Smith L. , 1999, p. 179). This has evolved because:

> Research is implicated in the production of Western knowledge, in the nature of academic work, in the production of Western theories which have dehumanized Maori and in practices which have continued to privilege Western ways of knowing, while denying the validity for Maori of Maori knowledge, language and culture....retrieve some space...(Smith L. , 1999, p. 183).

Smith further believes that Indigenous communities as part of the self-determination agenda engage quite deliberately in naming the world according to an indigenous world view. What researchers may call methodology, for example, Maori researchers in New Zealand call Kaupapa Maori research or Maori-centred research, This form of naming is about bringing to the centre and privileging indigenous values, attitudes and practices rather than disguising them within Westernized labels such as 'collaborative research'. (Smith L. , 1999, p. 125). Kaupapa Maori is a theorized approach (Smith L. , 1999, p. 132):

> Maori people's concerns about research focus on the locus of power over issues of initiation, benefits, representation, legitimacy and accountability being with the researcher (Bishop, 2005, p. 112).

According to Bishop, Kaupapa Maori challenges the dominance of the Pakeha world view in research (Bishop, 2005, p. 114). There are some like Irwin that identify Kaupapa Maori as its own research paradigm. Others are reluctant to engage in such a debate because it sets up comparisons with Western science, which is exactly what Kaupapa Maori is resisting (Smith L. , 1999, p. 190). Smith asserts that:

> Kaupapa Maori is more than and less than a paradigm. It sets out a field of study, enables a process of selection to occur, defines what needs to be studied, defines what questions to ask, has a set of assumptions, taken-for-granted values and taken-for-granted knowledge upon which it builds. Kaupapa Maori is more than the sum of those parts, it is a social project that weaves in and out of Maori cultural beliefs and values, Western ways of knowing, Maori histories and experiences undercolonialism, Western forms of education, Maori aspirations, Maori socio-economic needs, Western economics and global politics. Kaupapa Maori is concerned with sites and terrains of struggle. Kaupapa Maori research sets out to make a positive difference for the researched based on the assumption that research involves Maori people as individuals and as communities. Short and long-term benefits must be articulated, it must seriously address cultural ground rules of respect, working with communities and the sharing of processes and knowledge. Kaupapa Maori research incorporates processes such as networking, community consultations, whanau research groups which bring in to focus research problems that are significant for Maori. Researchers must share their 'control' of research and seek to maximise the participation and interest of Maori. Kaupapa Maori embodies an approach to training and supporting young researchers whose academic studies had not prepared them. Kaupapa Maori as a research approach provides a space for dialogue by Maori across disciplines about research (Smith L. , 1999, pp. 191-193).

Smith (G) asserts that Kaupapa Maori is related to "being Maori", is connected to Maori philosophy and principles, takes for granted the validity and legitimacy of Maori, the importance of Maori language and culture and is concerned with the "struggle for autonomy over our own cultural well-being" (Smith G in (Smith L. , 1999, p. 185).

Bishop identifies some "significant dimensions' of Kaupapa Maori that set it apart from traditional research including the following:

i) Operationalisation of self-determination by Maori people which captures a sense of Maori ownership and active control over the future

ii) Challenges the loci of power and control as it is located in another cultural frame of reference

iii) Challenges the dominance of traditional individualistic research that primarily, at least in its present form benefits the researcher and their agenda

iv) Kaupapa Maori is collectivistic being oriented toward benefitting all the research participants, ultimately the collectively determined agaenda

v) Define and acknowledge Maori aspirations for research while developing and implementing Maori theoretical and methodological preferences and practices for research

vi) Is a discourse that has emerged from and is legitimized from within Maori community

vii) The approach involves discursive practice which positions the researcher in such a way as to operationalise self-determination in terms of agentic positioning and behaviour for the research participants

viii) Challenges the essentializing dichotomization of the insider/outsider debate by offering a discursive position researchers irrespective of ethnicity

ix) The cultural aspirations, understandings and practices of Maori people are used both literally and figuratively to implement and to organize the research process

x) Issues of initiation, benefits, representation, legitimization and accountability are addressed and understood in practice by practitioners of Kaupapa Maori research within the cultural context of the research participants

xi) Challenges traditional ways of defining, accessing and constructing knowledge about Indigenous peoples; the process of self-critique and "paradigm shifting" used by western scholars as a means of 'cleansing' thought and attaining what becomes their version of the 'truth'

xii) Kaupapa Maori position is predicated on the understanding that Maori means of accessing, defining and protecting knowledge existed before European arrival in Aoteoroa

xiii) Kaupapa Maori analysis must benefit Maori people in principle and in practice in such a way that the current realities of marginalization and heritage of colonialism and neo-colonialism are addressed (Bishop, 2005, pp. 114-115).

xiv) Benefits all the research participants and their collectively determined agendas, defining and acknowledging Maori aspirations for research, while developing and implementing Maori theoretical and methodological preferences and practices for research. Emerged from and legitimized from within the Maori community (Bishop, 2005, pp. 114-115).

Figure 3.14. A Means of Evaluating Researcher Positioning

Source: Reproduced with permission from Bishop and Glynn (1999, p.129)

Kaupapa Maori has been applied across a wide range of projects and enterprises. Furthermore, not all Maori researchers would regard themselves, or their research, as fitting within a Kaupapa Maori framework (Smith L. , 1999, p. 184).

Kaupapa Maori, however, does not mean the same as Maori knowledge and epistemology. The concept of kaupapa implies a way of framing and structuring how we think about those ideas and practices....Kaupapa Maori is a 'conceptualisation of Maori knowledge' (Nepe in (Smith L. , 1999, p. 188).

Kaupapa Maori as an approach has provided a space for dialogue by Maori, across disciplines, about research....Maori interest in research has made research more interesting. Maori communities can engage in research in exciting ways if they are included in the research (Smith L. , 1999, p. 193).

Engaging in a discussion about research as an indigenous issue has been about finding a voice, or a way of voicing concerns, fears, desires, aspirations, needs and questions as they relate to research. When indigenous peoples become the researchers and not merely the researched, the activity of research is transformed. Questions are framed differently, priorities are ranked differently, problems are defined differently, people participate on different terms (Smith L. , 1999, p. 193).

From a pure Maori Studies perspective, the term Kaupapa Maori means the "ground work" or the "medium" from which Maori knowledge, including te reo me nga tikanga Maori, can be validated. Therefore, Kaupapa Maori research should be located organically from within the Indigenous worldview and not on the periphery as the other (Higgins, 2004, p. 8).

Kaupapa Maori is a collaborative, participatory epistemological model, characterized by the absence of a need to be in control and by a desire to be connected to and part of a moral community in which a primary goal is the compassionate understanding of another's moral position (Higgins, 2004, p. 8). Kaupapa Maori used by Maori rather than employing the word "Indigenist" (Smith L. , 2005, p. 90)

Model of Maoritanga and Maori Worldview

Higgins uses two theoretical frameworks in her PhD thesis; namely the Model of Maoritanga and Maori Worldview Model evolved by Rangihau and Ka'ai respectively (Higgins, 2004, p. 7). She describes these models as being based on a Kaupapa Maori paradigm. In these models Higgins asserts that the Model of Maoritanga centers Maoritanga and places the Pakehatanga at the periphery. This model illustrates an interlocking of relationships between some of the numerous concepts of Maori. Maoritanga is encased within aroha (profound love) from which other important cultural concepts are related to each other.

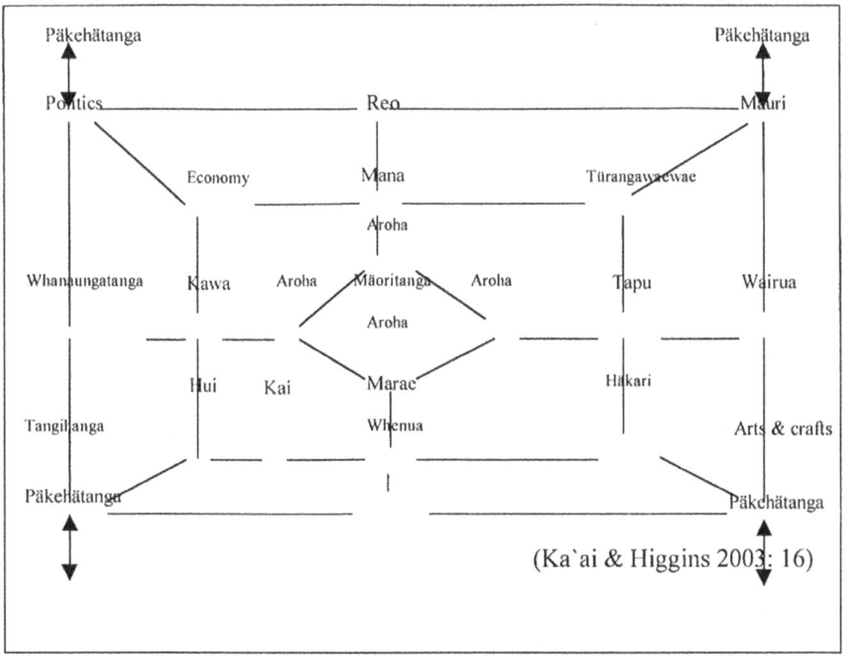

Figure 3.15. Rangihau's Conceptual Model (Higgins, 2004, p. 10)

Rangihau and Ka'ai have in the evolution of their theoretical frameworks "empowered Maori knowledge systems by locating Maori in the centre and Western knowledge to the margin" (Higgins, 2004, p. 8).

A number of Indigenous peoples are evolving models, paradigms, philosophies to lay the foundations for our research. The models all reflect local environmental factors.

CULTURAL INTERFACE: COLLIIDING TRAJECTORIES

This chapter has presented some Indigenous voices and views of a conceptual and theoretical aspect of research and in doing so has evolved and showcased a space that is clearly contested. I have visually presented this in the form of the Brick Wall and the sweet potato; the Waterlily being my final and local representation of research process and methodology. The previous chapter explored the non-Indigenous space; elements of the Brick Wall. It is now necessary to look at the contested space and the implications of such contestation. How we as Indigenous peoples have come to understand ourselves and how other Australians have come to see us as Indigenous peoples on a daily, lived basis is dependent on the outcome of the contest, indeed on the process and conceptualisation of the contest. As Indigenous peoples we have not made the rules, created the frameworks or boundaries. However, we live the daily reality of such articulations, such discourse. Nakata (Nakata M. , 2007) best describes this in relation to Torres Strait Islanders. He uses the term Cultural Interface to explore the contested space and the implications of this for Torres Strait Islanders. The Cultural Interface is "not restricted to cultural specificities", it "cannot be viewed solely in structuralist terms, is extremely complex and it cannot be understood in the present without historical specificities" (Nakata M. , 2007, p. 198). In essence, it is the space where Islanders live and act on a daily basis ... the personal and civic space where we make sense of our individual and collective experience. It is a lived location that cannot be described in purely physical terms. In exploring the complexity of the Cultural Interface, Nakata states that the complexities cannot be described in terms of the intersection between the theoretical and the 'real', expressed via the contestations and contradictions between textual and inter-textual representations of Islanders ...'. The complexities involve interwoven social, economic and political factors (Nakata M. , 2007, p. 198).

Nakata states unequivocally that his proposition is not simply another perspective it "is a proposition to expand assumptions underpinning theory based on a reading of how Islanders have been inscribed in Western systems of thought over the past century and more. It is a proposition to draw in to theory principles that give primacy to the Islander lifeworlds as a complex terrain of political and social contests" (Nakata M. , 2007, p. 197).

In defining the Cultural Interface, Nakata articulates this as a 'multi-layered, multi-dimensional space constituted by points of intersecting trajectories where there are many shifting and complex intersections between different peoples and different systems of thought (Nakata, 2007, pp.199-200).

Other Indigenous peoples have referred to cultural differences, "fluctuating boundaries and simplistic representations" (Cary, 2004, p. 79) and have served to dichotomise the debate. This has been and will continue to be necessary. In order to understand the Interface we need to understand the constituents, the 'bits'. Nakata has stepped back to explore not only the complex intersections but what he terms the Cultural Interface. It is "primarily a site of struggle over the meaning of our experience" (Nakata M. , 2007, p. 210).

This book and my place in doing the research for it exist within such a Cultural Interface, in terms of content and process. It is primarily a site of struggle, endeavouring to make sense of our lived experience as Indigenous Australians. Lilyology emerges from within this space.

Swisher (Swisher, 1998) argues "what is missing from the plethora of books, journals and articles produced by non-Indians about Indians is the passion from within, the authority to ask new and different questions based on histories and lived experiences as Indigenous peoples" (Swisher, 1998, p. 113).

Bishop clearly enunciates what a growing number of Indigenous researchers (Smith, Battiste, Youngblood Henderson, Mutua and Swadener, Anzaldua, Nakata, Rigney, Fixico, Hampton, Mihesuah and Wilson, De Loria, Cajete, Churchill, Moreton-Robinson to name a few) have articulated to varying degrees:

> Researchers in Aotearoa have developed a tradition of research that has perpetuated colonial power imbalances thereby belittling and undervaluing Maori knowledge and learning practices and processes creating a social pathology and perpetuating an ideology of cultural superiority. Traditional research has misrepresented Maori understandings and ways of knowing by simplifying, conglomerating and commodifying Maori knowledge for consumption by the colonizers (Bishop, 2005, p. 110).

> Traditional research epistemologies have developed methods of initiating research and accessing research participants that are located within the cultural practices and preferences of the Western world as opposed to the cultural preferences and practices of Maori people themselves; specifically, where there is a preoccupation with neutrality, objectivity and distance by researchers. These concepts have ultimately distanced Maori people from the construction, validation and legitimization of Maori knowledge (Bishop, 2005, p. 111).

Parallel Divide within the Brick Wall

There are some who might suggest that there are other places in the research methodology domain where contested spaces are apparent. Denzin and Lincoln (2005) identify this as the "the parallel divide between quantitative and qualitative research and that, that exists within each" (p.10). By acknowledging this divide and focussing on the diverse traditions and context they identify a new and vibrant theorising space: The Eight Moment (Denzin, N. & Lincoln, Y.S. 2005, p.20). The identification of this has opened up a dialogue between researchers, and between Indigenous and non-Indigenous researchers not previously engaged. This dialogue takes us to the space in-between, the zone of colliding trajectories referred to in this book.

There are many new, engaging, organic approaches to subjective research operating within the Brick Wall as well as within the space in-between. I am not storying Lilyology as something emerging from a unique set of circumstances, rather emerging from a context and epistemology outside of the Brick Wall.

REFLECTIVE OVERVIEW

This chapter has explored the contested space/contesting space in Indigenous research, specifically, methodology. A few illustrations of Indigenous thinking and Knowings about research have been presented. The chapter has explored the many dimensions of the sweet potato; the concept of Indigenous Knowings as distinct from the Brick Wall in the conceptualisation and performance of research. The previous chapter identified some western research paradigms and philosophies which we as Indigenous peoples have naturally gravitated towards and away from including feminism, post colonialism, critical race theory, cultural studies, grounded theory, rhizomatics, narrative, performance studies and decolonisation. It explored some western research strategies including action research, participant observation, focus groups, oral history and interview. The previous chapter explored some of the bricks in the western research Brick Wall. Before embarking on the next stage of the journey I stop to reflect on the words of a traditional owner and Elder from Derby in Western Australia, David Mowaljarlai, (Stockton, 1995, pp. 42-43) who offers profound insight into the contrast between Aboriginal and Western thinking; the Brick Wall and the sweet potato. It is necessary to be reminded of these words before journeying further into the domain of the Brick Wall, triangle thinking:

> Pattern thinking is Aboriginal thinking. There is no big boss. Patterns are about belonging. Nothing is separate from anything else. This land is not separate from nature, people, the heavens, and ancient stories. Everything belongs in the pattern. There is no 'ownership' in pattern-thinking. Only Belonging. Money cannot buy bits of a pattern. Power runs all through a pattern. It cannot be sold. It is not separate from the pattern.
>
> Triangle thinking is western culture thinking. There is always a big boss. There are other bosses who have power over people down the triangle. Triangles are about money and power. Everything in triangle thinking is connected with money and power. Triangle thinking separates everything in to layers of power and administration. 'Ownership' is a

triangle idea. 'Belonging' cannot fit in to Triangle thinking. 'Ownership' means 'rulership' by the owner. Triangles are separate from each other, and separate from patterns. Triangle thinking tries to squeeze patterns in to triangles. This cannot work. Patterns do not have rigid lines like triangles.

Our Knowing is pattern thinking. It is reflected in the voices of my Colleagues from Desert and Country, who share their Storys and experiences as the next wave to wash into our reflections, our reflectivescape about research and knowledge production.

In a traditional academic framework the next chapter is the report of the field research from which emerges the concept of Lilyology.

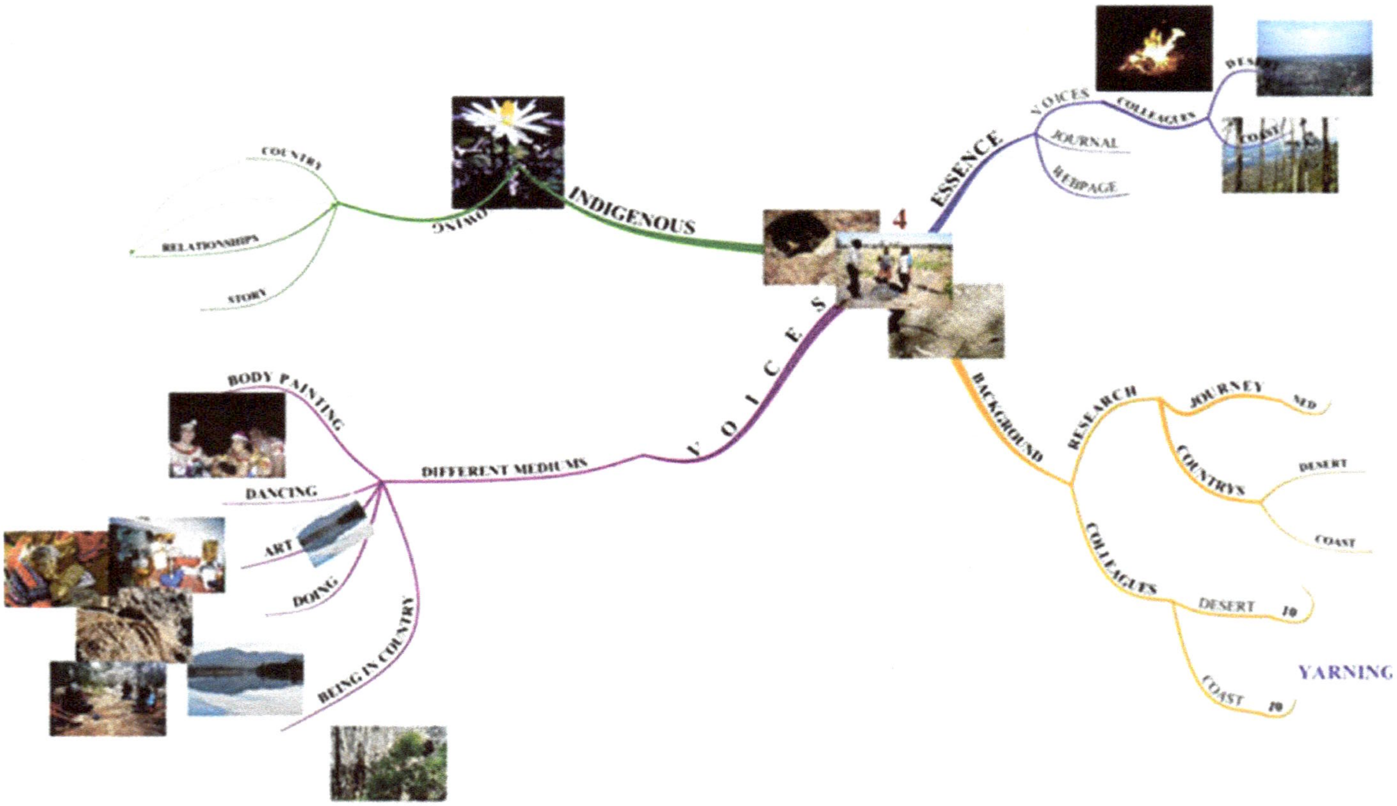

YARNING

JOURNEY
MED
DESERT
COAST

COUNTRY

RESEARCH

COLLEAGUES
DESERT
10
COAST
20

BACKGROUND

ESSENCE

VOICES
COLLEAGUES
JOURNAL
WEBPAGE
DES...
Foto...

4

VOICES

INDIGENOUS

...RING
COUNTRY
RELATIONSHIP
STORY

DIFFERENT MEDIUM

BODY PAINTING
DANCING
ART
DANC...
BEING IN COUNTRY

CHAPTER 4

Tellin' Me and Showin' Me!

This chapter is the essence of this book. It presents my Colleague's voices, those that I yarned with as well as my personal journal entries and the learning and Knowing experiences I had in each of the communities and Countrys I became a part of.

This chapter is a departure from the 'norm' and may be interpreted by some as lacking academic rigour. A departure because it presents the voices of my Colleagues as the starting point, whether it be their descriptions of the 'research sites' or their descriptions of themselves as community. Without this Indigenous Knowings, the core of this research is irrelevant. The descriptions are mainly narrative and have been derived from the yarns shared. To engage with this chapter, tune in to the webpage to listen to some of my colleague's voices then read this text as if listening to a conversation. Look at the images of Country to see where the Storys are emanating from. Watch the videos to see the relatedness of people to Country and each other.

The structure and organisation of this chapter does not follow the generic academic plan. Its structure and organisation reflect an insight into Indigenous Knowings.

The journal entries, identified as (JE) present as symbols, images, poems, reflections and descriptions. *The text from these entries is italicised* in order to differentiate it, not to make it more important – merely to identify the differing source. I have chosen not to edit the text though there are words, thoughts recorded in the moment that I would want to change upon reflection and engagement with them in a different space and time. This is part of the journey's process, warts and all.

The learning experiences for me as the researcher go beyond the yarns to visits to Country. They embody the experiential learning necessary for such a journey. In each community and Country visited, my Colleagues took me out to Country to yarn, to see places, to sit in Country and reflect, to actually do things. I choose not to present these in a linear, sequential way but to weave them through the dialogue as they occurred. The context is important and cannot be removed. The experiences cannot be decontextualised. In some instances these learning and

Knowing experiences are re-presented inadequately, as a medium such as this does not lend itself to the situation. For example, I cannot adequately represent the experiences I felt, shared and embodied when taken to Country to do body painting, to sing and dance. I choose to show some photographic images that with the permission of my Colleagues illustrate a superficial layer of learning.

I also present these experiences in a mixed medium where possible. An unedited video version of part of a trip out to Country to catch goanna; and to visit water holes were activities done before and after the yarns. The video presents layers of learning that linear text cannot.

Fabrics are presented in photographic form of the research experience as painted by my Colleagues from the Desert. My Colleagues came together (at their instigation) to share their journeys of the research experience and my place within it, on fabric. (Refer to Figures 4.3 & 4.4)

Colleagues from the Desert chose to redo an interview in language. I felt that the English language could not do justice to their expression of themselves, their Knowings perhaps an arrogant assumption but one we all reflected on for some time. How could I re-present Indigenous Knowings in English and in an academic linear textual frame? How could I re-present the rhythm, the sound, the timing of my colleague's yarns? The outcome is still limiting but goes some way towards re-presenting it in context. This is something I continue to ponder as the 'researcher'.

Student's songs are presented as I became involved in and out of the classroom in Desert. My involvement in the classroom was not as a traditional research experience to be documented and measured. It was not merely as a participant observer. It wasn't in fact intended to be a part of the research journey. It happened as so many of our learning experiences do. I was asked by my Colleagues to include the songs; their words and the CDs as part of my research journey for others to share.

Finally, images of Country are presented through photographs. The visual is the key to our understanding, our communication of our Knowings.

The mixed medium is presented in two ways; embodied in text and interactively on a webpage. I am not an IT expert. This webpage is about illustrating the presentation of Indigenous Knowings in a more meaningful way than linear text. It is NOT about my IT skills.

This chapter presents the following:

i)   some background to this research journey
ii)   some background on the research Country and communities

iii) some information about my Colleagues
iv) the voices of people, verbatim, in script form
v) Coast community - 'The Mountain Calls me Home'
vi) Desert community - Nyndirrum Inkyjuk : Body Painting

This chapter embodies narrative, Story.

There is a story I know.[1] It begins in a community in the Northern Territory. I travelled to this community full of anticipation, eager, enthusiastic, apprehensive and with time on my hands. I had taken 6 months study leave from work to 'conduct my PhD field research'. Lots of time and everything was so organised. Ethics had been achieved. The community had said yes, come and visit us, yarn with us. Land Council approval to enter the Country had been sought and approved...but wait; only part approval had been given I was doing research and needed to submit another application. My application was granted after much to and fro very much like the waves themselves. What to me at this point seemed bizarre was the fact that the community had authorised me to come to them. The traditional owners had given me their approval to come and 'conduct my research' with them. The non-Indigenous anthropologists from the (Indigenous) Lands Council had not yet approved my application and found the request complex. As an Indigenous researcher I felt:

> *Well, the last few days have been mentally tumultuous...I have tried to work through feelings of anxiety, frustration, sense of failure, impatience, - all a bit of a smoke screen, a haze* [JE8/09/02].

My contact from that community was a research student and friend and she invited me to stay with her, her partner and their puppy 'Trakka'. It was all set.

A change of Community Advisor by this stage however had left the community in a state of limbo. The earlier passing of an Elder statesman/traditional owner; Sorry Business, had left gaps in the community. The politics escalated.

> *Four weeks down the track 'I felt the highs and lows...The sense of failure and inadequacy have been acute. How can I teach what I can't do myself? Talking to [my supervisor] helped balance things out. Let go and move on!'* [JE20/09/02]

---

[1] This phrase and context is referenced to Thomas King (King, 2003).

Earlier I reflected:

> *I felt a bit empty, a lot tired and exhausted from plotting, planning and*
> *negotiating. I feel a failure (yes, I know, irrational, but it is how I feel).*
> *So let it go, get over it!!* [JE15/09/02]

The research did not happen here. I had to let it go and begin again somewhere else. Much less time. Panic set in. Funny how things have a way of changing. How the waves in this part of the ocean were tentatively drawing energy from disparate sources, creating an uneven wash. Is this where the story ends? No. So much learning happened here and is fundamental to the outcome.

I drew on friendships and networks and found the Country and community that was always destined to be. An early morning bus, plane and Toyota four wheel drive saw me arrive in Desert twelve hours after leaving home. Desert and the people in Desert welcomed me giving me a place in the community as Nangala to some; sister. The journey here begins.

> *How do I begin to describe today? Words are inadequate. My*
> *experience here is my thesis. I am learning and being learnt by some*
> *very special people.* [JE10/11/02]

This Story has moved ahead of itself. Coast was the other community and Country I became a part of. An Elder, a mentor from decades past was to guide me in this part of my journey. This was the second community/Country I became a part of. It is where the research journey 'proper' began. It is where the yarns began. It is where I was shown and told by my Colleagues.

> *As I drove down an eagle flew over as I reached the [x] River. A sign? I*
> *feel apprehensive, still deflated from my lack of 'success' in Darwin,*
> *basically flat.* [JE11.10.02]

RESEARCH COUNTRY AND COMMUNITIES

I spent time in two communities, two Countrys as a part of this research journey. One I call 'Coast', the other 'Desert'. I choose geographic descriptions as names rather than place names or words because they embody so much of the image of place. Both communities and Countrys are diverse within themselves and to each other. I do not compare the two communities and Countrys, as this is simply not possible. They exist in their own right.

These communities/Countries were chosen to explore any diversity and similarity from each other as I believed at the outset that they epitomised distinct difference; one community/Country being in the eastern part of the country, the other inland where colonising experiences had been different and time apart. The impact on people's learning and Knowing in these circumstances would be of interest. Historical, geographical, economic and political difference was I perceived greatest between such communities. I hypothesised, as I thought I must, that Indigenous ways of Knowing would not be terribly different in each community, no matter how diverse and geographically and historically apart they may seem.

Coast is an old mission where people have lived since 1891. Coast is a place where people were born but were affected by the Stolen Generation. Coast is a place where people were re-located to and from other places and in some cases have stayed. Coast is a place where the traditional language is being revived by a few and traditional cultural practice would appear from the outside to be non-existent.

Desert is a service centre where people come in to town from outstations for medical and education reasons, local government services, art business and extremely limited grocery shopping. Some people live in Desert for long and short periods of time. In Desert there are four homes that Indigenous people live in. There are many more homes for the non-Indigenous service providers. Desert is a place where 2 Indigenous language groups exist with both languages being taught in the school. People visit Country regularly, they hunt and care for Country regularly. Desert is a place where people were 'indentured' as labourers, housekeepers and stock people not so far from home. People have had access to their Country. People have strong Knowings about traditional cultural practice, family and kinship structures. People have been less culturally dislocated in Desert than in Coast.

I visited each community three times over a period of two years. Time in each community varied but ranged from two weeks to six weeks each visit.

I am reticent to describe participants as either subjects or participants. I have chosen to refer to people as Colleagues as this indicates more of a sharing relationship where learning took place for all involved in the research journey.

I yarned with eight Colleagues in Desert and ten in Coast. Who were my Colleagues exactly? They were Elders, youth, school teachers, education workers in schools, workers from Indigenous community organisations, unemployed, mothers, fathers, grandparents, uncles, aunties, retired, people who fished, hunted and health workers. Some of these labels overlap with individuals, sometimes more than one overlaps. I have given my Colleagues pseudonyms in the form of native plants. I have chosen plant names not specific to either Desert or Coast as the pseudonyms, so as not to inappropriately identify people. These names are for me more appropriate than English names like Joe, Jan etc. as they at least embody some part of Country and are Indigenous elements of this land. Where people are quoted in the text that follows the reference in brackets uses my transcript notation.

How were my Colleagues 'recruited'? In each community I phoned and sent a letter of introduction and an Information Sheet to explain my research and my intent. I met with members of the Local Council/Land Council to talk about my research and to seek approval for the research to take place. I developed a mind map (Figure 4.1 below) to graphically illustrate my intent and the process. Essentially, I intended to yarn about the research process including; research question and focus, ethics, yarn process, transcribing, feedback and reciprocity, my intended outcomes and the role of those willing to be involved

Figure 4.1. Mind Map of Research Steps

This map identifies the steps to be taken in the research process. From clockwise top right the first arm (purple) refers to the importance of meetings with community people and/or organisations. It also refers to the need to establish a Steering Committee to guide the research; it asks who would be involved and asserts the need to establish an agreed purpose. The third sub-branch of this arm refers to my agenda and background in terms of the personal and the research. It identifies the need to show people photos of 'my place'; including family as well as establish the fact that I was conducting this research for a PhD. It further identifies a few key concepts including; Knowings, mind mapping, Story and Country. The final sub-branch of this arm acknowledges the need for me to leave space for people's questions, their thoughts, experiences and reactions.

The second arm (red/pink) establishes the idea for a Steering Committee and introduces some ideas for discussion including; membership, purpose, ethics and a possible research plan. The Membership Branch asks who should be involved and how many people. The Purpose Branch identifies guiding the research purpose as well as skilling people up in the community into different aspects of research. The Ethics Branch identifies all of the factors necessary for University ethics clearance including; informed consent, information about the complaints process, confidentiality, the fact that people involved in the research can withdraw at any time, the use of recording machines and taking notes which will be appropriately stored in a locked facility. It also picks up the importance of Elders in the research process and the use of appropriate community protocols by myself as the researcher; with the establishment of these at the outset. The Research Plan Branch identifies the need for the Steering Committee to identify the venue, the number of and time for meetings as well as the overall time-frame for the research. A discussion about people's expectations; community, university and the researcher are identified. The next sub-branch identifies any limitations identified at this stage, possible outcomes, the importance of feedback. There is also space for questions, feelings, reactions.

Moving clockwise, bottom left as you face the map is a heading Yarn Times (blue). This refers to the 'interview process'. The sub-branches look at the recruitment of participants or Colleagues; whether I should be looking at individuals, groups, mixed gender and what age groups should be identified if any. The second sub-branch refers to the taping of 'yarns, the taking of notes, the option for people to draw or symbolically respond to the questions. The third sub-branch explains the anticipated number of yarns conducted and the time needed for each of these. The issue of language and translation is raised for people's thoughts, comments and guidance. The final sub-branch refers to the ownership of the material collected and opens up an opportunity for discussion about this.

The fourth branch (brown) identifies the use of Transcripts and the process for such use in the final research. It explains the importance for people who choose to be involved in the yarn to edit the verbatim transcripts which as the researcher I will send back and discuss with people on a special visit. It explores the fact that this process is two-way and often allows for further information to be added in to the yarn. As well as establish whether I have accurately recorded and interpreted the information they have so generously shared.

The fifth arm (green), top left hand side of the page refers to the importance of Feedback to the community as well as those personally involved in the research. It refers the importance of this feedback being ongoing and in mixed media formats.

The final arm (blue) refers to Outcomes. Some Outcomes being the research itself, publications, community links and skilling and any other suggestions.

In Desert I met with the Town Clerk who invited me to speak at a monthly meeting. I had previously sent an Information Sheet and letter of introduction to members of the Council to seek their approval prior to me arriving in Desert. I had spoken to the Town Clerk and emailed him on a number of occasions. The Council approved me coming up to Desert. A number of funerals and 'Sorry Business' impacted on the timing of my meeting with Council; once I had arrived. Meetings were postponed. During this time after many discussions with people who became my Colleagues and after much reflection the mind map developed above was transformed into something more relevant (Figure 4.2). The presentation to Council involved the presentation of the figure below on silk cloth; something transportable, visual and situating people, Country and relationships. The meeting with Council occurred at the end of my first visit. However, members supported and endorsed what I was doing, as they had done prior to my arrival in Desert. My Colleagues involved in the yarns self-nominated after introductions to people from my community facilitator and friend, and after I had 'hung around' and involved myself in the school, the main 'institution' in town.

Figure 4.2. Introduction to Research

Figure 4.2 was drawn by my Desert community facilitator and Colleague after a lot of yarning. It is not a map of Australia without Tasmania. It is a free flowing concept of a place with the blue circles representing locations of Desert and Coast, my Country or origin, work and residence. There are images emerging from the 'map' which appeared without manipulation; images of significance like the eagle (my totem). The 'map' is the presentation or the drawing on the ground. It emerged from the criss-crossing of language lines. Other images emerge from the 'map' for different people as they view it using their own lens, carrying with them their own personal baggage.

In Coast, community people were invited to participate in a meeting. Coast is a small contained community and when a call goes out for a meeting most people know. People self nominated as a result of this meeting and the subsequent time I spent in the community 'hanging around' and yarning with people. I had a strong community contact who also assisted with my introduction to Coast community. My own previous involvement in this community and standing as an Indigenous educator also assisted my 'finding a place' to speak to people initially.

In both Coast and Desert the Steering Committee did not eventuate. Colleagues were happy to guide the process themselves.

SENSE OF PLACE/COUNTRY:

It is imperative to illustrate a sense of place. It is imperative that this be done through the voices at the centre of this research. This is also a departure from the norm with geographical and demographic description traditionally provided through census data, Local Shire or Council data or Government department data none of which seem appropriate because my Colleagues have their own unique forms of description and belonging to the Country visited.

Country is central to the theory, method and Story of this research. Country and sense of place are therefore fundamental on this journey, though conceptualised in ways differing to my original thoughts. I have Storyd Country in more detail in the Prologue and chapter five.

How do I as a researcher talk to people about Indigenous Knowings? I chose to make use of 'Yarning' or 'Yarn Times' (Hanlen, 2002), (Bessarab & Ng'andu, 2010) as discussed in the previous chapter. The following formed the frame for the 'yarns':

Tell me about yourself, your story?
Prompts:

- Tell me about your Country?
- How do you know about your Country?
- How do you feel about being in this Country?
- How did you learn about your Country?
- How do you know about your Country?
- How do other people come to know about Country and culture in [name of community]
- Is story telling important to you, your family and friends? If, so, how and why?
- Could you tell me about your family and their Storys?
- What do you think is important about the way you fellas teach younger fellas about culture and Country?

A Consent Form was used prior to each interview. This form became important because it was a way of describing the research process to Colleagues. In all cases Colleagues responded well to the form and filled it out. I spent a lot of time talking to people before, during and after the yarning about research and research process. I discussed the notion of community, ethics and communities such as those Colleagues were a part of, developing their own ethics process and form for the multitude of researchers coming into their communities.

My assertion was that Indigenous Knowings were centred on the concept of 'Country'. In Desert it became very clear that Indigenous Knowings is centred on relationships; relationships of people with Country, Country with Country and relationships peoples have with each other.

> I guess when I think of my Country I think of my family tree and mum's done a painting of our family tree and it, it really shows that your Country is a part of other people, other individuals, other groups, other languages and I actually see, I guess, my Country as the whole of Australia. So, like mum's painting shows about eight different language groups that that are part of our family tree and so it's just kilometres and kilometres of Country but our Country joins on to someone else's Country… So, you've got to really think of other people in terms of Country and when I think of my Country and to describe it, there's all the laws, your behaviour, the way you think about yourself, the way you think about who you are, where you're heading, what you're going to do in life, your children, your grandchildren, your great grandchildren, in the past, it's all of that, it's very complex when I think of Country. Complex as…individual, the immediate family, mum, dad, brothers and sisters and it goes beyond that, the aunties and uncles, then beyond that when you then bring in the kinship, backing up with all these other groups through that kinship (Lotus).

WATERLILYS: THE VOICES

In an endeavour to re-present my Colleagues voices much reflection took place. How do I re-present people's voices, their quotes, their experiences, their expertise in such a way that the rhythms, colours and dimensions are not distorted? That the contexts are not violently mis-placed? That as the researcher my voice does not distort, contort and submerge those voices of my Colleagues. People's Storys I merely narrate. This misrepresentation of Indigenous voices by past and present researchers across all Disciplines was clearly articulated in the last chapter. This is not a research process I wish to embody.

Upon reflection the cloth done by Desert community as an illustration of the research journey for each and every one of them and myself (Fig.4.3) became a potential source for a framework. A way to re-present, to narrate people's voices in such a way as to be culturally appropriate and meaningful. In reality any illustration of Indigenous Knowings cannot be effectively presented in linear form. Indigenous Knowings are not linear. These are not written using words. As the researcher my dilemma became how to avoid being superficial and hypocritical in my re-presentation of the expertise so generously shared?

What of the process? I and my colleague/s find a place and space to yarn. They tell me their story. I listen, record, watch, experience, later transcribing, returning transcripts for my Colleagues to ponder and edit. As a facilitator I bring people's Storys together Storys not otherwise shared or told, around a central theme. In this instance; Indigenous Knowings become the central theme. This builds a whole picture about Indigenous Knowings; a picture with many parts.

In Desert, my Colleagues illustrated the shared research journey; telling their Story of the process (Figure 4.3). My Colleagues told me that this illustration shows each individual sitting down and yarning. The hands represent each person. The hands are coloured to represent relationships to each other; relationships to Country; for example there is only one grey hand, their totem also in grey is the dingo and there is only one dingo totem person. There are four red circles inside the space where the hands are; these represent the four different countries that people have come from. The circles in the centre is where we all gather, sit and yarn from different Countrys, different relationships. Colleagues relationships and place are illustrated through their totems; the brown snake, the dingo, the green bean. The feet represent me, the facilitator and narrator speaking to each, joining people and their Storys, their experiences together around a common theme. It further illustrates a sharing of ideas. It illustrates Desert. It illustrates relationships of people to people, people to Country and Country to Country.

Figure 4.3. Desert Colleagues Designing Research Process – Shared Research Journey

Figure 4..4 Desert Colleagues Research Process: overlay of people's names, Country & totems

This illustration was created from Desert, not Coast. It is not possible to use it as it is, to re-present Coast voices. However, two processes become cumbersome and merely over complicated. The Storys' from Desert and Coast overlap within and between each other. They repeat. They are both circular in narrative. They are clearly different geographical locations, joined as are many Indigenous communities by song lines, kinship and trade.

In looking at and reflecting on the above issues and the Desert cloth, a new image emerged - that of a Waterlily (Figure 4.5). My Desert Colleagues told me that I was the narrator travelling to and from each Story. Upon reflection I began to explore this as Waterlily where as the narrator, I travelled to and from each colleague like a series of petals on the Lily flower. The petals are not homogenous. Neither are my Colleagues or their experiences and expertise. The petals; the Storys, their experiences overlap. They have layers. The stamen holds all the petals together. The stamen re-generates life as I the researcher/narrator re-generate my colleague's Storys and their experiences.

Figure 4.5. Waterlily

The Waterlily has a strong, slender stem. It has wide flat leaves that float on the top of the water. The stem and the leaves could be conceptualised as Indigenous Knowings. There are many different types of Waterlily. Are there different Indigenous Knowings? This research supports the notion that there are different types of Knowings.

THE MOUNTAIN CALLS ME HOME

> I just don't like going from here, every time I go away, Mountain...calls us back. That's it [Eutaxia].

Coast is one of the places I became a visitor and yarned with people (Figure 4.6). Coast is 'beautiful Country, it's a, it's pretty hilly and there is a lot of coastline with a lot of beach stretches'. The community I was gifted to become involved with live on an old mission which is on 'top of a pretty big hill that's a, surrounded by a lake and um it's got beach views from there'. There are 'rainforests, pretty thick rainforests'.

> ... and um in the Lake, there's a island in the middle of the, it's a sacred Lake and island...it's the shape of a duck' [Eutaxia].

There are mountains of extremely special significance that surround this community; 'the mountains are awesome; so bold, distinct, organic, beautiful with a backdrop to the sea' [JE11/10/02]

Figure. 4.6: Coast Country

The mountains; two in particular, became essential learning sites for me; with yarns on them, around them and reference to them with reverence by all Colleagues:

Words cannot describe today adequately. My spirit has been revitalised. I now know what it is like to feel full again from inside out... We walked through the trees after the interview to an area of granite boulders that carried so much power and energy; fertility, mother earth, penis, fly over the mushroom, pointer shark, serpent, wedding rock, each one a different rock but related to each other. This was like pass the parcel - every step led to a new awesome, powerful, energetic treasure. So much to take in. A is a beautiful teacher. A Kurrawong watched us.

Songs from the valley/rocks, floated/wafted through the space. Sounds of creaking, opening,/shutting hit us periodically as the trees twisted, leant and moved against the rocks. The shark and serpent (rocks) were awesome....I felt 'blown away'...As we drove back the Korrituku flew across our path - A said it was blessing my visit. [JE23/10/02]

This part of the Story weaves personal journal entries, insights from Colleagues and personal experiences that embody the learning. My Colleagues took me to different sites in Country to learn beyond the yarn. I experienced the learning, the Knowing and this as important a part of the journey as the other contributions. My Journal entries took the form of descriptions of events, pictures, drawings and poems. One such poem follows and encapsulates my place in Coast.

Landscape
Country
Let me in,
When you are ready.
I hear your moans and groans
Trees speak
Trees sing these songs
I, so small
Amidst boulders so grand;
Balanced
Poised
My life is in this Country
I was invited in
I was invited in
This Country put me in this landscape [JE23/10/02]

My Colleagues are diverse in background, age and experiences. Grevillea is an Elder whose totem is the white pointer shark 'which is very important to me...the white pointer shark and its people'. Her Country is coastal, north of the Country the yarns were conducted in. Grevillea's mother 'comes from Peru. She's South American. She came here with her mother and her grandmother, my grandma. And when she came to Australia she was taken away by the Aboriginal Protection Board, they thought she was Aboriginal'. Grevillea was raised in a girls home separated from her family. Grevillea married a man from Coast and has lived in Coast for many years. Grevillea has been actively involved in Indigenous education and teaching culture for many years. Grevillea is my Master teacher in Coast. She is my facilitator for Coast community. Grevillea is softly spoken, strong and proud, a mother and grandmother. Grevillea embodies wisdom in every sense of the word. Our yarn was conducted in Country and my learning was conducted through visits to different Country.

Acacia is a young Aboriginal mother. A twin who has travelled across borders to 'do schoolin' '. Growin' up over the years I sort of, felt, there was some part of me missin' mmm...It's like I'm lost, lost between two different places where, they both have significance to me .... She has worked in Aboriginal education and in community welfare as well as having studied at TAFE and University. When she speaks she is energetic and passionate about education.

Callistemon is a strong, articulate Aboriginal mother of two. She has worked in Country, in tourism and in education. She has a silent but expressive strength. Callistemon 'I think, I think what is important to me...I grew up in the past with um my mum and my dad being very...much um in their culture and understanding more about their culture.... Callistemon is from Coast; 'my peoples, my father's, my ancestors all from down this coast' . Our yarn was conducted outside. *Callistemon 'is a gifted storyteller', so animated and so alive, she uses her hands and body as she speaks.' (JE 24th October 2004).* Callistemon has studied at University.

Banksia was born outside of Coast and has lived in Coast for three years. He was raised in an urban environment visiting the nearby 'mish'[2]. He went to school in this environment. 'My totem is a, a red kangaroo, on my mum's side. Dad was Irish'. Banksia is an Aboriginal man who has been taught and introduced into Coast by a community Elder no longer living in this space, 'I've adopted, this as my Country now ...'. He fishes and our yarn was conducted on his boat whilst he fished and I listened and wrote. He is direct and reflective.

Lomandra is an older Aboriginal woman working in a significant community position in Coast. She was born elsewhere, away from coast and married into Coast community. She is one of 8 children, a mother of three and grandmother of many. Lomandra has lived in Coast for eleven years. She has been actively involved in community health, training and tourism. Lomandra though feeling reticent about what she had to offer engaged in the yarn with warmth and nervous laughter. We yarned in her Office.

Hibbertia is an older Aboriginal woman who was born at Coast and lived in Coast all of her life. She is a mother of two and from a family of 7 children.

> 'About my Country . Well, I only learnt about my Country and culture when I was in my 30's, think it was. I was told, it was just as children we weren't allowed to hang around the old people and hear about, learn about culture?'

---

[2] Mission

Hibbertia works in a key position in Coast. Our yarn was conducted outside.

Myrtle and Melaleuca were born in Coast and are a married couple. They went to the Mission school. Myrtle spent her childhood traveling with her family following the fruit and vegetable picking seasons.

> ...we grew older we left that farm, mum and dad left that settlement because they wanted to do pea picking, and peas and corn...They did it until they got that sick they couldn't do it any more, you know work....

> Well, when I was growing up here in [Coast], it's really different from, of today. With my growing up on here, mum and dad used to go fishin', they'd have a big bowl of milk, we'd have scones, we'd walk, they'd walk....

> Oh yes, and we used to, every Christmas...we used to go to X. Before you go on the Station there, you'd have to report. Dad would have to report, to let them know we was going to see grandfather.

Myrtle and Melaleuca yarned with me in their home.

Leucopogon is a young Aboriginal man, a father, who was born at Coast.

> I'm but um the son of ah one of the last tribal Elders...yeah no, I just, you know I'm really proud you know to be a son of a tribal Elder that's ah...initiated me the right way.

Leucopogon is energetic, passionate, reflective and direct. Non-verbal communication was extremely important during this yarn conducted on the verandah of his home.

Eutaxia is a middle aged Aboriginal man who

> 'has lived here all our lives and,...Grew up here,...One day probably buried here....The Country is, I just love this place here. Our home, you know that yourself, you got your Country, you're happy in your own little area, you know. I like to go north too, travel here and there but don't stay too long because old mountain up there always calls me back home.

Eutaxia is a father. He is a straight talker.

NYINDIRRUM INKYJUK

I guess when I think of my Country I think of my family tree and mum's done a painting of our family tree and it, it really shows that your Country is a part of other people, other individuals, other groups, other languages...So, you've got to really think of other people in terms of Country and when I think of my Country and to describe it, there's all the laws , your behaviour, the way you think about yourself, the way you think about who you are, where your heading, what you're going to do in life, your children, your grandchildren, in the past, it's all of that, it's very complex when I think of Country (Lotus).

Desert is the other place I became a visitor and yarned with people. The community I was gifted to become involved with, 'live in', is a service centre where people come in to town from outstations for medical and education reasons, local government services, art business and extremely limited shopping. Some people live in Desert for long and short periods of time. The Country people describe includes the service centre and some of the outstations from a 40 kilometre radius.

… It's a smaller, area in the desert, dry, creek bed [unclear] it's usually dry during the [unclear] but sometimes after rain it's full up...and it's a swimmin' place. It's a really rocky area...Yeah, there's a lot of hills around it and some of my...old people told me that there's a few, natural springs around that are a Yeah...and there's a lot of kangaroos, emus, um...there's a lot of cattle round that area [Cassinia].

Well, it's got a, three big water holes and those three waterholes, that other waterhole the womens can't go there but we use other two waterholes...The people long time ago, like people used to grind seeds [Epacris].

Figure 4.7. Desert Country - Water Holes

My Colleagues are diverse in background, age and experiences. Lilly is an Elder, small in stature, brown snake is her Dreaming and she grew up on a cattle station that many local people had connections with in Desert. Lilly went elsewhere to 'work' where she looked after the nanny goats, sheep and horses as well as working at the homestead. She describes her Country as 'big creek and water hole, him's long creek'. Lilly is a language speaker and moves between living in town and in Country. She is a Master of dance and body painting. Lilly is a vast repository of Knowings.

Casuarina worked on a cattle station mustering and droving cattle. His Dreaming is Dingo. Casuarina is an Elder, a Master of language, song and dance. He is a traditional speaker. Casuarina moves between town and Country.

Lotus was born outside of Desert and is 'a freshwater person' who loves the water; 'the water is one of my Dreamings...I miss it sooo much....I could come down here to desert and I know my skin group...and these mob down here in Desert straight away, they fit me in to their family'. Lotus has a western college education and vast experience as a classroom teacher in three different States and Territories. She is young and speaks her own language as well as being instructed in Desert language. Casuarina is an artist. Lotus and I are Nangala (daughters, grand daughters) to Yam and Epacris. Lotus has been my facilitator in to community. She blooms through poetry, art, music, song, dance, - she is a creative element, a tangible holistic symbol of everything this research embodies..

Yam is a strong traditional woman Elder and teacher of dance, body painting and language. Yam is my main teacher, my Professor. Her Dreaming is snake Dreaming; brown snake. Yam grew up in and around Desert. She worked on a cattle station milking cows for the station manager, ironing, washing clothes and washing dishes. She is mother, grandmother, great grandmother, auntie and sister to many. Yam is my grandmother; Nakamarra.

Cactus says 'my mother's from 'ere and my father's from ere as well'. Cactus is an Aboriginal woman working as an Aboriginal Health Worker and studying in the field of health. Cactus walks in both worlds. She is reserved in her speech, quiet. Her face and eyes are highly animated as she uses non-verbal language so powerfully. Cactus facilitates my yarns with others as a translator of language and context. She is a strong and centred presence.

Epacris is a young mother who breast feeds her young daughter as we speak. Her daughter and husband from other Country, are integral to our yarns, though silent observers. She is an Aboriginal Education Worker studying to be an Aboriginal teacher. She is an artist, a linguist and a mediator between two worlds. Epacris' Country is 'west of the station, that's my father's homeland'. I am daughter to Epacris. Epacris has been my facilitator, my teacher; the person to ground me in both Country and context.

Cassinia was born at a station where her family lived 'I grew up there and, cause there was no school there, so we moved to Desert station where I am staying now and, uh, sometimes we go back to x station because that's where my traditional place is'. Cassinia is an Aboriginal Education Worker and studying to be an Aboriginal teacher. She is a painter, a dancer and a gifted storyteller. *Cassinia's energy is awesome, her body language is strong, powerful, expressive, mainly her hands and face (JE 18th Nov. 2004).*

Senna is an Aboriginal teacher whose Country is Desert; 'I born here'. 'My Country is west of...but I originally stay in Desert, grow up here, and lost my parents. I grow up with my grandfather and Auntie (Yam). She stayed with Christian families in a main city for some of her childhood. Senna speaks and teaches multiple languages.

Two of my Colleagues are female Elders who accompanied others during their yarn sessions. They didn't speak verbally or respond directly. They endorsed what others were saying in non-verbal ways. They 'all got same Dreaming, got same Dreaming, Snake'. They grew up around Desert. One worked at Desert Station 'to milk the cow for the station manager and worked as a laundryer washing things, dishes and maybe clothes and she used to do ironing'.

A number of children accompanied others during their yarn sessions and during our Country visits. They sat, played, listened when they chose to, mimicked, explored, experimented and belonged.

> *I am a learner in a wondrous world with sooo much beauty in the*
> *harshness, dryness. We miss much when we look around us* (JE Sunday
> 10th Nov. 2004).

Stamen appears in the text that follows; Stamen is me, the facilitator, researcher.

There are three other important characters or essences that flow intermittently in the sea that is this book; Trakka, Shadow and Jaambe. How can dogs possibly assume such importance in an academically rigorous piece of work? Conferences papers and articles have identified the significance and problems associated with dogs in Indigenous communities (O'Brien, 1979) and (Raw).

For the purpose of this book dogs are active members of the communities visited. I formed friendships with three such dogs who have patiently listened to my narratives, questions, frustrations and joys. Each of these dogs accompanied me on different parts of my research journey. They may not be warding off evil spirits but they have and still do provide comfort and warmth in an otherwise unstable and perplexing environment

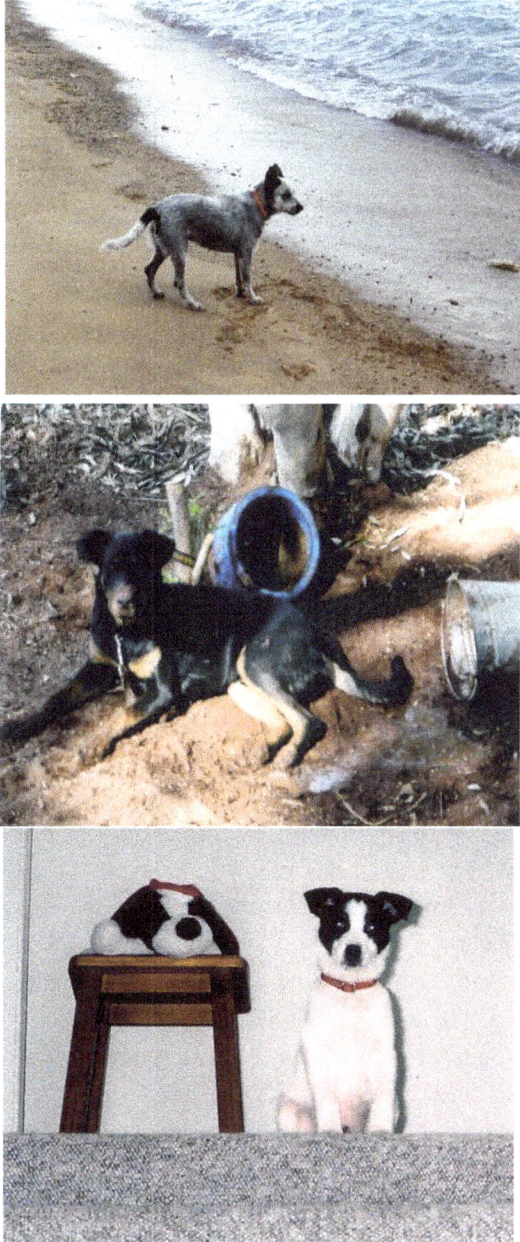

Figure 4.8. Trakka, Shadow and Jaambe

An image emerged after much discussion and reflection with Colleagues in desert; an image to help yarn about Indigenous Knowings. An image that drew on Colleagues voices. An image that played a part in the research process, the research journey that has its place in Desert (see Figure 4.3). This image was grown and represents one of the waves that washed ashore and left its mark in the evolution of the PhD thesis.

Indigenous Knowings are about Story. It is about one's Story being told by the custodian of that Knowing. It is pooled and shared. It is built on much like a wave in the sea. It gathers energy, power and force as each element injects its own essence. In this text my reflections and analysis are secondary to those of my Colleagues. The literature is also secondary.

Now my Colleagues tell their own Storys...verbatim.... They tell us about the following:

    i)   Knowing about Country?
    ii)   Feeling about Country?
    iii) Learning and Knowing about Country?

Listen to their voices, their words. Hear their rhythms and the colours of their words, their lived experiences. The language is Aboriginal English so remember to tune your senses in and to engage with the webpage for a deeper listening, understanding of these Storys, these Knowings. Read as if reading a play or picture yourselves in the following Yarn ...

KNOWING ABOUT YOUR COUNTRY?

L o t u s : Um, um, you see it being told, you know, to kids when they're very young, as you travel around you learn whose Country is...But another way you know is through paintings, you know, a lot of people have taken on contemporary ways, so, canvas paintings might show someone's Dreaming, so it might be bush tucker Dreaming and that person, you learn about that person's Country or your own Country if you learn this drawing, you know drawing ...about your Country or you learn about your Country and they might give you a painting, it might be bush tucker Dreaming and then, you know, you'll be trotting along and then they'll say – that's bush tucker Dreaming there. The painting you saw, you don't really know exactly where it is but you've seen what it looks like before you've got there and when you're there, then it all fits and then once you get all the different Storys of painting, things start piecing up everybody's Country. I mean,...that's one way of learning about other people's Country and your own....You can see this through painting or you actually go hunting, learn about Country and whose Country it is ...heaps of ways to learn about Country....when you go with the old people, they show you...and tell you Storys of how that was created, ...created .

S t a m e n : Storys are told. You go to Country...who with?

E p a c r i s : Well, first when I was little my father took me to my Country. And my family father, my father's father, and there was tellin' me, they was tellin' me and showin' me. The said to me – This is your Country, this your homeland. You go...the land, understanding...look after and maybe all my family, grandchilds can look after our Country. And,...they told me not to go further up to other waterhole cause that a sacred site only mans go there and not allowed kids, especially girls and young boys.

Cactus: Um, it was told to us...by grandparents who, um,...it was passed on through great grandparen' parents and mothers and great grandfathers and that's how all...everyone...which Country they belong to...different um, skin groups or that, different places and that's how the families passed it on from generation to generation and takin' the young kids and young boys, showing them all the secret sites, men's sacred sites and women's sacred sites and where men and women are not allowed to go, areas where all the men go, yeah....Yeah. ...

They, take us out, we walk along the bush, they show us that hills mens business, women's business or um... well that hills a, something Dreaming, snake Dreaming or kangaroo Dreaming. Yeah. Then...they show us, like sit down with us on the ground and they show just... show were all the place are like they draw a little map on the ground in sand and show us where we are and where all this other stuff and...waterholes and...all that...what they go and take us over there, show us what they are.

... They only show the ones that we can see not the ones we can't see, they usually just tell us, and maybe draw a map. Yeah

We walk along the bush they would tell us men's business or women's business along the hills and they would tell snake Dreaming or kangaroo Dreaming and they show us like they sit down on the ground and they show me all the places they do a little map on the ground in the sand and show us (unclear) or they go over there and take us and show us where they are.

... but if there's older people with kids then they, then the old people tell the, um, young adults, and they tell all the kids or grandkids...and it's really good to, um, if kids go over with old people and go, hunting with them and show them how to do stuff like, um, get bush tucker and stuff. Yeah.

[our] grandparents, father, uncles and um older people used to tell them about them.

Y a m : My older brother took him to his Country and he explained it and show her around Country what that snake had been doin'.

They past away a long time and they pass it on to [me]and [I] know the songs and body paintings that Elders pass it on to [me].

S t a m e n : Knowing is Knowing songs and body painting passed on …

S e n n a : How I know, because I grow up with my family and they teach me and I can look around with, I can look around and around the 'Desert' I know which way to go, which way song come from, where is, what's flower tells us, what roots tell us do, what times shadow tell us. Spirits, we feel it around here, that's why we can't leave this communities. We live with the little town but we still in Spiritual and we get Knowings strong here....We want the Aborigine kids to learn with the language, the first language, English is the second language for us. And, we know the place, what's to tell us...tree, clouds, birds, Spirit, when sunset and as we feel when we walk on the, without shoes, we feel it on the ground because the, we, um, we just like a Spirits people round here. But when, like you, come from another place, you like just a sister for us....And, yeah, we feel it and when we see the plant, new plant come up after the fire burn, we burn a fire for new plant, just like we, um, we, we are growed again, our bodies just growed again, like strong, Knowings, we get Spirit, our cultures are strong, yeah, round here. That's why we follow and old people when we go and visit them and talk about language and old people says – This is our Spirit growing now...that's the new …, that's the new leaves coming out, that's our body, we are strong.

S t a m e n : Knowing is feeling, Spirit, strong culture and language, all growing and a part of us, our bodies. Our bodies represent our Knowing …

C a s s i n i a : Well, um, our Elders tells us Storys. My father used to tell me Storys and my mother and my aunty and my grandmother, great great grandmother, yeah. And they used to tell us story just by telling us, on the sand Storys or by, um, doing body paintings. That's so when you...were used to paintings on our body to represent our traditional, um...Yes....for us...through the women, so, um, when they're dancing.

S t a m e n : Storys; embodied in song, body painting and dance show our Knowing, our relationships with and between each other, with and between Country …

L i l l y : [my] grandfather and father used to show them their Country around that, around her area, yeah. And show all the Dreaming places too.
Casuarina: same too.

S t a m e n : Different Country, different history yet dancing and songs tell and show us our place …

G r e v i l l e a : …we watched the big corroborees I could see the fires at the back of them and all these big, handsome, strong men were all dancing, dancing the songs that I know today as my cultural teaching that I've kept in my heart…. constantly we were told to sit still and watch and when we went home we'd get asked questions and that was the other part that the Elders knew which child was very interested and even though I always felt silly and inferior yet they gave me to, they said – Grevillea you've got to go on down because 'x' wants to talk to you… . And so I began to go down to x and sit down in his lovely cane chair with the pillows around me and a big bonfire and a black chain with soot and the black billy can full of lovely water boiled and he'd make a cup of tea, a mug of tea for us and he'd have two dogs there either fire side howling away while he played a violin….Well, well it was, it was written, I think, in the future by the Great Spirit that I would, I would, they were my people, they're my kinship system, marrying kinship system.

S t a m e n : Even when we move from our own Country our place is identified;

G r e v i l l e a : When I first came here she accepted me straight away and she was my Elder I didn't realise that…daughters didn't know me but then got to know me they kept taking me fishing and Auntie J, my Elder she was the one took me under her wing and taught me about this site up here this beautiful mountain called G she said to me out in the boat I had to go every day to see her and one day I missed and she was angry with me, oh God, and then I take her out in the boat every day and she showed me the sites and everywhere and I retained that knowledge because I realised then that this was my second Country because I was sent here by the Spirit and when I come up this beautiful mountain there was my totem further up there near the serpent the White Pointer Shark it looks like a shark and it looks like a dolphin but it comes from the ocean and that's where I fit in and it was the Spirit that put that printed that on that women's mouth. And the teaching of the women up here that's my totem the white pointer shark is here on the [Coast], got here before me... Yeah, we'll see that when we're 'oing.

S t a m e n : Knowing and learning ...

A c a c i a : it come from me own knowledge you know as campin' on the land and bein' one with the land, ...

S t a m e n : Knowing is belonging, being told, being given permission ...

B a n k s i a : ... I myself have come to the realisation I belong to in the whole of this land no matter where I go I know I realise that I must ask permission of the local people to be able to do this or do that or walk here or walk there to see (unclear).

S t a m e n : Knowing for some is not being told or shown ...

L o m a n d r a : My family never told me anything about my Country. They were back in the days when children were being taken, you know, and um, they never talked about it, never talked about culture or anything like that.
S t a m e n : Knowing is listening...and remembering;

H i b b e r t i a : Well, I first went up the, mountain there with Uncle, when I was in my 30's, and he told us some Storys up there and um went out with a, lady called Grevillea who ah, schools and things, and I just listened and I picked everything up by listening to peoples Storys to the old people to what they said. Never writ it down. I just kept it in my head. What they pass on to me I pass on to the young children. So, that's how I learned....

L e u c o p o g a n : It is important, it's something that you don't want to lose. It's so important that you remember it. You know? Like between now and years to come. Yeah. Because that's, that's what you can pass down. Yeah. What you've seen and what you know yourself. That what keeps you going, our culture ...You never really think about it you just live it. You just go through it.

S t a m e n : Knowing then, is remembering, going through it ...

E u t a x i a : go here and there.

FEELING ABOUT BEING IN COUNTRY …?

S t a m e n : I facilitated the Storys exploring people's feelings as these were so clearly integral to our journey together. Our feelings were felt at different stages through each of our senses. People told of their feelings as distant and not so distant memories. They told and we experienced together feelings as we yarned. People's feelings about being in Country, about Knowing and learning;

L o t u s : . . . It's great...I love it. Um, a sense of peace, of …, it's a little bit like the feeling here, you know, …sitting here and you hear, you hear different kinds of winds, it's a little bit like that. Just the soft, the softness in the winds.

Cactus: mmm feel proud and happy, healthy, yeah and just feeling good about bein' there, with all the family, all the relatives....

S t a m e n : Feelings about Country embody relationships, elements of nature;

S e n n a : We fee' like, like, we feel the wind blowing but my mind's always close to them, like, we follow the wind, we follow the shadow, we look at roots and trees …, we follow that, that's our culture when we follow. And we feel it, that's our home and that's our culture and that's our language. It's getting strong and strong.

S t a m e n : Feelings about Country physically and emotionally real …

G r e v i l l e a : I feel alive and I feel, oh, really good because this is my Country and I feel like there's spirits all around me and they're all here and they're seeing me and I can feel their presence and I find no problem with that.

A c a c i a : Sense of, just a sense of bein' here and being a part of it...you feel at ease, your mind...and...just,...I don't know, just, ya know bein' out in amongst the trees,...is a sense if being, being there with all the land...The joy...of...just bein', born to this land, (voice croakey) and...sort of...just feel, you feel love, joy ya know...just bein' here...… it's just like a, bein' born, and then rebein', being reborn...and all that sorta just, it makes you feel, at one with yourself.

S t a m e n : Feeling about Country is being in it, not separate from it. Country is 'lived in and lived with, it is a nourishing terrain' (Bird Rose, 1996, p. 7).

H i b b e r t i a : How do I feel, well I, feel a part of it because I was born here.

S t a m e n : We walked through the trees after the interview to an area of granite boulders that carried so much power and energy....So much to take in. Grevillea is a beautiful teacher. A Kurrawong watched us. Songs from the valley/rocks floated/wafted through the space. Sounds of creaking, opening/shutting hit us periodically as the trees twisted, leant and moved against the rocks (J.E., 23/10/02, pp.2-3).

S t a m e n : Feelings, spoken clearly as portrayals of Knowing which don't exist outside of our Knowing process.

LEARNING AND KNOWING ABOUT COUNTRY …?

S t a m e n : Learning and Knowing about Country through Storys, being taken out and shown if you are the right person to become the caretaker or custodian for that Knowing and learning. People have different responsibilities in this process.

L o t u s : Um, other ways, is through Storys,...sitting down around the fire and …Storys...Storys and that, your own Country,...The old people take you out,...I might take visitors back home, certain ceremonies might happen, welcome ceremony and where my old people take my friend and sits down to.... Whoever's chosen to actually do that ceremony, they take them...about Country that is the right people are chosen to do certain ceremonies. That's one other way of learning, through ceremony and the different roles people play and the responsibilities that....

S t a m e n : So show us around, tell us Storys …

C a c t u s : Through, by my grandparents at Desert. They completed my homeland when I was little, they show me around, they teach me how to look after things around water holes, rock …[6.8] they teach me how to find bush tuckers, cause there's other things similar like bush tucker, there's the poison things too round them water hole....And sometime animal comes and eat them, they die. Yeah. They grow like bush tomatoes. And animal...come and eat it....and...bush tuckers left in...And its causing, that kill animals. Yeah but never kill …[7.5] people only makes them really sick. Really sick and vomiting, really sick.

Well, they take us there. Sometime we camps around...and show us around, tell a story about spirits in there …[8.1] and then dance around at night, they show us a dance properly and they do body painting on our bodies and...and do like that with the …

That's through, um, like older people when they used to watch them...while women sit, while men used to make them get up and stand next to women...they used to sit them down and they used to show them dance...following them...standing behind and watch them how they use their feet and arms and you know their body, um, yeah.

S t a m e n : Body painting and dancing became a part of my own journey and my own way of learning. I was told. I listened. I watched. I danced. They laughed …with me as I became a part as I felt spiritually whole even for only a quarantined moment in time and space.

Figure 4.9. Ned with Colleagues from Desert during Body Painting

The webpage shares part of my journey; I have permission to share/show the photos and to play the song.

Yam: She said that when she's older her grandmother and everyone held to pass on the story of this Country and she know the song of this Country and dancing and also body painting [Yam sings traditional song on tape] Snake Dreaming.

S t a m e n : Listening, watching, being told and shown are the ways people share their Knowing. Relationships are fundamental to our Knowing. Relationships of the teacher and the learner, the custodian of the knowledge and the ascribed vessel of that Knowing. Relationships to Country and to each other.

C a s s i n i a : Yes, we learn, um, the other way that we learn is through dot painting, looking at the painting, looking at the land, through mapping, marking, marking the land where the place, the Dreaming starts and where it stops. Sometime might, um, jump over in to another, um, Dreaming....Yeah, like stepping over, say, say this is your area, so jumps over and makes another area there. Yes. And, um, they become families, relations. And, yeah, related to each other.

C a c t u s   t r a n s l a t i n g   f o r   L i l l y : Her (Lilly) grandfather wasn't round when she was round. Her father showed most of her, all the Country and knowledge…

Her other sister's Country is really close, they sort of close to each other. But there's still call that areas their Country, yeah, it's sort of close as well, yeah. When they have, like, Land Council meetings everyone from that area go to the meeting, yeah.

Everyone show their Country. Take everyone out and they show which Country theirs....Yeah, they used to draw and show them where their Country.

E p a c r i s   t r a n s l a t i n g   f o r   C a s u a r i n a : His father (Casuarina): showed him that Country, yeah. His Dreaming, dingo Dreaming. He was taken to that Country and showed them.

S t a m e n : Taken to Country and shown. Shown through body painting, dance, Story, song, mapping and painting. This is how people tell me and show me how they and others learn and Know about Country, about culture. I was shown body painting and taught about the seven sisters as we danced after being painted. My learning was reinforced later through a painting done by my Country mother, Epacris.

I was also taken and shown how to make a coolamon. This was done before the dancing and body painting shared above. It was done after relationships were identified. It was done after initial yarns took place. It was done prior to the research yarns. This experiential learning had many layers and many facets of time.

My research journey into the concept and practice of Indigenous Knowings/s as already stated took many forms; most unexpected. I use my journal extracts combined with still photos, video footage and music to be watched, read and listened to simultaneously.

There is a story I know...explaining this research journey as told through extracts from my research journal.

> *How do I begin to explain today? Words are inadequate. My experience here is my thesis - I am learning and being learnt by some very special people. Today, Yam, her grand daughter and old fella [Casuarina] took us to find a coolamon tree. We went to their camp first...and picked up some tools. That old fella show me the string he was making from hair - for belts and head bands. We stopped and found the right tree and Yam chopped the tree and cut out the coolamon. [Two children] watched Yam for a while then cut down their own tree and began to make coolamon. Watching Yam: patience, skill, sense of design, no wasted action, rhythm, harmony, holistic vision -. She used the axe to create the main shapes, the depth of inside (watching the bark come off was awesome - one piece as she hit the back of it). Then she used a file to work the inside. The coolamon dries in the sun for a week. Yam comes over later and finished Lotus's coolamon which Lotus [and her son] gave to me. (I am a very lucky person, a very blessed person). Yam set up a fire and had 3 wire bits with curves which she heated up in the fire - she marked the coolamon. The design was not a special personal Dreamtime design. Yam worked non stop, she would stop for a few seconds look at the whole coolamon then continue working - again no wasted movements - clarity, peace, purpose, focus, harmony. [Grand daughter] watched and made suggestions as Yam worked. She finished the inside of the whole coolamon I am overwhelmed - feeling inadequate, in awe - a few words that don't come close. Sitting on the ground, on the red earth and watching, trying to absorb, but so far away.* (J.E.10 November 2002).

The coolamon making happened prior to the goanna hunting and the teaching at the rock holes (the rock holes were significant in every colleague's yarn). We went to the rock holes twice; before the rain and after it.

> *What a day to remember. Yam, Epacris, Cactus, their mum, Lotus [and son] and [three young boys] and I went out to the rock holes (to look at the grooves where seeds were ground - they look like my photo of axe grinding grooves in Darkinjung Country). We stopped along the way to track goannas and catch them. It was a stinking hot day. These women astound me -their stamina, energy, vision. [Nine year old boy] tracked one goanna. Yam dug for the hole/tunnel. Goannas have back bones so you use the crow bar to feel for something soft in the tunnel. One person waits to get the goanna at the end - grab it by the tail and hit its head on the ground a few times. Young [non-Indigenous boy] caught one of the two goannas and he was so ecstatic he stood there holding it saying "I've caught my first goanna" - The women were trying to get him to kill it so it didn't bite him. He swung it around a few times and then hit it - the women laughed. At the next hole [one of the women] was digging and felt something which turned out to be a King Brown snake (soft and no backbone when digging and feeling) - the women's totem. The snake scared the shit out of all of us. It came out of the hole, and puffed up its body as it emerged.*

Goanna: yellow = eating, black = medicine

> *We found a clump of trees to stop, have a feed and do the yarns. I had bought bread rolls, chicken, sliced meat, tomatoes, cheese etc., - of course - cooking up the goannas (x2). None of us had matches and the car lighter - well it took three people (eventually Epacris got it - after Lotus and I) to get a spark to light the fire. The goannas went on the hot coals then were put in a dug out earth hole with coal on the top. One goanna was pregnant, so the eggs were cooked and eaten. These fellas rely on goanna (after lightning - the heralding of rain they come out of their holes). Best to catch early - mid-morning when sunning themselves. I tried some goanna - texture like calamari, chewy, ok flavour. I did the yarns while Lotus took the kids away for a while. We looked at the rock holes where seeds were ground by sitting next to the water holes. About*

twelve holes which women still look after - keep clean. On the way home we stopped for witchetty grubs - Yam is an awesome hunter. She got so many really big ones! They feel like marshmallows. We took people home giving them an esky full of food. Strong women, patient, persevere, insightful, skilled, amazing vision, perspective, eyesight...I felt exhausted, overwhelmed.

WORDS: Dimension, Space

Figure 4.10. Desert - Goanna Hunting and cooking

Lotus talked to (non-Indigenous boy) about looking and seeing goanna - using his eyes to scan the big picture, the whole scene - not just focusing on bits, small parts. I found it really hard to see the goanna - admittedly I was driving on dirt roads but - I have to let go, train my eyes (Tony Buzan has a sight exercise which relates to this). Seeing holistically, from above, an aerial view is so important in how these fellas paint, think, tell story.

Watching Yam dig for witchetty grubs was unbelievable - she worked her way around the base of the tree finding roots with grubs inside.

Words: tenacious, persistent, strong, silent, dignified, powerful. (J.E. 16th November 2002, pp.1-4)

Figure 4.11. Desert - Witchetty Grub Gathering

Figure 4.12. Desert - Witchetty Grubs

Figure 4.13. Desert - Research in Progress

It is so interesting that on tape Casuarina and Lilly speak a limited story but they as did Yam took me out after the interview and showed me more rock holes, Agie tree (berries) bush tucker - this is where the learning is.

Casuarina chopped down a sugar bag tree but there was no honey.

Figure 4.14. Desert - Cutting Sugar Bag Tree

They both tell yarns as you walk around with them. The experience of the talk is so important. They both used a lot of non-verbal communication during the interview, and referenced to directions with pointing. They drew in the ground. I come away feeling elated, filthy dirty, relaxed, tired, exhilarated. ...

Smells: rain, water in rock holes - stagnant/mosquito larvae, dust settling. Hot with a cool breeze. Ants as they squash. (J.E. 1st December 2002, pp. 2-4).

Figure 4.15. Desert - Water Holes After the Rain

Time as measured in seconds, minutes and hours had no place in any of the learning experiences. Time existed only in respect of the season, the rain, the position of the sun and the winds.

The experiences my Colleagues and I shared in this research journey culminated in a round table session to illustrate the journey we all shared.

Everyone one interviewed except Senna and Cactus (her mum did her hands for her) came over to Lotus's and painted their hands and put them on some linen - green = King Brown Dreaming, silver = Dingo Dreaming, Yellow = Lice, Red = Eagle (me). Epacris connected the hands using Nyndirrum Inkytjuk and me (footprints) and homelands (different ones). Such a powerful way to end - ...The process was toooo deadly - these fellas are so generous. (J.E. 4ᵗʰ December 2002, pp. 1-2)

The product of this session is illustrated below and has been used to develop my framework for this chapter, in some ways for this research. I repeat this image and the representation as a Story must. Story is repetition.

Figure 4.16. Desert - Indigenous Research Process

S t a m e n : Taken to places in Coast and shown and told.

> *Grevillea and I went to [X Cultural Centre] to pick up [the driver] and*
> *the 4 wheel drive. [The driver] drove us up to Mt. G. This is where the*
> *real adventure began.*
>
> *Iron barks; strong, tall and thin, white, green tree ferns, small, large and*
> *huge, windy, guttered road, lantana en masse - all marked our drive up*
> *Mt. G. Grevillea and I sat at the table at the top to do our interview. It*
> *was soooo windy and cold (it was hot below). Drops of rain periodically*
> *touched us. [The driver] slept and sat in the car....We walked through*
> *the trees after the interview to an area of granite boulders that carried*
> *so much power and energy* (J.E. 23rd October 2002, pp.1-2).

S t a m e n : Taken to places and told about learning as kids, together, Indigenous and non-Indigenous learning. So much learning intertwined over and between many different cultural paths:

G r e v i l l e a : Where I come from, we grew up with the understanding that all us kids played together, went swimming together, we swam in the river, shark infested waters, had no fear of the sharks. We fed on figs all day long while we sat out there enjoying ourselves and the figs was everything to us, it was food, medication, it was a necessary, healing fig that we all enjoyed and ate. We never went home in the day, we just went home in the afternoon and we were always in groups. The older girls and the older boys always protected the younger ones and wherever we went swimming in the rivers, there was only salt water coming in to our Country, never fresh water and wherever we went swimming or fishing, the older boys and girls protected us. So we got to know the areas very well and we felt their protection all the time. We learnt where to go for water, we learnt how to bring home some of the stuff that was needed. We learnt how the, that's the little lizards, built their nests, they were lumps...and we recognise what they were, we were taught by the Elders and they said to us – What's that little bit there? What's that build up in that dirt there? And we would say, oh, don't know – Would you just go and have a look, you start raking there. Is it the same as the other area? And we'd say, No not the same – So will you dig there? All right...And we'd start digging and out would roll these eggs and we'd be, well I remember the first time it happened to me and I was, ah, shocked and surprised and happy that I was able to do that, produce eggs that didn't belong to me. And we all had to be taught that way, bit by bit, foot by foot and trail by trail in the bush. And the bark and the trees and the plants were everything because that was there to protect the forest and to protect us as we survived thousands of years in this Country.

And we all learnt all about that and we could all swim like fish and we made our own little canoes and we lived in the mud and then we went home. It was beautiful. My mother used to take me fishing down at the same places and I noticed she'd take me, and never say a word and I'd say to her Mum, Mum what are you doing here? There would be a little creek, an inlet and that used to come with the high tide that would go out, flush out, like water in the tub, go out with the tide and she used to say to me – Never mind, don't talk. And she would have this special wattle on these special trees and she would gather it down and she would crush it all up and she'd get me, mind you, to swim in this water because it was low tide and I could see all the little holes at my feet and I'd say Mum, Mum this is frightening me and she'd say – No, you're all right. And so what I didn't realise was that I was putting plants in this water that my mother knew the tide would be up before about 3 or 4 hours and then that would service the feeding of the fish you know, make them hungry. And then the next morning early she'd bring me back with her. I had a little rod with a line and the hook that she put on, that we bought from Europeans, farmers, and she'd put that, attach that to my line. She would have a line and we'd be pulling in the fish all day until we had enough to go home. She was a very clever mum and I enjoyed that life and I learnt all the secrets of the old people because they were interested in me because when my dad, my Irish side, my dad he began to teach me and he taught me how to read...white literature. He used to buy me papers, he'd send me to town with my legs through the bar of the bike, a male bike, and I go in to town and buy two lots of papers, come back and we'd lean up against the beautiful house made of tin...that my dad built for us. And we'd be reading and I'd say to him, Dad what's that there? And he'd have a little pencil tied to a string and some little ball of paper in his pocket and every time I asked a question, he'd get me to write it down. You know I could read fluently by the time I got to school, a school and then we weren't allowed to go in to any white schools and we had a teacher that was sent from x place every morning on a push bike, he was a very nice man, we all liked him. A young Salvation Army, a Christian young man and as we listened to what he had to say, it was very important because we were brought up traditionally and our brains were working from the time we were born and so when he began to teach us white ways and the way to read or write or whatever, the consonants and the vowels that is taught in every school, I caught on quickly and all of us our brains were just like hitting a tennis ball against the wall, we were so adaptable. And that's the beauty of Aboriginal people growing up and teaching and keeping their own cultural way of teaching that's been lost today. But you know the heartache of most of us because our Elders have died and have taken that with them. And I regret that because I could speak my language when I left home when I went to college I...for myself and I couldn't, um, I lost the idea of my culture because there was no need for it after a while you had to learn English you had to learn all sorts of things that didn't belong to you. …

Yes, you knew that people were from other countries or you was from another Country or you came from a Country …because people brought people messages, there were constant corroborees and those corroborees were really large corroborees. I remember as a little toddler, the rest of my gang that I grew up with, my children like in the area, like I grew up with my cousins and the people there and we watched the big corroborees I could see the fires at the back of them and all these big, handsome, strong men were all dancing, dancing the songs that I know today as my cultural teaching that I've kept in my heart. And so, there were the Elders at the back with big fires and here's these men, fire would be dancing...with their spears and they would be activating culture that was taught to them in their initiations. And so then I knew what that was because constantly we were told to sit still and watch and when we went home we'd get asked questions and that was the other part that the Elders knew which child was very interested and even though I always felt silly and inferior yet they gave me to, they said – Grevillea you've got to go on down because [Elder] wants to talk to you. Now [Elder] was, he was very happy to talk to me and when I'd go down to his little house with my mum and my dad and my Uncle C., see the Uncles, my Uncle C. was a brother of my mama, he was the one who guided his sister, my mama, and talked to her and helped her with all of us in the family. He told my mother that this and that has to be done for us because he was following the words of the rest of the Elders and then he said to me, to my mama [Elder] wants to talk to [Grevillea]. And so I began to go down to [Elder] and sit down in his lovely cane chair with the pillows around me and a big bonfire and a black chain with soot and the black billy can full of lovely water boiled and he'd make a cup of tea, a mug of tea for us and he'd have two dogs there either fire side howling away while he played a violin. He would be playing the violin away because he was a white skinned Aboriginal and for many years I heard growing up that America was afraid in Pearl Harbour, that the Japanese were defeated by the atom bomb...that I learnt later on in life. [Elder] was fathered by a Japanese one generation, two generations back and I never knew that until I grew up because we had more people coming to this Country to visit us and they all went back. They had a great respect for ours, for this Country, they went back to their Country and left us behind and said goodbye, they respected our places. Now, close waters until we met Captain Cook who didn't respect that, he came in to close waters, he was told by my mama's people South Americans don't go in there there's close waters and they put their, the date of their entrance in to our Country on the top of Cairns and they went back home again. So, the Japanese and the Portuguese all these people and the people in Asia taught us how to make big boats, big long boats. We only had little canoes and so we benefited from all countries from everywhere only except.... So that's another story to tell...as time that our children need to know about...connecting....

S t a m e n : You move to this Country and find out about this Country through …

G r e v i l l e a : Well, my Auntie F. and my Auntie K. and, and all the people like the C family that used to, they come from here and Auntie N. was related to L. L. was married to T. when they were very young when I wasn't born at Coast and her sister J. who married T's brother A. When I first came here she accepted me straight away and she was my Elder I didn't realise that but when I used to go and visit her and P. and P. was living up the [coast] married in to my kin again up the [coast] and came back, brought her children back, and H. and X were living there already. J.'s daughters didn't know me but then got to know me they kept taking me fishing and Auntie J. my Elder she was the one took me under her wing and taught me about this site up here this beautiful mountain called G. she said to me out in the boat I had to go every day to see her and one day I missed and she was angry with me, oh god, and then I take her out in the boat every day and she showed me the sites and everywhere and I retained that knowledge because I realised then that this was my second Country because I was sent here by the Spirit and when I come up this beautiful mountain there was my totem further up there near the serpent the White Pointer Shark it looks like a shark and it looks like a dolphin but it comes from the ocean and that's where I fit in and it was the Spirit that put that printed that on that women's mouth. And the teaching of the women up here that's my totem the white pointer shark is here on the south coast, got here before me…

S t a m e n : Other people know about this Country too eh?

G r e v i l l e a : They know by people who...and intermarry other countries and other tribes and they know by traveling and when families travel they re-meet others and scientists, anthropologists are only just recently knowing the fact that Aboriginal people after much massacring which has happened in our Country they thought the Aboriginals were small in number and eliminated but finally anthropologists found out that we still exist by trade route so all tribes re-meet at certain, so many years apart and they still go traveling around Australia in the trade route area and they camp at these places and meet other tribes and they carry different stones and implements and different kinds of animal...animals with and they leave these with adjoining tribes. So all the tribes of the southeast coast, right up the top, going right all over Australia, those are different tribes that live there all the time and they come out and exchange goods and stuff with the traveling tribes...trade route...and I don't know how many years, maybe it's five or ten years apart, I don't know but up the top in Arnhem land at this moment...the Aboriginal people up there know me and know all my tribal names. It's fascinating and that's another story that anthropologists will have to find out for themselves.

A c a c i a : it come from me own knowledge you know as campin' on the land and bein' one with the land,....

S t a m e n : Knowing and learning using all of our senses:

Callistemon: Did mum get you to get a rock? Yeah, when they all get a rock, they put it down there and, and not only does it symbolise ah, that they were there, but, it symbolizes the learning processes of, the five senses and we as you know like sp', our spirits come. The red hand in the caves symbolises our five senses of, touching, feeling, hearing, smelling, you know (increase in tone at the end of these two last words) and listening and all our senses are there on G. And when we pick up the rock we can feel it, we can smell it, we can even taste it, you know, and they put it on, the, on the pile of rocks and it symbolizes that, that G is a very special mountain and ahm, it's special because, not only do we go there physically but one day now when you go home back to Newcastle, and then you know, people from Germany, that I took up, when they go home, when you go home, you could be sitting down like this you know, and ahm, or sun baking, or you know, working in the office and (clicks fingers) just at that instant you'll get touched again with G and you'll think 'oh, yeah, I remember that place' you know, and that's the magic of G. Because it's, it's in your heart and it goes in to your mind and it goes because we have the senses to be able to feel it all and that's the most impor' important thing is because we have these sense we can, we can learn so much, see! And that's why when we go up to G they learn all that on those teaching rocks and they learn that they can be a part of it and they can share just as much as anybody else and **all** over the world because that's all we are because we've got you know, we're gone you know? When our spirits are not with us so, and that teaches us that sp' the Spirit keeps us alive you know, um. If, we didn't have a spirit we wouldn't be here and ah, that's the beauty and we say, there's a saying that 'when you go away, the mountain calls you back', and it's, it's true, because that's the magnet, that's the beauty, of it and she'll call you and you come back and, see it again and go up and you'll learn something different you know? And, that, that's the main beauty, is that we can feel, we can cry, we can laugh as long as we have those senses like the red hand print on the cave (crescendo in tone), tch. We're also, acknowledging the Great Spirit, who made us with our 'ands as an identity and our senses to help us in this life that we are all in, you know.

S t a m e n : The process of Knowing also acknowledges the Spirit, through the intermingling of our senses, our energies, just as the waves along the coastline do. For some Knowing was complex because of cultural intrusion:

L o m a n d r a : My family never told me anything about my Country. They were back in the days when children were being taken, you know, and um, they never talked about it, never talked about culture or anything like that.

S t a m e n : Being shown and told Storys in Country;

H i b b e r t i a : Well, I first went up the, mountain there with Uncle T, when I was in my 30's, and he told us some Storys up there and um went out with a, lady called Grevillea who ah, schools and things, and I just listened and I picked everything up by listening to people's Storys to the old people to what they said. Never writ it down. I just kept it in my head. What they pass on to me I pass on to the young children. So, that's how I learned.....

L e u c o p o g o n : . . . You never really think about it you just live it. You just go through it....It is important, it's something that you don't want to lose. It's so important that you remember it. You know? Like between now and years to come. Yeah. Because that's, that's what you can pass down. Yeah. What you've seen and what you know yourself. That what keeps you going, our culture.

E u t a x i a : go here and there.

S t a m e n : Learning and Knowing by being a part of and living in two culturally different worlds …

C a l l i s t e m o n : Tch, um, obviously and fortunately my dad being bought up the way he was and me being so small I was able to participate in a lot of the things that he did um, a lot of his cultural camps ahm, the same with my mum she had Dreaming camps and guess like I went to those and learned about what it is like to probably...I guess my mum was involved a lot in, ah, in ahm working with kids Yeah, she had ah, youth group um kids, we'd mix with the kids and we'd go and ah, do all sorts of, we'd go, camping you know we'd have big bonfires and ah to get to know the kids and you'd get to know the families and things like that and you get to know Storys ah, our Dreamtime Storys when she used to teach us um...drama classes and we'd go in the hall you know, and we'd do the, our Dreamtime story which was um, Toonka and Nati you know, and the, and the waratah, and she would um pick a you know, a group of kids from after school and we'd put on this play and oh it was just fantastic and the parents could come and they could sid'own and watch you know, and their kids up doing this play. So we learnt more about our Dreamtime Storys like that too. Yeah. Plus singing [strong increase at the end of this word], I think singing as well and um and coz kids have a lot of energy and doing sports and running and doing all those other activities and swimming you know across the Lake for Bimballas and stuff like that was really, really important too, so I guess I sort of learnt um...by doing those things...

Yeah, just you know hands on things. Yeah, just something that you never forget I guess when you're a little kid...You know you always remember it. Yeah.

S t a m e n : Learning by doing and remembering. Listening ...to Storys ...

H i b b e r t i a : Oh, just sat down and started talkin' then a lot of stuff comes out (laugh). Yeah. Just talkin' and I keep it all in. I didn't ask questions. I just kept it in my head and it stayed there, cos I got a, I didn't write it down. I just kept it in my mind. Yeah well I don't write anything down, because I listen to people and Uncle T. said to me you, you got to listen you know and it's, this when it stays in your mind. When I listen I don't take note pads or anything with me and, and I just listen. It stays there. If I forget it I forget you know, but it'll all come back Cos as children we, the old people didn't tell us much. They just oh, we used to go fishin' and that with them and they'd tell us about the fishin' - 'shorty and talley' and all those things you know (laugh) So, as kids you know they'd tell the Storys or they'd be sayin' "oh shorty and talley' 'll get you" and things like that....

Well, well it's, it's mainly been um bein' passed down about um, Storys and uh and places, shown places, sites and stuff - um that are about your history, and your people. Yeah. Within your tribe.

Yeah, yep, told Storys um. Even in school, in high school and that or primary. We take daily excursions to sacred sites and that. Yeah, and ah even the white kids could come along and that, you know, it wasn't nothing really specific it was nothing like uh, you know, closed doors to the, you know, average person, so it wasn't anything that you know that you'd, you'd learn just for yourself, you know your group, your people it was learnt for, it was learnt by people you know. Other than that, like mainly white people or anybody you know who wanted to have an interest in the culture or in our area. Yeah, so yeah, that was pretty much it.

Yeah, well ah, after my initiation, when I turned 12 it was really a big part of it to um, to walk from uh, Coast to [city] coz ah, that's what me and my dad and my grandfather done when they were you know, when they were, when my dad was only my age and my grandfather was dad's age and uh, they walked from here to [city] and it took us, ah, 4,5 to 6 months yah know, nearly to walk all the way up that way and we went the coastline coz that's our our traditional trade routes, coastline so,...we followed that um...that's where most of us Yuens live (Laugh) Go coastline! And ah, yeah they were there they were our old trade routes but as a part of initiation that's where we done our walk, oh, it's just a specific walk for...for me and my family...that's what we do.

Um...The experience was to know my...culture more by um by how, how my culture worked between trade routes and um and to, to **know** where you um, you know where you could where you walked, and ah, where to go and that and to know that it's a part of your culture too if you could do that walk again then you know, you're doing what is a part of your culture, your heart. Yeah, and um that's really good coz you know, I'd, I'd like to do that again with my son, Yeah.

Yeah, um, it was mainly ah, more or less it was like ah, survival skills actually. When you you're on the road or you know, on the track (laugh) you may as well say in this term, um, yeah, coz you really have to fend for yourself when you do something like that it's, it's going back to tradition, it's um, not dependent on what we have now. It's sort of, um, just hunt what you can, and um, and fish what you can, you know, even though, even though you use modern day fishing lines and stuff like that it's, its still the same thing you know, but it's all about survival...yeah, and learning your trade route to stick with it and pass it down coz I think that's important because, um, if you have knowledge of...your culture that's been passed down to you that makes you feel like you're a part of your community, or your culture, of where you are, because you know where you stand and that, you know, and that and what you've learnt to be a part of um where you are.

S t a m e n : Country as 'a nourishing terrain' (Bird Rose, 1996, p. 7).

S t a m e n : Knowing and learning through Story telling:

L o t u s : My mum told me story happen in my Country, there's this rock, it's in the shape of a head and it's got etchings on it and one of our Dreamings is pelican as well, so this pelican came down in a raft, flew down, came down after it laid the egg and then those etchings there, they say it tells us how we were created and our Country, so through the Storys we learn about ourselves, about our Country, how our Country was created and how we were created...you know, how, who you are and...tell us a lot about your personality I think, you know, I'm like water,

I see water as truly destructive at times, it can be very soft, it's cleansing...it's um there, if you know where to look, there's waterfalls, there's a stream, it can be like a billabong at times where it's just...small...and then it fits in to any shape, you know, sometimes you take on whatever your Dreaming is, you take on...

Yes, I think it's a key way of learning, we just love Storys, up at home, us mob and I think that's something that even people that may be away from Country and may not have much language left still have that...of story telling and love sitting down yarning, especially funny Storys, eh, every black fella, I don't know one black fella that doesn't like a good yarn, you know, they love it, love it. And, um, but when, it's yes they learn culture and about Country, about Storys.

S t a m e n : Storys are told by the older people through family, through relationships

C a c t u s : Because, um, if you're with your family...more...like give you good things, grandparents would be there telling old Storys, um, like if there's only young people gathered there's nothing really achieved just talking normal young people things but if there's older people with kids then they, then the old people tell the, um, young adults, and they tell all the kids or grandkids...and it's really good too, um, if kids go over with old people and go, hunting with them and show them how to do stuff like, um, get bush tucker and stuff. Yeah.

S t a m e n : Storys are more than sharing words - they speak to us through pictures, ceremony, ...

C a c t u s : Yeah, it is, very important because that's the only way that they've done it. From generations to generations, pass messages on...Yeah. um. Like I said before there is this, sit, sit us down, on the ground and draw maps of all, all your family, like, um, trees or hills, stuff we had to know about and all...we weren't allowed to go and where we were allowed to go umm. Sometimes, um, it was... through paintings, rocks, um, rock paintings, um, like if one like...one, like one area of rocks, were there paintings, and all those paintings tell story of some sort of these are all families, and most of 'em all passed on the through that, and tell you Storys. ..., some like all the ceremony things were passed through women through um... teaching young kids, young men and young women through um dancing, singing, all the songs um that we, young girls were shown, through dancing,, and they had like designs on their body, and it was, um, it represented their Country, their totem like of what their Dreaming is.

Epacris translating for Yam: Important, important, yeah.

Important, well Yam said she about number 7 question that he passed on his story to his family and friends so they could know when Yam saw family and friends can know his Storys and like Dreaming things like dancing and body painting.

S t a m e n : So Storys involve song, dance and connection through the earth, drawing on the ground.

S e n n a : Yeah, Storys are important, just like, we, we, today we writing but long time there was just drawing for us, in the grass, in the ground, and teach us. That's way I learn, I did learning with pen and paper, I learn it from ground. My dad used to be telling me draw, he was read and write but he was just teaching me with the ground. That's why I got strong and strong. And she, he used to take me to his Country and show around Country, visiting, tell me the Spirit things. You see that shadow, this is the time for us and when wind blow that's your Spiritual he going to take you wherever you go, and Spirit with you all the time. And language and dot paints and body paint that's your, like mother and father when we going.

Yeah. And dancing is important too. Dancing and singing is lot like telling Storys. While I'm telling Storys, just like I feel it, just like I feel it, just like I go back and look those people die long time ago before me, after me, like, um, like mum. When I Storys she come back to, like picture for me, and tell me when to tell more.

Yeah, because she teach me to tell Storys. And my dad teach me on the ground. I got read and write just from ground, telling, he write it time, what time was morning, what time was lunchtime, what time was smoko. He write it in our ground. I still get that board [17.9] from long time, 1974. Still got it in the …outstation. I should have get it, I should have show you….Yeah, beautiful …, she can bring it over. We can look. This my dad photo and my mum and my brother, my sister, me and my young brother and another young brother and my young sister and these all got Storys. Just writing it in on the ground. And we get glue from spinnifex, glue, glue, I like glue...and you go like this, telling Storys. One day, maybe next week, I'm going to show you. We'll just go, drive down Gn… Road, we can get that swags....And I got to show you that, um, wax, …look like a glue. It's my grandmother's, grandfather's, and grandmother's, no grandfather's Country. My mum's Country's …

Yeah. These people, like white people have memory like photos, …but us we have memories in our memory, you know. When someone like you come now, we just tell Storys straight from our head.....

S t a m e n : Storys help us Know things at different key times in our lives;

S e n n a : It's, this is really important for me to paint because I'm teaching one young girl, like, …my niece, I'm teaching her because she wanted know how to relate to …countries, Spirit, secret woman's, like, Spirit, and secret when they are pregnant like 13, 12, that's why I'm teaching that painting. I'm not doing it for fun, I'm just telling the Storys for young girl. She's 10 years old and she listen to me. When she turn 9 you got to teach it through dot painting....

S t a m e n : Storys help us to Know things and learn things in different ways, covering different periods of time.

L o t u s : Well, like there's Storys over different periods of time, like that story I told you about the pelican, that was in the time of our ancestors. I mean, over time things happen and those Storys, recent Storys are still part of our way, part of our life...so, there's things that have happened in our Country like massacres so we hear these Storys but then …second generation...you know like pelican story...creation story, teaching different...as well...

S t a m e n : Singing and painting

S e n n a : Really important for dot painting and body painting that's to tell your Storys and singing. Sometime I singing, with my mum, my grandmother teach me. I sing it for cloud, I sing it for sun, make, um, one day I'll tell you when we just weekend, we'll go Sunday weekend somewhere. When I walk around I'll see maybe...later...you start singing again, yes, I like it. And he join...with me....He talk language with us. We teach him everything.

C a s s i n i a : Painting is the meaning behind it, tells the Story. It's not just there as a, um, pattern, it's a pattern there but it's got a meaning there. And people have, um, story behind it and talk about it. Story is told all the time round the camp fires. We talk about it a lot. We share ideas, agreements, disagreements, family talks, cultural business, we have things like that....Everyone show their Country.

Take everyone out and they show which Country theirs. Yeah, they used to draw and show them where their Country.

Stamen: Singing and mapping:

Cassinia: By telling, telling them over and over during, um, ceremonies and then they map it out on the ground. Mapping and singing as well, singing, yeah. Mapping through by talking and giving directions, I suppose. And pointing and then sand drawing as well. Yep.

Stamen: In Coast, another geographical and historical location, Storys portray cultural background and relationships;

Grevillea: Yeah, because the story that I told must be told before the children lose vision of their culture, their cultural background and the ways of the old people and to look after the land...

Because they [Storys] continually tell us the names of our ancestors, they tell us the names of those who've gone on before in spirit. They tell us of our past and who we are, they tell us how, who are our kinship, and who to marry or not to marry, they tell us about the medication and everything else that has kept us going and we've survived by those issues, they pass them down to all of us and every tribe is expected to do the same. So that maintains our health and our survival even in a tribal area. And we learn the boundaries of that and everybody else's tribe and we learn to look their totems as well. And we respect each other's boundaries because you can't go to a rainforest...because it's a different kind of gathering. The women out there dig underneath the earth because it's flat soil and they get everything else from under the soil in front of them. Where here in the rainforest everything is provided for us, we can go up there, we are collectors in the rainforest and we have water running, we have everything available for us in the rainforest. So it's a different kind of way of working together. In the rainforest by the way men and women work together gathering. Out in the desert only women and children and their sons and their daughters work. So it's a different kind of system but they're all maintained by identity and we have to pass over each other's boundary and we have to have acknowledgment...accept us then it's all right to walk over their area. This is very, very important and that's only the time, if we break those rules then our effective near family, like the seven people in one tribe, becomes affected because they're all intermarried from other areas. So, it's very, very important back there. When I think about, again, what happened to our people, pre, European invasion how much of our culture was lost and our teachings and when I look at the land, the land is desecrated because of that and I do believe that today and I still will always believe that and that was a desecration of our people. Does that help?

Yeah, the Storys we're told around the big fires at night as the mother gathers...all around the same area, families doing similar things, the same way. But it's also passed down by corroboree, by singing, by dancing, by working by collecting food and given sovereignty and worship to the trees and everything else in the trees that gives life. All those trees in the forest has to be maintained, its got to grow, its got to be there for the purpose of survival and that's what we had to learn.

S t a m e n : Storys about protecting and growing the land and our cultures to enhance our survival;

A c a c i a : Yeah, yeah. I think, tellin' a story,...and all the knowledge you've got you Know it should be, told rather than kept...where in other ways,...it's hard to tell a story when (laugh) you know certain people like they want to 'ear it to a certain extent but they don't want to Know about it?

S t a m e n : Storys help you Know ...

C a l l i s t e m o n : Oh, oh yeah, definitely. I mean, if you didn't have Storys (laugh) you just wouldn't know ... and ah if you didn't have like the landscape or the, paint or, the clay or whatever it is that you want to make or understand, if you didn't have that you just wouldn't know what it's about you know, so yeah no, I think um yeah that's, that's really, really important, way of learning, is to be able to, to see um, what it is. Yeah.

L o m a n d r a : In every tribe there was always a person who held the whole history for the tribe people and usually somebody was always trained to follow him, to know all the laws, well not all the laws, but all the old time, Dreamtime Storys from, right from the past down to the present, and he was the last one who had that knowledge ...Oh, yeah, yeah. Well some of it's fun, some of it's relaxation, some of it's party and...always come in as part of it, as history and, um, these party things, you might call it traditional culture but it was part of our culture back then.

S t a m e n : Storys teach us as well as building respect …

M y r t l e   a n d   M e l a l e u c a : … otherwise we wouldn't know today and we still hear that from lots of places where we go to meet but it's some of the young people love to learn, love to learn and respect you with them times Storys.....

S t a m e n : Storys show our cultures …

L e u c o p o g o n : Yes, Storytelling is good. I think that Storytelling um, keeps the culture alive...I think. I think it um, it portrays our culture...you know in our areas you know how we were and that and that and that um,...you know that comforts a lot of us...that we have storytelling coz um, it's a big part of our culture I think being passed down and everybody should know all their Storys you know, all their areas and their tribes and...their, their towns and that, you know.

S t a m e n : Story telling keeps the cultures alive.

When yarning with my Colleagues asking them if they can share Storys, some told Storys, some told Storys just for me, for my learning only. Others told Storys to share. Others yarned about Storys and their significance in learning and Knowing culture; general and ceremonial/secret/sacred information.

To this point this chapter has presented peoples voices; their thoughts and their experiences about Knowing and learning and using Story in this process. Now I would like to share a story or two from each Country visited; from Coast and from Desert. The Storys as told to me are not re-presented here as a means of illustrating the moral of the Story. They are re-presented as a means to show how Story impacts on the way we learn and Know. They stand in their own right as illustrations of Knowing and learning, as illustrations of Indigenous Knowings since time immemorial.

Storys

Casuarina's Dreaming: Desert

Casuarina's Dreaming dingo, emu and kangaroo....And little bird Dreaming
And the little bird sit in one of the plains there, it sit on the ground, it's like a little rock but it shaped like bird, yeah, and people not allowed touch that, this little stone like bird, yeah. If they touch it they get sick, yeah.

And that emu, there's emu Dreaming from there too and there's rocks like eggs, emu eggs, yeah.

And anyone can have a look, man and all the women, kids have a look. They're not allowed to climb on it.

His father's show him all this Dreaming and he used to look after them, these three Dreaming and not to, you know, touch or look at other people's Dreaming, just to look after his own.

Yeah, it's important to look after Dreaming.

Snake Dreaming: Desert

About that snake we saw, behind, they can only hear it because they're sort of, um, they're totem, yeah, we can't hit the snake or they get somebody else to hit it if they don't want to hit it, yeah (laugh). Yeah. They only scare it away. Or just leave it there. Yeah. If they were to hit it or killed it then they'd get sick. Yeah.

They also do snake, Dreaming dance. They dance like a snake, move everyone, make a line like a snake and they dance up and back and sideway, yeah, and they do, um, designs on the body, snake Dreaming.

Bird Learning: Coast

When my mama and other women took us out, took children out, the children that couldn't be looked after by their fathers or their brothers who are working, we all went out to the bush and we were sat down and we were told to look at different things around us and whatever it was, it made us become interested in those issues. One of those things I remember was...our language from [my community], it means a bird and this bird does come from the rainforest at home, where I come from is a great big rainforest and this bird, goodness me, now what is it, it comes from the rainforest and it's called, it's a grey thrush and this bird calls out and now we've been taught how to recognise the sound of every kind of bird. At times when a bird comes and visits me at home, one bird when it came to visit me came all around the window and when it circled the window made a square travel around the window and...I thought it was looking at the spiders and every other edible food but the bird was saying to me when it left and when it went down the hill a bit my niece [ ] was outside sitting in a position and coming back she said Auntie [ ]could you hear the sound of that bird and I said yeah that's X and she said what's X and I said, he's a messenger bird from home and I said you listen carefully he's saying something which way the story's coming from and I tried to teach her that but she didn't understand that. We were taught at home that when that bird called out we listen carefully sometime the bird continually, continually called out just one lot of calling you know the sound and then we listened for the next one and we were told when that would happen, it was a change of the wind or maybe it was the way we had to situate ourselves and remember then we had to sit in a certain position called the X, you've probably heard of that, white people are just finding out about that now but all nations throughout the world were aware that so if you are sitting in the songlines in the direction that bird knows that and then the bird keeps calling. Now, the direction, that bird knew, you almost hear it say west, east, south, north and you know that we said that in our language not in a way Europeans say it's south east west and north in that direction it's a...dialect their language. In us, with us we had our own dialect to explain the bird was telling us which direction we had to go home...died, who it was and a certain place we were intermarried into, White Pointer Shark tribe, from the black duck tribe, these people, this bird was saying come on, come on now someone has gone into the spirit world. So that was, we would dread, and the little bird used to be up in the tree and it would go round and round the tree trunks and then it would come out again and look at us and then start calling out. And this bird, and I remember my mama saying to this bird, she was talking the language to the bird, the bird was nodding its head, yes and it was saying no and I couldn't get over.

Toonka & Nati: Coast

Um, (cough) yeah, some. I know the ah story of um Toonka and Nati our Dreamtime story, uhm and [Mountain] which is behind us is ahm, is the mountain that Nati the Dreamtime story she climbs up onto um, because she, she can't find ah, ah Toonka um and ah [mountain] is a very special mountain and also ah, not just for Nati as a creation story but it also tells us that the creation of the people and the Country here ah, because it was ah, a volcanic mountain, so it was like a, like a um, like a fertility or a, a woman or she's been born into this world and she comes out and creates this wonderful land and places and that's, all that is a part of that Dreamtime story and um, Nati um, is the lady in the end um, that after she couldn't find Toonka um, he went out and ah wanted to some hunting and because he got very impatient and just you know, didn't understand to um, just take his time and learn. He got very angry so he grabbed a spear and, and aiming it at a star, he threw the spear and the Great Spirit caught it and he bent it over his knee and he threw it back and, and that was the beginning of the boomerang, Yeah. And so um, tch, and then he was, he punished ah, Toonka because, he didn't have the patience to, to learn and then he put him up into the moon and, and that's why sometimes you hear the Storys of the man in the moon, you know...And um, and that was that's interesting too because that's another, a story from my mum's Country in [x], white pointer shark? And so while Toonka's up in the moon Nati looks for him everywhere (cough) coz she has a gunyah at the...bottom of the mountain and she has, a, fire going. And then she started to wander and she climbed the highest mountain which was [mountain]. And she climbed up right up to the top and she was so, exhausted and tired that she just fell down and she cried and the tears came down the creeks and down the rivers and that's why today the creeks sing peacefully you know when you're sitting by, you can hear the creeks singing and peacefully, and it created the creeks and the, and the sea and everything like that and um. If ever Toonka should return Nati left her heart, um on the mountain for him to find and today our emblem is the waratah...yeah, so and that's...and which is very interesting because about 10 years ago we had a few young boys who, like you know, like myself and my brothers years ago we'd venture off you know, to [mountain] you know. These young guys went up there and they came back, they were excited they'd found one waratah bush...growing up on [mountain] and, normally they normally don't you know uhm grow down this area mainly up in the city or (intelligible word or two) Eora around there but uhm, yeah, there is um, one warratah tree growing on top of [mountain] which is fascinating, mmm, and so I mean that story just ahhh (deep sigh) is just you know a part of our, our culture, the story of our land and the creation of our land ....

The Red Coats Came ...

And another thing I want to tell you too is the, um, I don't know if this is a story that'll be told but from my father about his grandfather, about his grandmother. It was his great grandmother, I think it was his great grandmother, anyway the boys, all the boys went out, went out fishing and, uh,...that was her name, they had their names then...one day they went out fishing, the red coats come in and they try to tell them to get off that land, this is land that...for us because it's all our land and we know for a fact that it is our land. But, anyway, when the boys went fishing, the red coats come there, they must have done something to her, they killed her, raped her, whatever and they cut her head off. When the boys come back and seen that they just all split up, you know, just went, you know,...there, there or there, you know. They was going to do the same to the rest of the boys because they was out looking for the boys at the time but the boys wasn't home, they was going to kill the boys, you know. Like this is all dad's grand, grand peoples, brothers and that, great grand peoples brothers and all their kids...so it has been...But today we know that great grandmother's head is over there...in England and still over there in Buckingham Palace...because one of our, one of my cousins went there over to try to retrieve it back and they wouldn't give it to him. You know, what are we going to do about that, you know, that just makes me real upset, you know, for them white people to go and take me great grandmothers, an ancestor's head, you know. They've still got it in a big jar over there. We're just trying to work out how we're going to get it back. They wouldn't give it us. But he died now my cousin, he was older than me, he was about 60 something and this is back in the '80s he went over there to retrieve that head. They wouldn't give it to him, you know....we want to work out a way how we're going to retrieve it back. That's ours, that's our history, you know, put her back up there where she is. She's in the grave up there with no head....My brother knows, my brother knows where that grave is because dad said years ago when he went back there looking for it, back in '70s,...you find little white rocks, little pebbles, well that's where our great, great grandmother buried. And he found her for dad, eh, and dad real happy, eh, found them graves back in the scrub, you know, that's where the Kooris used to live.

... Well, that's the thing that I was telling you about my great grandmother's head, you know, I just, we want to try and work out a way to get that back. Because, it's just not right, you know, for someone to do that. What if they went and killed John Howard and took his head how would they feel.

Storys cover periods of time:

S t a m e n : Story telling keeps our cultures alive for our young people, our future generations. Storys are told and shown in Country. Tellin' me and showin' me.

G r e v i l l e a : And what happened one day, [my son], he's a gentle giant call him today, he was only about 10 or 11 I think years old and in the kitchen one day when nobody was at home but just us two and he walked past and he said mum what did you do, did you know your culture back there, what did you do when you was a kid he said where you come from. I said, well I said we had to be told about our culture if we were really interested and we would sit down and talk about it. And he said, yeah well did you speak your language when you was home. I said yeah, I used to speak my language but I can only remember it when I go, when I go back home it comes back to me cause I hear people talking and shouting and all that. And he said uh oh yeah and he said mum what was you taught and I said now...and ask me a question about culture. I can sit down and I can tell you because that's what I have to do. So I sat down, [my son] and I, and I told him about my culture. I told him that when I saw the men dancing, doing the corroborees, these great, big giants, these beautiful men like big, tall, strong men and I saw this chief and the Elder on the other side sitting in a little humpy with a big fire and I saw them in their canoes and the story of the songs is, it takes in all the cultural teaching from where they go and what they do and whatever they call that, like collecting.

... Yeah, I showed him, and I got up and I said – You sit down there. And it was a lovely summer's day in my big kitchen and I began to tell him. This is what I saw and I showed him and explained it to him....

C a l l i s t e m o n : I know at the moment a lot of our Elders have passed away and the language is really harsh, but, I don't know for me, for me it's, different, I think. Maybe it's because for me it's different to learn, maybe it's cos my father knew it! My mum knew it! But, and also when I go out in the bush um, you just um...it just comes to you. I ah, it just comes to you and, and I was like I've been given some Storys by the Spirits.

L o m a n d r a : . . . I think any teaching has got to be hands on stuff, you know, it's just like a...you've got to be able to look wholly, look at it, you know, look at it if it's the Country, well, they should go to it so they can see for themselves and, um, here, while they're actually at the place, the Storys relating to them and they can see for themselves what's there.

L e u c o p o g a n : Well, like the like the first you know like that, that question. I will, you know, hand down my Storys that my fathers taught me and know about, you know. But what basically, what I've learnt off dad, passed down from him, everything that I've known that I will try to teach [my son] and try and make sure that he gets it all and I'll, I'll bring him up to know his surroundings and know his sacred sites and his area and um, you know ...

Oh, I'd take him places. I'd take him out there, um, I'd take him to all sites and tell him what they are, and what they are by their language. Yeah. And um, you know...show him things. My father showed me how to throw a boomerang when I was, you know 10 and I, I wouldn't leave it alone for months on end, you know (laugh). Yeah. And um, just stuff like that...any little thing and um,...Yeah...just teach him that way by taking him out and showing him the sacred sites and the areas and what Storys are behind it. Yeah.

Well,...(clear throat) Indigenous knowledge, that's a tricky one! Um, I don't know...it's, it's mainly all comes down what's passed on to you. It's um, it's what you've taken from your Elders, is what you get from them that… That may be it, um, because ah, nothing would be passed down without our Elders, Yeah. Or we'd be nowhere without our old people. That's what I think….Oh, right, like um…well, when I think about it [Country], I think about our surroundings more like more like um, influences us a lot, um being near the water.

It is important, it's something that you don't want to lose. It's so important that you remember it. You know? Like between now and years to come. Yeah. Because that's, that's what you can pass down. Yeah. What you've seen and what you know yourself. That what keeps you going, our culture….Yeah, it was mainly just um, like I said, it was mainly just remembering things. You never really think about it you just live it. You just go through it. Yeah. It's just, just something that you do because I agree with you. I had no, you know, I had no thoughts of doin' it and one day me and dad just jumped up and did it. Yeah.. and um and that's something that I, it was spontaneous, yeah. So it's, it's something that I wouldn't jot down or you know write down or anything like that, yeah….It'll just be in my mind. Yeah. That'd be it. Yeah.

S t a m e n : Storys keep our cultures alive. Storys portrayed through dance, singing, body painting, drawing on the ground, art on rocks, on canvas, natural fixtures. Indigenous Knowing in Desert and Coast is telling and showing me. It is embedded in Country, in relationships, in experience. It is watching and seeing. It is listening and hearing. It is doing; 'hands on'. Indigenous Knowing is ongoing, cyclic with different purpose; general and ceremonial. Indigenous Knowings is survival. We must look after our Dreaming; our Knowing, our Country. All of our senses are involved and they cannot be separated from Country, nature, body, spirit and relationships. Indigenous Knowing is overlayed, is rhythmic and reflective. It continues to exist even where cultural intrusion has endeavoured to quash all that is significant. Indigenous Knowing is told, stored in memory and shown.

Figure 4.17. Coast - Teaching and My Teacher

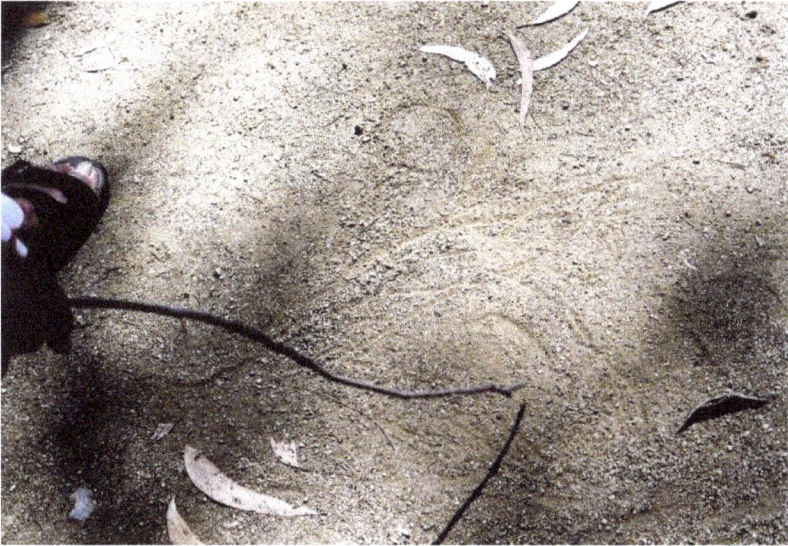

Figure 4.18. Coast – Teaching

There is a story I know. Indigenous Knowings and learning like the Waterlily is layered, delicate yet strong - it stands tall immersed in Country (water) that nourishes it and affords a strong and powerful base. Yet, it is flexible adapting to seasons/environmental changes or variables. Indigenous Knowing is rooted in Country. It is built on relationships; relationships between and within individuals, clans, nations and Country. Lilyology is born – to be explained in the Epilogue ...

There is a story I know. Many voices have told this Story. It may not have been in a conventional way. It may have appeared to be disjointed. It may have been strange. But I ask you to stop and remember the rhythm of the words the tellers of the Story told. The words are telling the Story of Indigenous Knowings. The voices are telling the Story of Indigenous Knowings. No one voice is stronger than the other. No one voice is more valid than the other. They all tell a Story about Indigenous Knowing. It was the job of this research to listen to these voices, to privilege these voices. It is the job of this book to 'tell 'em and show 'em'; to tell you and to show you! You can 'draw your own conclusions and gain life lessons from a more personal perspective, - getting away from abstractions and rules Storys allow us to see other's life experiences through our own eyes' (Wilson, 2008, p.17).

MIND MAPPING

NEW TERRAIN

OXYMORON

EMBEDDED

CULTURALLY TEACHING

LIBRARY

GENRES
NARRATIVE
SONG
ORAL HISTORY
POEM
DRAMATIC PERFORMANCE
BOOKS

INDIGENOUS LITERACIES

KNOWING
COUNTRY
ELDERS
START NARRATIVE
SCHOLARS NARRATIVE

RIGHTS INTELLECTUAL PROPERTY
ETHICS
USED HOW?
SOVEREIGNTY
ACADEMY THE
INDIGENOUS TEXT
RESEARCH
KNOWING THOUGHTS

KNOWLEDGE

CHAPTER 5

Reflecting: Literature, Textual Sources & Literary Genres

> In the context of Indigenous knowledge, therefore, a literature review is
> an oxymoron because Indigenous knowledge is typically embedded in
> the cumulative experiences and teachings of Indigenous peoples rather
> than a library. (Battiste, 2002, p. 2).

This chapter is in essence the 'literature review" of the PhD dissertation. In
presenting this chapter for this book I am highlighting the issues associated with
the doing and presenting of a literature review as part of a dissertation as well as
using this space to identify some of the voices playing in the dialogue that is
Indigenous Knowings.

Battiste (above) succinctly describes the challenge I faced as an Indigenous
researcher doing a PhD dissertation. In this context I am writing about Indigenous
Knowing, endeavouring to privilege it. Yet, I am structuring and framing this text
in a way that negates the essence of wholeness, the very concept I have advocated
is 'Indigenous Knowing'. I do box, label and categorise themes for the purpose of
the dissertation, reflecting on, being mindful of, and constantly drawn back to the
caution presented by Battiste. It is the Academy, the conveyor and embodiment of
the Eurocentric knowledge system that requires and determines such
categorisation; thereby requiring a dissertation to follow these rules. A book such
as this also requires categorisation in order to structure an understanding of what
has been written.

A LITERATURE REVIEW FOR THE PHD DISSERTATION:

The 'doing' of the Literature Review was a major stumbling block for me and
caused me to wallow for many months in a quagmire of rules and expectations, of
thinking, versus my own gut feelings. The Faculty required a Literature Review
early in the journey because it traditionally contextualised and identified themes
that would then frame the work I was undertaking as an academic. This was my
challenge because for me the central piece of the 'document' was the voices and
expressed experiences of my research Colleagues in Desert and Coast. I didn't
feel I could proceed with a Literature Review before the 'field research'; before

my Colleagues voices were heard. In privileging Indigenous Knowings these voices must be 'the doing'. A Literature Review even when I use Indigenous scholarly voices privileges the Brick Wall; the Academy. My Knowing was affirmed by the 'field research'; with the issues my research Colleagues raised being very different to those of a traditional literature review process. This explains the location of this chapter after the listening to and the hearing of my Colleagues voices in the previous chapter and on the associated web page.

The requirements of The Academy; the Brick Wall and associated framing contexts are a subterranean theme within this chapter. This research took place as I and others doing similar research 'struggle to disencrypt discourses underpinned by investigatory research; process and outcomes that have sustained colonial oppression, discursively and materially' (Mutua, Decolonizing research in Cross-Cultural Contexts, 2004, p. 1). It is set against a background that as Spivak notes in her discussion about decolonization, evokes a very real ambivalence in Western universities about the legitimacy of Indigenous knowledge, one that privileges Western knowledges over Indigenous epistemologies (Spivak, 1999, p. x). This book and the associated Doctoral dissertation privileges Indigenous Knowings but it is constrained by Western Eurocentric parameters at every contact point. It is constrained by the very essence of the concept 'research', the process of 'research' and the difference between 'Knowing' and 'knowledge' as discussed later in this chapter. Hokari clearly identifies this major difference; 'the (Gurindji) art of knowing is not always the way of searching, but often the way of paying attention (Hokari, 2000, p. 2). Here the Gurindji search for history involves paying attention where you see, listen and feel the history around yourself if you are sensitive to know it' (Hokari, 2000, p. 3). Research within a Eurocentric domain is essentially about 'searching' for an answer to a question not 'paying attention' to what is around you:

As Battiste asserts for Eurocentric academics the search involves posing a "problem", presenting a "question," or constituting a "case." In searching for the answers for others, they believe they maintain a universal discourse, and speak the language of objectivity or impartiality (Battiste M. , Indigenous Knowledge and Research, 1996, p. 229). Deloria (1999, p.11) argues 'the idea of forcing nature to tell us its secrets [in the form of a question] has an alternative in other cultural tradition of observing nature and adjusting to its larger rhythms (Deloria, 1999, p. 12).

I participated as a student and supervisor of a postgraduate student, at a summer school for Indigenous postgraduates. It was organised and run by Indigenous peoples. The first session we attended asked us to say who we were and tell everyone what our research question was and how we intended to answer it. I said I have no research question and have no intention of having a question and looking for answers. The chair for the session, a well known and respected Indigenous academic condemned me for such naivety. I suggested I could not explore people's Storys of Indigenous Knowing by creating an artificial question and framing responses. The chair shook her head and moved on. Deloria and Battiste offered a form of vindication in my quest to 'Know'. Our way of Knowing is not question and answer based.

At this stage as an Indigenous scholar we have a dilemma engaging paying attention rather than searching and the need to pose questions and answer them in the search. Another dilemma is in the choice of literature; does it have to be scholarly academic journal articles written within the last 12 months or can it be seminal works created and performed by Indigenous peoples since time immemorial? The validity of oral Story becomes questioned as written text is seen as the only valid form of knowledge. The material I chose to draw on encompasses differing genres of literature including narrative, oral history, poems, film, art, dramatic performance, song text, in essence 'Story' by Indigenous community peoples, Indigenous scholars and non-Indigenous scholars as well. I centre and privilege Indigenous literacies (Hanlen, 2002).

Many of the sources cited are books, sections in books, literary pieces. They are not journal articles and they are not always current. This is the case because in an Australian context publishing for us as Indigenous academics is problematic. Books tell whole Storys from different perspectives, different parts that belong to the Story. Journal articles categorise and dissect knowledge and apply many constraints as evidenced at the most simplest level including discipline; categorisation; specialisation; and Eurocentric parameters involving language and article structure; some of the bricks in the Brick Wall. The audience for academically produced materials is not necessarily the same as ours. Our audience includes equally community peoples, Elders, developers and decision-makers, practitioners not theorists and/or philosophers operating from within the Brick Wall. I reflect below:

> My Colleagues and I have sat in many Indigenous conferences lamenting the dilemmas facing us when submitting articles for mainstream, registered, refereed journals of international repute. The editing teams and peer reviewers (usually non-Indigenous people) of such journals question our use of the 'first person', our use of an uppercase 'I' or 'A' for Indigenous or Aboriginal; two fundamentally

important factors for us in our writing. Use language that is softer for example, 'settlement' not 'invasion', 'separated' not 'stolen' etc. We are told to validate our sources with work done by non-Indigenous anthropologists or historians; though hesitant and reluctant in the hope of publication we seek and find non-Indigenous scholars wanting to charge us for their life's work; even though our need for information is about our own family history...[personal communications at various Indigenous conferences between 1980 and 2008].

Our desire to feed back to our communities influences what we choose to produce.

In an Australian context, the literary focus has been on historical, anthropological and linguistic discourse. There is a growing discourse engaging literature by Indigenous peoples in the fields of education and research method and process, but it is limited. Very little has been written that is multidisciplinary as we try to fit in to The Academy, the Brick Wall. Even less has been written which embodies Indigenous essence in the arena of Indigenous Knowing and the challenges this poses for us as Indigenous researchers not just Indigenous people doing research about Indigenous issues. As Indigenous scholars in the field where do we go to engage, to reflect the literature, textual sources and literary genres?

HOW TO READ THIS CHAPTER

I have chosen to quote at length in some cases throughout this chapter because to shorten takes away the spirit of the narrative, the telling of the Story. The telling of the Story the whole way. I have tried to remain true to my conceptual journey by including people's Storys, in text boxes; keeping Indigenous voices alive and speaking throughout the document. They appear in dimensional text boxes because there are many dimensions to the Storys being told.

The following themes have emerged and are explored in this chapter:

- Concept of Country
- Concept of 'Knowing'
- Elders as traditional scholars
- Story and Storying

Cultural Interface and Colliding Trajectories

- How Indigenous Knowings have been used?
- The Academy : Indigenous Knowings and Research

- The Academy : Knowing – Thoughts as Text, Thoughts Embodied
- Sovereignty and Self-Determination
- Intellectual property rights and ethics

Creating and Establishing New Terrains

- Decolonisation
- Mind Mapping and other alternative forms of Knowing/thinking

In the above list I have included what I term sliver inserts. In the first instance 'cultural interface and colliding trajectories' and next 'creating and establishing new terrains'. These are sliding thoughts, thoughts that frame the abovementioned themes but which are not headings that assign hierarchy to our thoughts; they are more transient and organic in nature as are the themes. These are thoughts that sliver in and out of my thought process. This work is very much like a sand drawing; a mimetic moment is created and enacted (Benterrak, 1996, p. 62). The sliver inserts may also be likened to threads weaving in and out of a tapestry. Perhaps they are more like song lines (Randall, 2003, pp. 22-23) weaving across the terrain moving throughout and unifying all things that form this chapter.

CONCEPT OF 'COUNTRY'

We were introduced to the concept of 'Country' in the prologue. I want here to bring our focus back to the concept of Country and Indigenous Knowing, adding depth, another layer to our understanding. Remember, Country is alive as is our relatedness to it:

> ...the earth itself is alive too. ... Jimmy Mangayarri, a very old man in Dargaragu told me this. He picked up a handful of sand and taught me that you may think this is *janja* (soil) was just soil, but this was a 'man'. ... the Earth tells you the Right Way. (Hokari, 2000, p. 4)

Australia was one of the last of the lands to be conquered after America, Canada and Aoteoroa (New Zealand). It was one of the last frontiers and as a result the invaders already had a concept of how Indigenous peoples should look, live, feel about Country and how they fought for territory. The British expected open warfare as they had experienced in other parts of the world as they marched colonising country after country. Aboriginal Australians took them by surprise because of the extent of their guerrilla warfare (Reynolds, 2000, 2007, Evans et al

1988). Aboriginal Australians didn't 'fit' their expectations. In Australia, pre-invasion, Country could not be bought and sold, it could not be fought over because we are so much a part of it. Hokari gives a tangible understanding of this:

For the Gurindji people, 'home' is not a small box called 'house' ... they use their house almost like a storeroom. ... They keep few valuable things in the house, but they spend most of their time outside ... The outside of a house within the community is a kind of 'living room' in which you can eat, play, talk and sleep. ... their 'home' is their Country itself. There are so many other 'rooms' you should visit and stay such as 'fishing rooms', bush plum rooms, or 'ceremonial rooms' and so on. ...The world is alive and full of life in the Gurindji Country. Therefore it is logical to say that their home is not only huge, but also shared space. That being said, the relationship between you and your 'home' cannot be like that between owners and their private property. When you move around your Country, whatever your purposes are, you should always beware that you are surrounded by your 'home' which is full of life. You are not the owner of your 'home', but part of it (Hokari, 2000, p. 6).

Langton (2000, p.259) through a discussion of the works of the artists from Papunya, in the Western Desert, Australia, powerfully illustrates a connection between Country and knowledge, ongoing practice in the form of paintings, a specific style:

The artists represented by Papunya Tula...are intimately connected to their traditional land estates through a set of beliefs in the sacredness of places and the necessity of celebrating that sacredness through ceremonial acts. These places, they say originated in the primordial adventures of spiritual ancestor beings whose 'creative dramas' established the appearance and patterns of life experienced today... They share the idea of a sacred landscape and, in most cases, an artistic style derived from ritual adornments of ground sculptures, bodies, sacred boards, rock faces and ceremonial objects such as decorated poles. The features of the style are typically; the birds-eye view, abbreviated cartographic representation of landscapes whose places and species are familiar and familial. The paintings are iconographic, gender-specific responsibilities influence the choice of subjects... The great majority of Western Desert paintings represent the extent of the landscape and its sacred elements biota and geographic features for which the painters are responsible as traditional owners (Langton, 2000, p. 259).

It is apparent then that Indigenous Knowing around the world has developed its own cultural literacy ones based on continuity where knowledge is a "sinew that runs throughout the ages": Knowledge is not something that is reinvented every generation (Meyer, 2001, p. 127). Continuity is critical and cyclic, it is sustainable:

> Holistic systems are often thought to be closed and therefore incapable of incorporating new elements. In fact, quite the opposite is true for Aboriginal understandings of country. ...Virtually everything can be accommodated, from tin cans to Toyotas, but everything must be accommodated according to the logic of country. This logic is that each country is its own centre, holds its own law, and is subservient to no other country (Bird Rose, 1996, p. 41)

Countrys are ecologies entirely dependent on relationships within them and around them. The last word on Country should be left to an Uncle an Australian Aboriginal Elder since passed:

'Because you love it this world.
Yes, this country, your country, my country...I love im.
I don't want to lose country, somebody take im.
Make you worry.
If somebody take im your country, you'n'me both get sick.
Because feeling...this country where you brought up and just like you'n'me mother.
Somebody else doing it wrong...you'n'me feel im.
Anybody, anyone...you'n'me feel." (Neidjie, 1989, p.152)

CONCEPT OF 'KNOWING'

Unlike others who have explored this issue of Indigenous knowledge and heritage, we are not concerned with a lack of a comprehensive definition of Indigenous knowledge. We are not creating a grand theory or a universal conceptualization of Indigenous knowledge or heritage. We are intimately aware that each Indigenous regime is characteristic of the creative adaptation of a people to an ecological order. Given the ecological diversity, a corresponding diversity of Indigenous languages, knowledge, and heritages exists. For any research to seek to give a comprehensive definition of Indigenous knowledge and heritage in any language system would be a massive undertaking, which would probably be misleading.

Other scholars have also reached the conclusion that comprehensive definitions cannot contain the diversity of Indigenous peoples or their knowledge, as does the United Nations working paper on 'On the Concept of "Indigenous People" [1996a],which concludes that the best practice is to allow Indigenous people to define themselves (Battiste M. &., 2000, p. 31).

Here 'Indigenous Knowings', are made visible through not so much an explanation of 'what they are' but through the stated assertion that Indigenous Knowings exist as valid entities in their own right. I discuss and celebrate Indigenous Knowings, I try not to fall in to the trap of 'them' and 'us'; a comparative analysis, establishing and positing a dichotomy between Indigenous and non-Indigenous or more specifically Eurocentric worldviews.

Battiste and Henderson's reflection above about the diversity of Indigenous languages, knowledges, and heritages cannot be overstated. Locally, nationally, internationally our diversities enliven what we each think of as Indigenous Knowings. It cannot therefore be my aim or intent to define 'Indigenous Knowings'. It is my aim to explore the implications of the different elements and concepts, to look at the impact on the transmission of our Knowings in our own communities and in the communities at large. I will discuss the space between the 'two worlds of Knowing'; Indigenous and Eurocentric Knowings and knowledge. A space Nakata refers to as the 'interface of colliding trajectories' (Nakata, 2007, p. 197). This space 'slivers' throughout this discussion as it does the book. I cannot discuss Indigenous Knowings as if these were 'frozen in time' (Battiste, 2002, p. 4). They are not and cannot be. Colonisation has without doubt impacted on 'systems and structures' of Indigenous Knowing and as such this section and indeed the book itself cannot be read without some understanding of its impact.

Elements and Concepts of Indigenous Knowings

Where do we begin? Our focal point rather than a starting point is with a description of some of the elements and concepts of 'Indigenous Knowings'. In this context a focal point is more significant than a starting point because one of the essences of our Knowing is the circular notion of Knowing, where there is no centre, only a web of connections without a centre (Hokari, 2000, p. 8). Where constant motion or flux (Little Bear, 2000, pp. 79-80), the ethics of spatial movement (Hokari, 2000, p. 8) do not stop for a beginning.

Different peoples, different voices, have articulated a number of concepts which I introduce here including that of time, ecological connection, experiential and participatory learning, innovation, relationships and connections across many dimensions, language, a holistic nature, learning propelled from the ground upwards where the initiative to learn lies with the learner, with this in some way being driven by the need to deal with real life issues, and the transmission and renewal of knowing through ritual and ceremony.

Time is discussed by people in the same breath as space and it is imbued with energy and real movement. Time is dependent on the moments and movements of the ecologies that are our understanding of 'Country'. Different Indigenous authors speak in different voices from Countrys/nations within Australia (Randall, 2003, pp. 16-17), Hokari (2000, p.10), from Canada (Youngblood Henderson, 2000, p. 265),(Battiste & Henderson 2000, p.48) and from North America (Little Bear 2000).

> There are only moments in Aboriginal life, our time is not the same. Everything is happening now. The past, present and future are all happening now. There is no time to waste, it's like ocean tides (Buchanan, 2007. p.3).

> If our 'existence consists of energy then everything is alive and imbued with spirit' (Little Bear, 2000, p.78). Our Knowings therefore are impacted by everything being in constant motion and in flux like the waves. They are impacted by the importance of relatedness and relationships. It "results in a concept of time that is dynamic but without motion. Time is part of the constant flux but goes nowhere. Time just is" (Little Bear, 2000, p. 78).

Without diminishing the uniqueness of each situation Indigenous Knowings across the globe speak of space rather than time, as well as fluid, cyclic movement and energy that relates to the ecological environment communities and individuals existing within.

Ecological connections or connections and relationships with Country are well articulated as 'empirical relationships with local ecosystems' by Youngblood Henderson, as 'spatial movement and the maintenance of the world through a web of connections' by Hokari,(2000, p.8) as involving a 'sanctity of personal and community relationships to the natural world' by Cajete 2004, p.248-249). The imaging of the spider and sweet potatoes is important to reflect on in this context.

Relationships are the 'cornerstone' of our Knowings (Meyer, 2001, p. 134), (Arbon, V. 2008. p.34), (Martin, K. 2008. pp.69-70), (Kovach, 2009, p.47) (Wilson, S. 2008, p.58); relationships with each other, with our Countrys and with our spiritual ancestors. Our teachings, our Knowings are informed by these relationships, and our Countrys. Ceremonies are a means of communicating with all of these elements, a means of nourishing, growing and practising our Knowings (Wilson. S, 2000), (Arbon, 2008. p.41), (Kovach,2008, p.67) (Youngblood Henderson, 2000, p.261) and (Battiste & Henderson, 2000, p.43).

A significant element of this relatedness is the centering of 'self' (Hokari, 2000, p.8), (Kovach, 2008, p.50), (Martin, K. 2008, p.78) where "we are the relationships that we hold and are part of" (Wilson, S. 2008, p.80).

The circle is a fundamental part of American Indian Knowing as it is with Indigenous cultures globally (Fixico, 2003, p.59). Kanyini and Yalka as metaphor (Arbon, V. 2008. p. 24) demonstrate this from within an Australian space. The circle embodies relationships, continuity, holism and spirit:

> The circle of life is inclusive of all things, including the physical, metaphysical and time. All things exist in a spiritual energy ... (Fixico, 2003, p. 59).

In the South Pacific we see reference to the importance of the spiral (Stewart-Harawira, 2005, pp.50-51) and (Sullivan, 2005, p.27) instead of the circle as a metaphor for conceptualising, and practising Indigenous Knowings. Circles and spirals are very different forms to the linear form of Western Knowledge or that in the Brick Wall.

In embracing, time and space, holism, circles and relatedness Indigenous Knowings therefore engage movement, dynamics, and an exploration and full use of all of our senses. Cajete and Meyer emphasise this below:

> Native science reflects the unfolding story of a creative universe in which human beings are active and creative participants. When viewed from this perspective, science is evolutionary – its expression unfolds through the general scheme of the creative process of first insight, immersion, creation, and reflection. Native science is a reflection of the metaphoric mind and is embedded in creative participation with nature. It reflects the sensual capacities of humans. It is tied to spirit, and is both ecological and integrative (Cajete, 2006, p. 249).

> The separation of mind from body is not found in a Hawaiian worldview. Intelligence, for these 20 Hawaiian educators, was not separate from feeling. Indeed, intelligence is found in the core of our body system ... feeling comfortable is part of Hawaiian intelligence. ... how "feeling" shapes the process and product of knowledge production,

> and whether one was innate (feeling), or learned (emotion). ... Knowing something is feeling something, and it is at the core of our embodied knowledge system. ... being metaphorically housed in our stomach region ... feelings precede emotions, then wisdom develops (Meyer, 2001, pp. 141-142).

Meyer asserts the significance of activity, engagement and application in Indigenous Knowing:

> Our empirical rapport with the environment is not something passive. We are active in our understanding. We are engaged in it. Knowing something becomes something *we create* (Meyer, 2001, p. 132). Knowledge is *valued* when it is applied (Meyer, 2001, p. 137).

The association of the natural world with Knowing and a sense of space rather than time directs some Indigenous peoples toward 'patterning' in their Knowing as so powerfully articulated by Mowaljarlai, an Elder and lawman I have referred to earlier in this book (Chapter 3). Continuing referencing throughout this book creates a pattern of its own; an element woven through the entire reflective journey. It is an element I am constantly drawn back to, to further engage and develop ideas. Mowaljarli is not alone in his articulation of patterning as being a significant essence of Indigenous Knowings. Little Bear, (2000, pp.79-80) explores our focus on the 'totality of the constant flux rather than individual patterns', Watson and Chambers (Watson H. C., 1989, pp. 31-41) discuss the importance of finding patterns that make sense of the world linking nature with family/kinship. (Watson H. C., 1989, p. 39) Patterns, therefore, play a fundamental role in Indigenous epistemology – a role that networks and relates ideas and themes, one that offers a sense of Belonging[1].

> Clearly, Indigenous epistemologies, throughout Australia have an absolute sense of *Belonging*, of relatedness through language, use of metaphor and story. Networks and patterns are fundamental to the expression of thought. These refer to the spiritual essence that imbues the relationship of people to their country with meaning ...a religious expression of fundamental spiritual origins and the place of phenomena in the world. (Langton, 2000, pp. 260-261).

---

[1] Belonging is a link and relationship to Country, family, community.

In Storying about Indigenous Knowings, we see these are imbued with a sense of continuous flow which has been clearly identified in earlier chapters through models and images presented. 'Garma' as evidenced in Chapter Three is a powerful metaphor conveying this flow through the meeting and mixing of two streams which flow – one from the land, the other from the sea. Garma much like Mowaljarli's pattern and triangle thinking that I find myself constantly pulled back into. It is a pull like a rip in the sea at the beach – a space that demands release, being able to 'go with the flow' and constantly turn ideas around in my mind. Garma is aptly the space I think of and refer to as the zone of colliding trajectories (as evidenced in Figure XX).

Cajete (2000, p.181-182) highlights metaphor as a tool, as a significant element of Indigenous Knowings.

> Cajete identifies metaphors –' represented in words, images, and symbols – as providing food for thought and a way to reflect on how we can use the tools of education in this process of reinventing a contemporary philosophy of Indigenous education' (Cajete, 2000, p.181).

This book is driven by metaphor; that of Waterlilys, Brick Walls, colliding trajectories, spiders and sweet potatoes.

It is apparent that space, patterning, connections and relationship to Country, family, kinship are significant elements of Indigenous 'Knowing'. Metaphor and story are expressions and forms of transmission of such 'Knowing':

> In fact, one aspect of the Indigenous worldview is that it takes a thousand voices to tell a story. (Wilshire, 2006, p. 160).

This Story has involved many voices and its ongoing journey will involve many more.

STORY AND STORYING

The truth about stories is that that's all we are (King, 2003, p. 2).

Indigenous Knowing across the globe is as King states 'all we are'. Story explains, explores and projects our being, our connections and relationships. Fixico,(2003, p.21, p.37), Battiste, (2002, p.25), King, (2003), Hokari,(2000, pp.8-9) Little Bear, (2000, p.81) and Chamberlin share their sense that Indigenous Knowing is dependent on story to transmit and grow, that the storytellers and the listeners are connected through Story and that Storys have many dimensions, many perspectives which all contribute to Indigenous Knowings.

Hokari explains a difference between Waterlily Knowing and Brick Wall Knowledge of Story that is fundamental:

> Different stories which contradict each other, do not conflict, but simply coexist. ...A story is told, the information is exchanged and discussed. However, the discussion was not for finding a single 'right' story, but for exploring the several possibilities of the cause ...maintaining the knowledge did not mean finding a 'right' story but widening the possibilities of stories. Information of different variations is preferred, pooled and maintained as a bundle of possibilities without judgement. It is an open system...The Gurindji knowledge system is not only open but also flexible (Hokari, 2000, pp. 8-9).

Storys are not generally explanations or descriptions but focus on the process of Knowings (Henderson, 2000, p.266), (Denzin, N. & Lincoln, Y.S. 2005, p.933). Storys are therefore not just about content. Storys are much more than hearing a fine entertainment account (Fixico, 2003, p.37). Storys, as King states are, 'all that we are'. Storys are the vehicles that transmit Indigenous Knowings: the flower of the Waterlilys. Storys have many dimensions and perspectives; the petals on the different lilys, involving patterning and repetition as they 'grow from the inside out' (Denzin, N. & Lincoln, Y.S. 2005, p.933).

Kwaymallina succinctly Storys this sense:

> I come from generations of storytellers who told tales in words, painted them in art, and sang and danced them in rhythm with the seasons and the sun and the stars. The people were one with the stories and the stories one with the people, and every tale both embodied and sustained the whole. The Indigenous peoples of the globe have always understood the universe to be a continually enfolding and unfolding place where everything holds everything else. We had no fractured stories, until the colonisers arrived, bringing with them tales that divided people from people and people from the earth. Indigenous peoples learned to navigate these stories too; we had to if we wanted to survive (Kwaymullina, 2014).

Storys from an Indigenous centre are:

> gifted through and as part of ceremony. Story can be sung, drawn, danced, performed, spoken and is multidimensional involving all body/mind senses whilst being shared on many canvases. The canvas can be the human body through painting and/or on rock, sand, bark whatever the terrain asserts is the appropriate medium. Each of these mediums has different space and is dynamic, transitory and fluid. Where to every action there is a story. (King, 2003, p. 29)

Story has structure, a number of voices and movements. Storys have layers; layers that a few people may Know and more layers that everyone Knows. The storyteller is often the listener at the same time they are the story teller. The story teller is often the one being spoken to as Armstrong identifies:

> 'through my language I understand I am being spoken to, I'm not the one speaking. The words are coming from many tongues and mouths of Okanagan people and the land around them. I am a listener to the language's stories, and when my words form I am merely retelling the same stories in different patterns' (King, 2003, p. 2).

Storys become more and more important as people realized the strength of the authority with which the words are uttered (Benterrak, 1996, p.258). It matters who says what, where and when and to whom.

When we think of Indigenous Storys we often think quaint Dreamtime stories, oral story, memory, Chinese whispers and fabrication. In Indigenous communities around the world, memory is the repository of our Knowings. Uncle Rueben Kelly once said to me 'when we started to write things down we forgot how to use our minds' (Kelly, 1984). His words haunt me as an Indigenous academic indulging in knowledge so 'textcentric'. His words bring back the power of Indigenous Knowings, the power of the mind. Cajete tells a story to showcase this further:

> I remember a quote from Vine Deloria. He had asked an Elder what it was that allowed him to know his environment and how he knew things without being in a place or even ever having been there. The Elder told him, "I have a map in my head." Indigenous curricula are maps. ...

The maps we are operating with now support the very system that colonized us. Indigenous people are working with maps that are not of our own making. We are working with the colonizer's maps. It's only when we become our own "cartographers" that we will be able to find our way through the territory and move once again in to the Tao of teaching, in to Indigenous education (Cajete, 2000, p. 188).

The use of memory is pivotal in Storying, and learning from Indigenous Knowing. Trudgen (2000, p. 104) refers to Yolngu from a very early age being taught to carry and repeat messages accurately. Here it does not matter that they may not understand and they know not to ask for meaning because it might be something they should not Know about (Trudgen, 2000, p. 104). Bunge (1984, p.76) a Lakota Indian and scholar writes about the notion of what is 'true' and its connection to Lakota Knowing.

Rains, a Native scholar from North America explores links between memory, Country and age whereby:

> 'because we are old, it may be thought that the memory of things may be lost with us, who have not, like you, the art of preserving it by committing all transactions to writing'. We nevertheless have methods of transmitting ... an account of all these things. You will find the remembrance of them is faithfully preserved, and our succeeding generations are made acquainted with what has passed, that it may not forget as long as the earth remains (Rains, 2000 , p. 337).

Buzan, the creator of the Mind Map® reinforces this timeless wisdom in his search for meaning and contribution to global mental literacy:

> Multiple evidence indicates that by using the brain well and properly as you get older; you physically challenge it, improving and streamlining its synaptic connections and hence its power of association. ... memory ... (Buzan, 1996, p. 8).

Engaging with oral cultures, oral Knowings requires a different skill set to those required for engaging with written text.

> Learning the existing oral legacy involves intimate and endless listening to stories and dialogue with Elders and parents. This process takes time and patience. It is iterative rather than linear. The stories are told in a

circular or spiral theme, with each thematic repetition or spiral adding a
little. This can be contrasted with the step-by-step, linear progression of
an Aristotelian argument (Youngblood Henderson, 2000, p. 266).

What frame of reference do you use to engage with Story? There remains one
final element of Story to share and that is premised on how we listen to Story, so
differently conceptualised. What is our strategy for listening? If we centre
Western Knowledges and Western concept of Story Benterrak suggests that we
only 'hear' what we want to hear about what shapes our disciplines (Benterrak,
1996, p. 62), answers our questions directly. The iterative process, the endless
need for listening, the repetition and spiralling of Story Henderson spoke of
before is challenging; it is a part of the contested zone that requires reformatting
if we are to 'come across'. Dadirri (Ungunmerr-Baumann) embodying the
concept of 'deep listening' is what we need to engage with Indigenous Storys.

David Unaipon asserted that story telling is more like a dramatic
performance and it contains the truths of his people (Bell, 1998, p.394). To
understand these truths we must first appreciate and then respect the different
centres. We must then let go of the recipe we have for hearing Indigenous Storys
and craft a new set of skills to listen holistically, watch holistically engaging all
of our senses; the senses we need to experience dramatic performance. In order to
Know then we need to 'be still and pay attention' (Hokari, 2000, p. 2). In being
still and paying attention one is totally reliant on the interplay of each of our
senses.

A visual representation of the significance of Story and all that has been
stated and reflected upon before is presented below where through symbols
drawn in the sand, Pintubi women discuss journeys of their ancestors, the two
sisters, as they travelled across the desert to Kintore looking for bush food. By
means of such teachings, children learn about the Country and gain their world
view (Isaacs, 1990, pp. 47-48). Here there are many layers of Story: Story
through body, sand, performance and Dadirri.

.

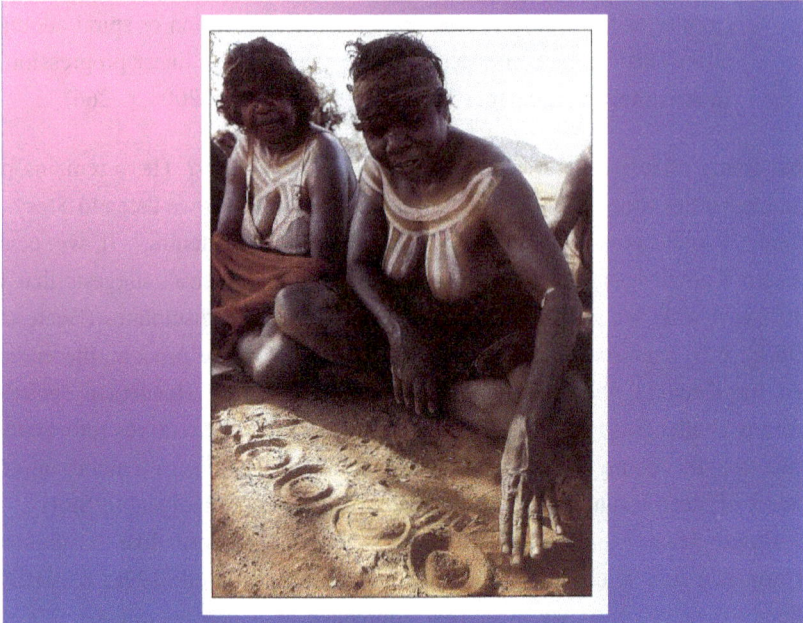

Figure 5.1. Indigenous Knowing: Women in Country

Photography, Reg Morrison. Reprinted with permission Jennifer Isaacs, Papunya Tula Artists October 2015.

.

Other Indigenous scholars such as Moreton Robinson (2000, pp.1-4) use the term 'life writings' to discuss 'story' to capture the collective nature, self-presentation and subjectivity as well as relationality through Story. Archibald (2008) has created Indigenous Storywork which has become a powerful means of engaging with research; a research method, and research framework.

ELDERS AS TRADITIONAL SCHOLARS

Elders have a pivotal role in the transmission and sharing of Indigenous Knowings, in traditional and contemporary contexts, in community, corporate and academic environments in Hawaii, Australia, Canada, and North America. Our Elders are our teachers, our facilitators of Knowings (Churchill, 1996, p.510). Discussion about Elders invariably invokes reference to the concept of wisdom and the impact this has on Indigenous Knowings. Deloria speaks of wisdom in terms of our maturity; 'within life history of maturity one can be said to travel from information to knowledge to wisdom' (Deloria, 1999, pp. 13-15). In Inuit culture, Nunavik speak of wisdom going hand in hand with independence where Elders are the source of such wisdom (Nunavik, 1992, pp, 2,11).

To be able to actively learn from Elders we must remember:

> Just as it takes years of training to address and understand a Canadian Supreme Court Justice, for example, so it can take many years of apprenticeship to hear the words of Elders and traditional teachers. These teachings do not come in the prepackaged form to which students are accustomed (Peter Kulchyski, 1999, p. xv).

Themes explored so far include the concepts of Country and Indigenous Knowings, the role of Elders as traditional scholars and the significance of Story. These themes form an essence of Indigenous Knowings which find themselves entrapped in a cultural interface where trajectories collide. These elements in the context of research theory and practice are being tussled in the whirlpools of Garma. This discussion is a sliver weaving in and out throughout the entire Story, growing it and grounding it through a need for constant reflection, re-energising and draining. Discord is created.

Cultural Interface and Colliding Trajectories

The discord between Aboriginal and Eurocentric worldviews is dramatic. It is conflict between natural and artificial contexts. Aboriginal worldviews are not reductionist. They have always stressed similarities rather than differences (Youngblood Henderson, 2000, p. 261).

It is now useful to look at Indigenous Knowings in that space of muddy terrain, the space Garma describes above as where fresh and salt water meet. It is not a simple meeting point where sameness and difference converge, mix and settle. It as and Youngblood Henderson succinctly describes above, "dramatic". Nakata stresses that we have developed "a reading of ourselves at the interface of colliding trajectories" which highlights the role of The Academy in defining Indigenous Knowings; to our detriment (Nakata M. , 2007, p. 197). Battiste refers to cognitive imperialism and a 'decaying colonial mentality' to illustrate the space of inappropriate reclamation and territorialisation that we find ourselves in:

> From Saskatchewan where I boarded to the unfamiliar airports to the crystal shores of Australia, I was to enter in to a strange journey into the "soul of darkness". The "soul of darkness" is a metaphor seeking to explain an Indigenous journey through the decaying colonial mentality.

My voyage was a journey into the old colonized empires that are becoming mastered by the Indigenous soul. From the eagle feather headdress of Saskatoon airport to the airports of Vancouver, Hawaii, and Sydney, Australia, I witnessed the extensive appropriation of Indigenous art to create national or regional identities of the colonizers. Expressions of Indigenous art and spirituality were used to create false reconciliations with Indigenous peoples as the colonialists sought to reconstruct their regional or national identities. One could not be but awed by the magnificent Indigenous jade rock carvings in the Vancouver airport, or miss the market places displaying Indigenous legendary characters of the raven and bear or the totem poles being used as local souvenirs of Vancouver. Each airport made me aware of the presence of Indigenous peoples whose painted designs, art, and sacred objects would be dotted among the hotels, restaurants, and airport shops of Australia. ... Every expression of the Indigenous soul was a silent witnessing of an emerging post-colonial world that is escaping the circularity of Eurocentric colonialism (Battiste M. , 1996, p. 224).

In this space of colliding trajectories I now look at five elements that demonstrate the muddiness, the drama, the impact of emerging and existing in such contested space;

1. How Indigenous Knowings have been used
2. The Academy: Indigenous Knowings and research
3. The Academy : Indigenous Knowings – Thoughts as Text, Thoughts Embodied
4. Self-Determination and Sovereignty
5. Protection of Intellectual and Cultural Property

HOW INDIGENOUS KNOWINGS HAVE BEEN USED?

Historically the muldarbi has positioned Aboriginal Peoples in a space that is short of invisible, and if to appear at all, it has been at the lowest point in its hierarchical ordering of life. The muldarbi has positioned Nunga women, men and children through its way of seeing, and its way of seeing us is through a white male dominant and race lens. In the eyes of the muldarbi-colonisers being indigenous was to be 'known' by them as inferior, while they were 'known' to themselves as a 'scientific fact' to be superior. Their construction of who we are and where we are placed in their hierarchical ordering of life continues. They continue to name and define who we are. How we should look. How we should act. What our culture is and should look like to them, etc etc etc. The power of 'right-knowing functions on different levels. The state and its agencies construct 'the Aborigines' and other groups also have their own way of knowing who we are and how we should be (Watson I. , 1998, p. 30).

Indigenous Knowings have been used by Eurocentric scholars to elevate and position themselves in a superior stage of humanity as Watson articulates above. They have been used to objectify, silence, oppress, marginalize, subjugate, submerge and in some instances erase and eradicate our own lifeworlds. Cavender Wilson (2004, p.79) and Fixico (1998, p.93) condemn historians specifically for researching and writing in such a way as to create a 'great conspiracy' whilst subjugating Indigenous peoples, our histories and Knowings.

Our own Knowing has been turned on us through the fragmentation of it under Eurocentric microscopic gazing. It has been used to create the 'other', the marginal and the inferior. Trask has echoed Watson (above) in an assertion that defining, constructing who we are, are acts of colonization that have had enormous impacts on us in terms of accepting, and denying our Indigeneity; our cultures, our being:

> Because of colonization, the question of who defines what is Native, and even who is defined as Native has been taken away from Native peoples by Western-trained scholars, government officials, and other technicians. This theft in itself testifies to the pervasive power of colonialism and explains why self-identity by Natives of who and what they are elicits such strenuous and sometimes vicious denials by the dominant culture (Trask, 1993, p. 43).

This gaze was evidenced in the Prologue when Storying my fathers and my own personal experiences. W. E.B.Du Bois captures this internal mental, emotional and spiritual chaos best in his notion of 'double consciousness':

> This sense of always looking at one's self through the eyes of others, of measuring one's soul by the tape of a world that looks on in amused contempt and pity (du Bois, 1969, p. 45).

Battiste illustrates this notion of 'double consciousness' in the context of seeking universality. According to Battiste and Youngblood Henderson this Eurocentric quest for universal definitions has raised suspicion among Indigenous peoples, who do not want to be assimilated into Eurocentric categories (Battiste & Henderson, 2000, p.37). This is where the collision of trajectories becomes more intense; where all peoples have a fundamental human right to practice their own culture and one group contrives, manipulates and constructs knowing of and about the other from their own frames of reference; reinforcing marginalisation. The making invisible of Indigenous Knowings, Indigenous being and Indigenous peoples is the result of such manipulation:

> Eurocentric thought asserts that only Europeans can progress and that Indigenous peoples are frozen in time ... These strategies have caused Indigenous peoples to be viewed as backward and as passive recipients of European knowledge. Indigenous knowledge became invisible to

> Eurocentric knowledge to its development theories, and to global science (Battiste, 2002, p. 4).

Smith (1999) maintains that this push to see Indigenous people as passive recipients continues through the philosophy of 'Modernism' to colonize indigenous people as these adhere to the belief that humans progress via a linear, universal, predetermined process (Cannella G. , 1997) . Constructed as a "truth" then, Western knowledge has been legitimized as the standard for "normalcy." Thus, other understandings of human relations become marginalized and in need of control, surveillance, and colonization (Viruru, 2004). Seeking universality and establishing 'normalcy' through such benchmarking has no meaning for us as Indigenous peoples.

Eurocentric scholar's assessment of Indigenous Knowings through the universalisation of it (Battiste & Henderson, 2000, pp.36-38) has led to a 'mis-diagnoses' of exactly what comprises Indigenous Knowings. The universalisation of Indigenous Knowings has placed it where 'Eurocentric arrogance and sense of superiority of their own world view imposes it on Indigenous peoples' (p.37) .

Indigenous Knowings have been made invisible and advanced through and by The Academy; the Brick Wall (Youngblood Henderson, 2000, p.265). Research has been conducted by various scholars across a variety of disciplines which effectively reinforces such invisibility. It is useful at this point to look at Indigenous Knowings and The Academy and research conducted through it. Battiste and Henderson articulate some problems in understanding Indigenous Knowings through Eurocentric lenses specifically language and understanding of concepts such as 'culture' and 'Indigenous knowledge' (Battiste & Henderson, 2000, p.37). They argue and I agree that the difference between the two worldviews can be seen in asking two questions: firstly: "What is Indigenous knowledge?" and secondly "What can savages know or how do they think?"

In this juxtaposition of thinking it is clear that we cannot define Indigenous Knowings through Eurocentric lenses; there is no easy definition and certainly no thinking across conceptual boundaries. Many of the scholars housed within the Brick Wall place Indigenous Knowings with the context of culture which Battiste & Henderson reject because Indigenous Knowledge exists as a manifestation of particular ecological orders seeing a 'mysticism' being created around some Indigenous Knowledges leading to a massive economic industry in 'new age' possibilities.

Battiste & Henderson (2000) further argue that Indigenous Knowledge cannot be categorised (p.35) in to the Bricks of the Wall nor can it be 'separated from the bearer because it is a part of us and unidentifiable except in a personal context' (p.37). To do so while the principles of universality and diffusionism exploit Eurocentric concepts of superiority is a destructive process described best as "ontological imperialism" (Livinas 1961) and "cognitive imperialism" (Battiste M. &., 2000, p. 37).

Indigenous peoples are speaking back about how we have been exploited by the very conduct of the majority of research; whether it is done by anthropologists, archaeologists, historians. Martin (2008, pp.26-29) succinctly articulates the early patterns in the dispossession of our Storys through research. What is clear is that we have not only been silenced but our spirit has been trampled on by many researchers (Trask, 1993, p.127). One Story I know illustrates this:

> Sally Morgan, a renowned Indigenist writer, educator, artist and Professor, and I chaired a talking circle session at one of our National Indigenous Research Forums. She responded to an Aboriginal woman who shared her experience. This woman like many Indigenous peoples was researching her family. She discovered a non-Indigenous academic who had done a lot of research in her country and held a lot of information about her family. This woman approached her about accessing the information. The academic told her 'I can't just give this information away, this has been my life's work'. The Aboriginal woman after feeling confused, angry and frustrated asked what it would take to get the information she needed about her family. The academic said it would cost the woman $x. Sally Morgan who was chairing the session said 'gee the price has gone up since we approached her for information, it has xxx!'

Fixico (1998,pp.84-85) discusses certain moral ethics and responsibilities in the field of American Indian history leading ultimately to convince historians and others of the importance of upholding such ethics and fulfilling responsibilities pertaining to the proper study and writing of American Indian history.

Von Liebenstein & Slikkerveer (1993) identify that 'until the 1980s Indigenous Knowledge surfaced in very few academic disciplines, but now is in many scientific and academic circles (p.1). De La Torres (2004) explores the discipline of political science stating 'it not only omits Indigenous knowledge but also attempts to alter Indigenous knowledge to fit in to the theoretical paradigms of the discipline (De La Torre, 2004, pp. 181-182). This is not a new experience and in fact is experienced in any discipline that Indigenous Knowings have been identified as 'significant'.

> Deloria Jnr (2004) posits we need only to read Stephen Jay Gould's The Mismeasure of Man to understand the degree to which racism was embedded in science and what a task it was to raise these issues.

> Gould outlines the history of the study of human skulls and demonstrates that where data was not deliberately faked to conform to pre-existing doctrines, scholars showed obvious bias and were oblivious to their own racist assumptions. The idea that measuring the shape of the human skull could determine intellectual and cultural potential and accomplishments and even identify race was absurd from the beginning. Yet for the better part of a century scholars devoutly believed this nonsense (Deloria Jr., 2004, p. 19).

> Deloria Jnr (2004) acknowledges that we are often our own worst enemies because our response to such cognitive imperialism has been piecemeal (p.21). He found in his criticism of anthropologists in Custer Died for Your Sins 'Indian scholars were the most vocal against his stance, being content to be good house pets in anthropology' (p.29). I agree that in an Australian context many of us as Indigenous scholars fail to question discipline knowledge. We fail to centre our own Indigenous Knowings, instead centering knowledges within the Brick Wall and somehow trying to fit Indigenous Knowings within it.

But what happens, or what do we need to consider, when Indigenous Knowledge is brought into relation with the disciplines in The Academy? In their differences, Indigenous Knowings and Western scientific knowledge systems are considered so disparate as to be 'incommensurable' (Verran, 2005) or 'irreconcilable' (Russell, 2005) on cosmological, epistemological and ontological grounds. Nakata (2007) argues the lived space of Indigenous people in colonial regimes is the most complex of spaces and the reader, the listener of our Indigenous Knowings 'must be persuaded that understandings of the Indigenous position must be 'complicated' rather than simplified through any theoretical framing (Nakata, 2007, p. 12).

This leaves us as Indigenous peoples in a challenging situation. One that demands that we centre our own Indigenous Knowings, using language and structures that facilitate 'creative learning' (Cajete, 2004, p. 25). We need to move beyond defending our position and strengthen our own life worlds, not lose ourselves in the process (Nakata, 2007, p.9).

In moving on we must come to terms with The Academy and its role in the disembodying, and disparaging of Indigenous Knowings, peoples and cultures. We must honestly as the growing body of literature asserts move beyond the contested space, move beyond "ontological imperialism" (Livinas 1961) and "cognitive imperialism" (Battiste 1986). Colonization and The Academy as its prime enacting agent have much to answer for. The next section explores how our spirits as Indigenous peoples have been silenced by practices created, enacted and endorsed by The Academy. I speak in unison with the voices of my Indigenous brothers and sisters as they explore the main features of Indigenous Knowings, as they identify what has become Known in the contested space between Western and Indigenous Knowings. This is what I have also referred to as colliding trajectories and again slivers appear throughout the next section, namely that of the impact of colonisation.

THE ACADEMY: INDIGENOUS KNOWINGS AND RESEARCH

> It is important to understand what happens when Indigenous Knowledge is documented in ways that disembody it from the people who are its agents, when the 'knowers' of that knowledge are separated out from what comes to be 'the known', in ways that dislocate it from its locale, and separate it from the social institutions that uphold and reinforce its efficacy, and cleave it from the practices that constantly renew its meanings in the here and now. And it is also important to consider what disintegrations and transformations occur when it is redistributed across Western categories of classification, when it is managed in databases via technologies that have been developed in ways that suit the hierarchies, linearity, abstraction and objectification of Western knowledge – all of which are the antithesis of Indigenous Knowledge traditions and technologies (Nakata, 2007, pp. 191-192).

Much of our energy as Indigenous scholars has been trying to 'fit into' the Western Eurocentric (Kovach, 2009, p.31), (Wilson, 2008, p.127), Arbon (2008, p.27) Brick Wall. In this process we see the dislocation, reclassification and disintegrations of our Knowings as referenced by Nakata above.

This section explores this space; the cleavage between two distinct systems of Knowing. It explores what people require in advocacy for Indigenous self-determination; one that privileges Indigenous Knowings and calls on the process of decolonisation

This part of the Story begins where the embodiment of nature; the environment, Country and ecology embedded within Indigenous Knowings, with webs of connections is centred rather than a system that classifies things hierarchically as Western knowledges do. This has significant impact on how Indigenous peoples 'research' or conceptualise 'research' and the development of new knowledge:

Little Bear asserts that Eurocentric values of 'linearity and singularity, a static nature and objectivity manifests in the thinking processes of Western Europeans in concepts such as one true god, one true answer, and one right way (2000, pp. 82-83). This singularity results in a social structure consisting of specialists. ... Specializations are ranked in terms of prestige.... Such focus on categorisation and specialisation repels the creative spirit so much a part of Native Science and relies on the commitment of Western science to increasing human mastery over nature, to continue conquering until everything natural is under absolute human control (Cajete, 2006, p.250, p.253).

These become the bricks in the Brick Wall.

Such embeddedness in Indigenous Knowings of Country, and ecologies finds people sensually developing their skills, their Knowing by "tuning in" to the natural world (Cajete, 2006, p.254), and by listening and being observant (Meyer, 2001, p.129), deep listening or Dadirri (Ungunmerr-Baumann). I remember returning home after being in Desert for a month and sitting on my balcony noticing things I had never seen before. Things that weren't new I just hadn't tuned in to the fact that they were there; things in the trees and Country surrounding me.

Indigenous scholars such as Battiste and Youngblood Henderson, Cajete (2004, p.26), Wilshire and Trask (1993, p.121) further explore this connection, the bond between people and land also lament the lack of this element in Western knowledge. It is surely one of the main reasons for the disparity, the cleavage the diametric trajectories between the different systems of Knowing:

> But because the West has lost any cultural understanding of the bond between people and land, it is not possible to know this connection through Western culture. This means that the history of indigenous people can not be written from within Western culture. Such a story is merely the West's story of itself.

> Our story remains unwritten. It rests within the culture, which is inseparable from the land. To know this is to know our history. To write this is to write of the land and the people who are born from her (Trask, 1993, p. 121).

This has led to basic grounds of complete unknowing. In this state and space as Trask asserts 'historians, I realized, were very much like missionaries. They were part of the colonizing horde. One group colonized the spirit; the other, the mind' (Trask, 1993, p. 114).

The West then having a knowledge system based on linear time, sequence, categorisation and development, having no bonding with the earth so much a part of our being, classifies and separates out domains of Knowings. In essence there are two distinct domains of Knowing/Knowledge and many domains, within each. There are other elements that Indigenous voices articulate as disparate, profoundly conceptually different, including the importance of the whole experience, that, that is holistic for example.

Indigenous scholars speak of the importance of subjectivity over objectivity (Cajete, 2004, p.26).

> The mindset associated with fragmentation, dissecting the world, research and knowledges into bits to be analysed and categorised 'impedes progress towards inwardness that our ancestors undertook ... With holism, an environmental ethic is possible (Ermine, 1998, 102-103).

Authors such as Cajete (1986, p.124) and Battiste & Youngblood Henderson (2000, pp.36-37) examine some of the challenges associated with Indigenous Knowings being fragmented and classified, framed within Eurocentric categories when the belief systems are so different. They look at the process of understanding being more important than that of classification.

Deloria Jr. contextualises such fragmentation within the concept and experience of racism within The Academy: one we are all too familiar with as Indigenous scholars, where:

> Academia has often been a hotbed of racism because scholars are taught to pretend that they can observe phenomena objectively. In fact they observe data through culturally prescribed categories that restrict the possible answers and understandings to a predetermined few selections. With Western thought primarily a binary, yes/no method of determining

truth, so much data is excluded, and so limited are the possible answers that Western Knowledge might be regarded as a mere classification system devoid of valid conclusions (Deloria Jr., 2004, p. 19).

The impact of the interplay and assertion of 'a truth' in Western Knowledge has led to dangerous and damaging knowledge for us as Indigenous peoples about ourselves and how the West perceives us:

> Suddenly the entire sweep of our written history was clear to me. I was reading the West's view of itself through the degradation of my own past (Trask, 1993, p. 117).

> Anzaldua (1990) refers to "internal exiles" (Bacca in Anzaldua) continually challenging institutional discourses and being suspicious of the dominant culture's interpretation of "our" experience, of the way they "read" us (Anzaldua, 1990, p. xxv).

Let us explore at this point a few other elements contributing to us seeing Indigenous Knowings as a separate domain and what some Indigenous scholars see as stages and elemental characteristics of Indigenous education.

The secular nature of Indigenous Knowings aspires a living process to be absorbed and understood creating the context and texture of life not a commodity that can be possessed or controlled by educational institutions (Battiste and Youngblood Henderson 2002, p.17).

Cajete refers to the participatory nature of Indigenous Knowings, an aspect that demands subjectivity and creativity (Cajete, 2006, pp. 258-259). Cardinal also speaks of a 'unique creative process' through the 'centrality and power of "visioning" (Cardinal, 1991).

None of these elements of Indigenous Knowings; neither the interrelationships with Knowings, land and people, subjectivity, non-linear concept of time nor participation and experiential learning (Battiste, 2002, pp.14-15), exist on their own. They are intertwined, they form patterns rather than the triangles Mowarljarli referred to earlier which are hierarchic, linear and time-bound:

> Wholeness becomes paramount in Indigenous Knowings as evidenced earlier in this chapter. Little Bear likens wholeness to a flower; it could be the Waterlily flower:

> Wholeness is like a flower with four petals. When it opens, one discovers strength, sharing, honesty and kindness. Together these four petals create balance, harmony and beauty. Wholeness works in the same interconnected way. The value strength speaks to the idea of sustaining balance. ... Understanding the four interrelated petals of the flower demonstrates why collective decision making was and is such an important Aboriginal custom (Little Bear, 2000, pp. 79-80).

Fragmentation was and remains a legacy of colonization:

> Colonization created a fragmentary worldview among Aboriginal peoples. By force, terror, and educational policy, it attempted to destroy the Aboriginal worldview – but failed. Instead, colonization left a heritage of jagged worldviews among Indigenous people. They no longer had an Aboriginal worldview, nor did they adopt a Eurocentric worldview. Their consciousness became a random puzzle, a jigsaw puzzle that each person has to attempt to understand. Many collective views of the world competed for control of their behaviour, and since none was dominant modern Aboriginal people had to make guesses or choices about everything. Aboriginal consciousness became a site of overlapping, contentious, fragmented, competing desires and values (Little Bear, 2000).

The space we as Indigenous peoples currently inherit; the space of endeavouring to privilege our Knowing and translate complex, bombarding, disparate elements of Knowing has found expression in some Indigenous scholars work as 'testimonials of survival'. Anzaldua (1990, p. xvii) is one such author. In discussing her anthology she diminishes the significance of objectivity and breathes in notions of the chameleon, our vulnerabilities and exposure as Indigenous peoples in such environments. Here the chameleon and masked beings image a dynamic, raw and deep reaction to this space of colliding trajectories where "We are all bleeding, rubbed raw behind our masks." After years of wearing masks we may become just a series of roles, the constellated self, limping along with its broken limbs (Anzaldua, 1990, p. xv).

This 'bleeding' and being 'rubbed raw' is an engaging way to illustrate what I described earlier as the box with different shapes. At what cost do we as Indigenous peoples develop and embody our own space, our own Knowings?

This question is a constant throughout this book and as yet I have no one answer and probably never will have one universal response. There will be many layers to any responses. In interrogating the question further I illustrate through a brief description, Australian Indigenous peoples experiences of education, of a context whereby frameworks of Western knowledge have standardised approaches to Indigenous education, establishing binaries through tables of difference and a notion of Indigenous pedagogy.

In the 1970s and 1980s, Bourke, (Bourke, 1975) (Bourke, 1979), (Hughes, 1984) (Hughes P. , 1997), (Hughes, First Indigenous Researchers Forum, 1998), (Harris, 1990), (Harris, 1982) and (Watson, 1988) developed the discourse on Aboriginal pedagogy and Aboriginal epistemology. They argued that the principles and practices informing Aboriginal pedagogy are:

i)   experiential learning;
ii) learning perceived as an end in itself;
iii) Aboriginal learning oriented toward the present;
iv) learning as a community activity where co-operation and group learning are fundamental; and that
v)   the transmission of knowledge is not the sole responsibility of one individual, nor is
vi) it a one way process.
vii) learning is holistic.

This was an era developing and assessing 'learning styles theory'.

The research in the 1980s and 1990s was according to (Hughes, First Indigenous Researchers Forum, 1998) 'based on our own collective knowledge', rather than 'actual research'. This literature and research focused primarily on language, linguistic differences and impact on the classroom and learning outcomes. Christie, (Christie, 1985), Harkins, (Harkins, 1994), Harris, (Harris, 1982), (Harris, 1990) and Eades (Eades, 1988) were prominent contributors to this era of discourse. Out of this era emerged the discourse on 'two-ways' or 'both ways' education. Two-ways education is an approach to cultural interaction and cross-cultural learning, bringing together the Aboriginal traditions of knowledge with Western education traditions (Harris, 1990).

Stockton (Stockton, 1995, p. 39), in an assessment of research into Aboriginal modes of thinking and learning conducted by Harris in Arnhem Land and Lex Grey in Sydney, determined some of the basic differences. Stockton asserts that, though polarised, most individuals "fit within" the following range of characteristics:

Aboriginal	European
Right cerebral hemisphere dominant	Left cerebral hemisphere dominant
Global mode (Gestalt – synthetic)	Propositional mode with comparison, classification, analysis and verbalisation
Words recall experience when used	Words have conceptual content
Non-verbal thinking (images, feelings juxtaposed)	Verbal thinking
Present time oriented	Future/past oriented
Person oriented	Information oriented
Learning by observation, imitation, trial-and-error	Learning by instruction and demonstration
Non-competitive, co-operative	Individualistic, excelling, standing out
Real life performance	Practice in contrived situations
Context-specific skills	Context-free principles, universally applicable
Separation of domains of thought	Single domain
Three-dimensional thought (visual, spatial)	Linear or two-dimensional thought

Practitioners took up the concept advanced by these academics and embodied the principles in curriculum design and policy at state and national level. In South Australia, the Education Department (South Australian Department of Education, 1991, p. 21) stated:

> … from the evidence we have from Aboriginal and similar cultures,…it is reasonable to suggest that Aboriginal learning style differences occur often enough to be a significant factor warranting careful attention by all

teachers and in all schools....there appears to be a fundamental dysfunction between the teaching/learning styles in tradition-oriented Aboriginal learning society and the Western school classroom.

In traditional (Aboriginal) society children learn by observation, manipulation and experimentation but in the school classroom they must learn by response to verbal instruction, reading and writing. This creates a discontinuity in the enculturation process of the children. This discontinuity applies for children from tradition-oriented communities and lifestyles, and is indicated to a reasonable significant extent for urban Aboriginal children as well.

Government policies, at all levels, responded to the research of the 1980s and 1990s by developing the National Aboriginal and Torres Strait Islander Education Policy (AEP). The AEP identified eleven recommendations to provide alternate structures within the mainstream structures to better cater for Indigenous students' needs (Christensen, 1997/1998). In New South Wales teachers were expected to implement policy which sought culturally appropriate teaching strategies and assessment methods.

According to Hughes: (Hughes, First Indigenous Researchers Forum, 1998)

For years we had been arguing that we as Aboriginal people could take control ourselves and do things the 'Aboriginal way'. However, when others said OK what is the 'Aboriginal way' we could not come up with any statements that could help.' Hughes goes on to argue that as Indigenous educators we developed some useful 'Aboriginal way' statements that could be used politically - we effectively made it up as we went along. Further we, did not base our actions on actual research, we relied on our own collective knowledge. This became the basis of government policy on Aboriginal education.

More recently, research has begun to focus on the notion of Indigenous epistemology; specifically, concepts such as patterning, language and the use of metaphors.

Globally we as Indigenous peoples began to pick up Western concepts and constructs. Concepts such as 'epistemology' joined that of 'pedagogy' in our repertoire amidst our efforts to skate around the fringes of Western knowledge, drawing on 'double consciousness'. We began to explore our own sense of Knowings within the bounds of Western knowledge.

Some Indigenous scholars advocate for the need to engage in western constructs. Bunge discusses six distinct types of knowledge discernible among the Lakota so that he can make Lakota philosophical assumptions intelligible to minds accustomed to thinking in the categories of traditional European tradition. He does this engaging with the language of the coloniser and within the frames or reference of Western knowledge. In doing this he does assert the existence of differing Lakota techniques of knowing. He states:

Deloria in his assessment moves beyond some of the more obvious western frames and links the concept of quantum physics with Indigenous epistemology; a positioning between epistemology and metaphysics ... (Deloria, 1999, p. 13).

Mignolo (2000) uses the term 'epistemology' as a survivalist strategy as a way to assert difference between the knowings referring as Deloria does to metaphysics as an element of congruence (p.259)

If we revisit Hughes assertion that in Australia we were looking for Aboriginal 'ways of knowing' (p.36) and had no research beyond that, then perhaps if we had known more about decolonising our minds, our language and centring our own systems of Knowing we could have accepted our experiences as a separate domain of Knowing. This is an illustration of how we as Indigenous peoples grapple with that space of colliding trajectories.

The issue of language is one that has concerned Indigenous scholars 'Storying' Indigenous Knowings. Specifically, if Knowing and knowledge has a different domain it is expressed through its language of preference. Little Bear (2000, p.78) and Youngblood Henderson (2000, p.263) emphasise the verb rich aspect of Indigenous languages implying action and process rather than naming in noun-centred languages associated with Eurocentric knowledge. For Yolgnu the English language is seen as a ' a collection of detached objects' yet Yolgnu language embodies the 'flowing face of nature as is seen in a state of relatedness' (Watson et al., 1989, p.15).

This feature of linguistic difference is an essential element in the context of how 'The Academy' has attempted to translate Indigenous Knowings and create an opposing binary, one that has silenced Indigenous voices and languages of Knowings:

> Thus, language already has both knowledge and law enfolded in it. Without access to their Aboriginal language, Aboriginal people can neither create nor sustain a postcolonial order. They can have access to Aboriginal cultures through English, but they cannot grasp the inherent

beauty of Aboriginal worldviews and language through English. They end up living a translated life (Youngblood Henderson, 2000, p. 264).

Linguicide, a term coined by Skutnabb-Kangas (Mutua, 2004, p. 14) is a direct result of the impact of colonisation. Mutua and Swadener identify a 'growing body of scholarship that asserts language is playing an increasingly important role as a means of control and domination'; it is evoking 'linguicide' which disconnects peoples from culture, from Knowing. wa Thiong'o (2005) illustrates this lack of association and connection with language and culture with a Story about the child, the colonial child being assimilated to use the colonisers language and finding themselves taken further and further away from themselves and their worlds; the child living a translated life (pp.14-19).

Cultural Interface and Colliding Trajectories

As Arrows states 'the language of conquest is ultimately a language of deceit. It echoes in the corridors of every American institution, building illusion upon illusion while robbing all of us of our collective Indigenous wisdom' (Arrows, 2006, p. 18). Total miscommunication can exist in the space of colliding trajectories and we as Indigenous peoples must inhabit and reinvigorate this space, by privileging our own Indigenous Knowings, by decolonising our minds, our language.

The Academy has created and perpetuated this travesty, this entrapment through deceit. It does this not merely in terms of the language used; the words used but the very essence, structure and format of the concept, 'language'. Tony Buzan, at a workshop asked his audience what is your primary language? What is my primary language? As one of the participants I was enthralled to hear him say his primary language is not English but the language of the brain; it is the language of images. This offered me a new dimension to the construct 'language'.

How then do these languages of images, patterns, performance and verb rich aspects play out within the defined space of The Academy; this being the 'truth of the written, linear and categorised text' as opposed to the non-truth of the oral and memoried Story? The next section of this chapter explores this through Story and an array of Indigenous experience and voice.

THE ACADEMY: INDIGENOUS KNOWINGS – THOUGHTS AS TEXT, THOUGHTS EMBODIED

When we started writing things down, using words, we began to lose our memory. (Rueben, 1984)

Kelly's words often haunt me as I, an Indigenous person and academic indulge in Knowing so 'textcentric'. In Eurocentric worldviews or knowledge, thoughts become validated when words are created and written as linear text on a canvas of paper; a book, an article, a newspaper. These thoughts become truth. They become thoughts transmitted and stored in libraries. They become in an academic arena publications where the aim is for others to cite such words in an analysis of their own thoughts. Knowledge becomes shared and grown using others' thoughts. In Indigenous Knowing thoughts and indeed visions become 'validated' when images, words, patterns, sounds, smells, tastes are felt and transmitted through an array of canvases including, sand, soil, bark, the body, rock ... . Performance, movement, art, story all become embodied. The memory is the 'library' or the repository of such thoughts. These thoughts become shared and grown using others thoughts and visions, Country, connections and relationships. Indigenous Knowings

Responsibility is significant within Indigenous Knowings, whereby 'within an oral culture, knowledge is restricted to certain persons; for the system to work, those who are not privy to the "inside knowledge" must accept the authority of those persons who are, and honour the wisdom of the restrictions' (Bell D. , 1998,

p. 406). Battiste (2002) goes further stating that the knowledge holders and workers have a status and responsibility to uphold (p.13).

The use of all of our senses in the creation and transmission of Knowings has been clearly articulated by Trask, Fixico (2003), Meyer (2001, p.125) and Hokari (2000, p.2). Meyer illustrates from Hawaiian language how the word 'ike' means "to see" and also "to know" showing how vision educates, how looking teaches, how watching informs (Meyer, 2001, p. 131). In being still and paying attention one is totally reliant on the interplay of each of our senses.

Fixico (2003, p.2, p.17) further elaborates the significance of visualization and seeing as well as holism in Indigenous Knowing. Chamberlin(2000) draws on the 'world of our imagination' which is not a world in which we escape from reality but one by means of which we engage reality (p.127).

Cultural Interface & Colliding Trajectories

In the cultural interface where Knowings have been and continue to be dichotomised 'people are inclined to think of oral traditions as less evolved than written traditions and of communities in which oral traditions flourish as correspondingly less developed – socially, culturally, and perhaps emotionally and intellectually' (Chamberlin, 2000, p. 139). Non-Indigenous people, academics specifically ascribe not only issues associated with human intellectual development and evolution in this interface but a notion of what is 'truth', what is 'fabrication'? One of course leads to the other. Ultimately we as Indigenous peoples find ourselves battling notions of subjugation and living as 'the other'.

In order to illustrate how the space I refer to as colliding trajectories impacts on our sense of self I present some Storys from Australia. Storys that debate what is 'truth', what is 'fact' and what is fabrication. These Storys illustrate the notion of Story through written text and oral genre; something that gives oral history greater dimension than written history (Fixico, 2003, p. 36).

There is a story I know ... a story that relies on written history to formulate true history of a nation. During the last decade in Australia there has been much said about a 'black armband approach' to Australian history; an approach that in the words of the former Prime Minister John Howard he 'profoundly rejects' (Howard, 1996):

> I have spoken tonight of the need to guard against the re-writing of Australian political history and, in particular, to ensure that the contribution of Robert Menzies and the Liberal tradition are accorded their proper place in it. There is, of course, a related and broader

challenge involved. And that is to ensure that our history as a nation is not written definitively by those who take the view that we should apologise for most of it. This black armband view of our past reflects a belief that most Australian history since 1788 has been little more than a disgraceful story of imperialism, exploitation, racism, sexism and other forms of discrimination. I take a very different view. I believe that the balance sheet of our history is one of heroic achievement and that we have achieved much more as a nation of which we can be proud than of which we should be ashamed. In saying that I do not exclude or ignore specific aspects of our past where we are rightly held to account. Injustices were done in Australia and no-one should obscure or minimise them. But in understanding these realities our priority should not be to apportion blame and guilt for historic wrongs but to commit to a practical program of action that will remove the enduring legacies of disadvantage. I think we have been too apologetic about our history in the past (Howard, 1996, p.9).

What resulted from such a sustained assault by the former Prime Minister is what has been termed the 'history wars'. This decade of vile, racist, mean spirited dialogue in our history is a classic illustration of Knowing, of Knowledge in the interface of colliding trajectories. It also illustrates more specifically one element of this collision; the issue of written sources being the 'right' information, the 'truth' and oral sources being fanciful, dependent on memory and therefore less 'truthful'. The debate highlights how written sources such as diaries, letters, newspaper articles and reports are perceived as containing factual information about the numbers of Aboriginal peoples murdered in massacres in different parts of the Country. Oral accounts from Aboriginal peoples are seen by a large number of academic scholars and policy makers to contain no truths.

Windschuttle, an Australian historian, in his discussion about the history of conflict between Aborigines and colonists asserts much in terms of 'the standard of proof required for the writing of history';

On the contrary, the standard of proof required for the writing of history is not legalistic but journalistic. That is, for a claim of killing to be credible it needs either first-hand reports from eyewitnesses, second-hand reports from those with direct contact to the participants, or accounts by those who saw the bodies afterwards. These reports should be reasonably contemporary with events and provide specific details like names, dates, places and numbers. The informants should be credible

witnesses. Anyone with an obvious agenda to mislead should be treated
sceptically. In most cases, criteria of this kind would satisfy normal
historical enquiry (Windschuttle, 2002, p. 165).

Non-Indigenous historians have played out the war with many Indigenous
scholars and community peoples seething on the sidelines, unable and unwilling
to engage in a debate that so clearly illustrates the cleavage, the chasm that exists
between the two Knowing/Knowledge systems.

A further illustration in Australia of this cavity was played out in the various
legal court jurisdictions and a Royal Commission regarding the building of a
bridge to Kumarangk, Hindmarsh Island in South Australia on Ngarindjerri
Country. Bell, a non-Indigenous anthropologist herself depicts 'Ngarrindjeri
culture as a weave of diverse strands, personalities, histories, experiences and
stories, where the whole is stronger than any one part but where the whole is
rarely more than ever glimpsed (Bell D. , 2001, p. 131)'. A travesty was played
out in which Royal Commission found fabrication in the traditional women's oral
stories, parts of stories as opposed to 'truth' in the written text of predominantly
male anthropologists, scientists, government officials and legal professionals. A
finding which gutted Ngarindjerri peoples, leaving peoples dispirited, broken.

Watson (1998) an Indigenous scholar and barrister laments the exercise of
'right-knowing' in the High Court decision to validate Commonwealth legislation
that would enable the building of a bridge to Kumarangk. She does this in the
context of the introduction of gender as a creator of division, a sustainer based
primarily on the research of white male anthropologists, and in an Aboriginal
context is meaningless but which increases the chasm and which illustrates
dramatically a collision of trajectories (p.30)

Bell raised the gendered nature of 'women's business' and in identifying a
principle of feminist ethnography states 'decentring the male is not just a
methodological move, it is a profoundly political move' (Bell D. , 2001, p. 123).
This element, these elements in the debate form the muddy water that Garma so
aptly represents above.

The impact of such debate is such that the Ngarrindjeri of the first written
records rarely speak in their own voices. They are rendered passive, mere
shadows in the landscape; they are stereotyped as the wild and violent men of the
Coorong ... (Bell D. , 1998, p. 425). History, anthropology, government systems
and practices and the legal profession teamed up using non-Indigenous,
Eurocentric knowledge as their frame of reference without any regard for
Indigenous Knowing, without any regard for centring and privileging the

Knowing of those most impacted on by the violation of such Country. Bell simply states:

> I have not attempted an exhaustive account of such trajectories, but rather indicated how contemporary beliefs and practices are a complex weave of knowledge from the old people; a continuing dialogue with the land through story, song, weaving, feather flowers, visiting places, burials, respect for Elders, a privileging of the spoken word and personal experience, accommodation of changing circumstances and a fierce determination to care for place they hold dear (Bell D. , 1998, p. 482).

If Indigenous Knowing had been centred in this situation, if it had been seen as alive and not frozen in a seemingly irrelevant past the outcomes may well have been different.

Trask a Native Hawaiian scholar personally accounts the impact of a written record on her sense of self and place, on her culture's sense of self and place:

> For so long, more than half my life, I had misunderstood this written record, thinking it described my own people. But my history was nowhere present. For we had chanted and sailed and fished and built and prayed. And we had told stories through the great bloodlines of memory:geneology (Trask, 1993, p. 118).

In order for Trask to know her history, she had to put away her books and return to the land ... (Trask, 1993, p. 118). Nakata reinforces Trask's spirit:

> ... when, as a student, I first came to read the historical literature and the educational literature on the Torres Strait Islanders, I did not read them from a position of 'ignorance' or 'neutrality' or as an 'onlooker'. Rather I read them from a position of awareness that this literature was an attempt to re-present my experience and my forebears' experience, as well as an attempt to re-present an analysis of my or my fellow Islanders' situation. This brought to light a significant omission. The readings and analyses brought down through family and collective consciousness, from which my position was derived, were invariably absent or bypassed, or, more often, re-explained in such a way as to negate the validity of my own understanding as an Islander.

It was from this lifeworld that I emerged to confront the knowledge inscribed in academic institutions (Nakata, 2007, p. 8).

Nakata illustrates his challenge in an analysis of the Cambridge Haddon-led expedition in the late 1890's to the Torres Strait Islands. Its aim was to 'recover the past life of the [I]slanders, ...' (Nakata, 2007, pp. 27-128). He describes some very morally and ethically corrupt research practices by Indigenous and non-Indigenous standards; practices such as the manipulation of data to suit the desired findings and a reinterpretation of some findings so as to better fit the final assessment.

> It was as if Indigenous people were an object of study viewed from the confines of a fixed vantage point. Our perspective – the Islanders' point of view was mostly obscured from view and, it would seem, irrelevant as it could always be explained away by theoretical knowledge (Nakata, 2007, p. 2).

When he and indeed other Indigenous peoples try to redress corrupt practices of academics they are accused of "getting it wrong"

> because, it is said, we do not fully understand all that has influenced the context that shaped our experiences. The implication is that, in the passing down of our understandings of events via the oral tradition, 'popular memory' distorts, exaggerates, misunderstands, fabricates or simply 'forgets' the actual 'facts' of what was experienced. This growing awareness of the uneasy relationship between my lived experience and that ascribed to me by the texts produced about Islanders led to the focus of my studies over the years (Nakata, 2007, p. 3).

What emerges from this interface is the challenge for us as Indigenous peoples to center our own Knowings whilst 'sensing' what we choose to use from Eurocentric Knowledge; from written text and theory. Of determining ourselves the Knowings we choose to share, the Storys we wish to share, the histories we wish to share.

Watson establishes and summarises what I believe is our challenge:

> The muldarbi uses its power (acquired by force), to shape the way we know, and the way we know shapes social power in terms of social inequality. So we struggle with the muldarbi against the shaping of our being with its way of knowing. We struggle with the thinking and

language of our rapist. We struggle to see the horizon, as we know it
from Kaldowinyeri[2], and to stop it dissolving into the imposing
muldarbi. We struggle for that place that is free from this 'right way of
knowing' to be free to know in the way of the grandmothers. And as a
process of healing and creating that space, bel hooks suggests we
dissolve white thinking. For me that is a process of decolonizing the
mind, and dissolving dominant colonial thought patterns. So that I can
see the horizon from an indigenous place and space, and know the
mother beneath my feet (Watson I. , 1998, p. 31)

Anzaldua (1990) engages her readers in the notion of theorizing in the dominant
academic community where the disparity of worldviews is most profound but the
opportunity to articulate new positions, be visionaries "in-between", Borderland
worlds can loosen and empower us rather than gag and disempower us (pp. xxvi-
xxvii).

In opposing the structure and Eurocentric values of The Academy, Cavender
Wilson seeks a reaffirmation of Indigenous epistemological and ontological
foundations in contemporary times offering a central form of resistance to the
colonial forces that have consistently and methodologically denigrated and
silenced them (Cavender Wilson, 2004, p. 71). In doing this we have a
responsibility to be 'respectful of the wisdom embedded within our traditions; we
must find answers from within those traditions, and present them in ways that
preserve the integrity of our languages and communicative styles. Most
importantly, as writers and thinkers, we should be answerable to our nations and
communities' (Cavender Wilson, 2004, p. 72).

Reclamation and/or recovery of Indigenous Knowings has a further obstacle
in our contemporary world. This obstacle is that of the globalisation of
Indigenous Knowings; a more contemporary version of colonisation which is in
fact "the latest great resource rush", reinstalling the predatory mentality of
Eurocentric thought, raising questions about the ethics of the new global
enterprise and about Indigenous peoples' ability to survive it (Battiste M. &.,
2000, p. 11). A renewed interest is creating a new industry.

Indigenous Knowings has become more fragmented and specialised as
scientists and humanitarians pick at the bits and pieces that fit with their interests
and disciplines (Nakata, 2007, p.184, p.187). Indigenous Knowing today as it is

---

[2] Kaldowinyeri meaning the beginning of creation (Watson I. , 1998, p. 29).

filtered through Western frameworks is poorly represented (Nakata M. , 2007, pp. 190-191).

SOVEREIGNTY AND SELF-DETERMINATION

Sovereignty is the bedrock upon which any and every discussion of Indian reality today must be built (Lomawaima, 2000, p. 3).

Across all levels of government; local, regional, state/province, Nation State to international the issue of self-determination and sovereignty is fundamental; it is the bedrock upon which Indigenous issues and Indigenous Knowings in contemporary terrains and domains flourish. Dodson, the inaugural Australian Aboriginal and Torres Strait Islander Social Justice Commissioner (1993), Cavender Wilson (2004, pp.75-76), Battiste & Youngblood Henderson (2002, Moreton-Robinson (2000p. 164), Watson, I. (1992 pp.180-181), Swisher (1998, p.193), and Martin (2008, pp.57-59) underline their writings, their reflections with this very issue. The notion of sovereignty and self-determination is highly political and the politics of the world we exist in today demands such reflection. It is not a political statement as such, it is what infuses discussion about our needs as Indigenous peoples today. It dominates our reflections about our own imaging and impacts significantly on our ability to give real significance and meaning to our own knowledge and knowing. I present a number of varying views from Indigenous scholars, leaders, community peoples, artists and professionals below.

To begin we must start on the same page with an understanding of what we mean by self-determination and sovereignty. This is critical because this issue has been hotly contested within the international governance arena where it is argued by some Nation States that where it is a fundamental inherent human right for all peoples to self-determination recognised in international law by the International Covenant on Civil and Political Rights (ICCPR). ... it does not apply to Indigenous peoples because they argue, we are populations, not people.

To understand self-determination we must understand the notion of human rights:

Human rights is the foundation on which social justice rests, encompassing virtually every sphere of life – social, cultural, economic, political and civil. Name any issue of concern to Aboriginal people, and it relates to human rights, because at the heart of social justice issues are the experiences and suffering of Aboriginal peoples and Torres Strait Islanders (Dodson, 1997, p. 13).

If this is so at a most tangible level:

> Social Justice is what faces you when you get up in the morning. It is awakening in a house with an adequate water supply, cooking facilities and sanitation. It is the ability to nourish your children and send them to a school where their education not only equips them for employment but reinforces their knowledge and appreciation of their cultural inheritance. It is the prospect of genuine employment and good health: a life of choices and opportunity, free from discrimination (Dodson, 1993, p. 10).

Sovereignty and Self-determination as constructs must inform and be informed by our own Indigenous Knowings.

Self-determination is about the power of decision-making which may be applied to all aspects of life. The right to self-determination is seminal to the exercise of all other human rights (Dodson, 1993, pp. 41-43). A lived and tangible consciousness of the concept of self-determination will assist us to decolonise our minds, our actions and to look at the 'truths within our own forms of knowledge' (Cavender Wilson, 2004, p. 75).

A way forward must see 'this act of intellectual self-determination, through Indigenous academics developing new analyses and methodologies to decolonize themselves, their communities, and their institutions' (Battiste, 2002, p. 4). This is an ongoing and tension ridden act as we tear our reflections and ourselves in so many differing directions; colliding trajectories, within the cultural interface.

Indigenous Knowings must be informed by the concept of Self-Determination. It is time for us to 'release our dependency on Western research traditions' and move beyond merely assuming an Indigenous perspective on these non-Indigenous paradigms' (Wilson, 2001, p.176) – an ultimate act of self-determination. We must define education in our own voices and on our own terms, because it has been, and continues to be, a grand story, a search for meaning, an essential food for the soul (Cajete, 2004, p. 28).

PROTECTION OF INTELLECTUAL AND CULTURAL PROPERTY

Any discussion about Indigenous Knowings is incomplete without a reference to the protection of intellectual and cultural property. This is distressing because we should not have to be on guard, we should not have to protect our Knowings from appropriation and vandalism.

Battiste and Youngblood Henderson identified an operational definition of Indigenous knowledge and heritage articulated in principles and guidelines drafted in the nature of an internationally recognised Declaration. These principles and guidelines are aspirational rather than existing as a binding convention (Battiste M. &., 2000, p. 66). They describe how Indigenous scholars and human rights experts in the United Nations Sub Commission on the Elimination of All Forms of Discrimination and Protection of Minorities elaborated and ratified the Principles and Guidelines for the Protection of the Heritage of Indigenous People.

Much work has been done at different levels of government and community to contribute to and implement such principles across many Nation States. In Australia, Janke an Indigenous lawyer and author researched and produced a National Report entitled 'Our Culture : Our Future'. This report establishes aspirations within an Australian context for the protection of our intellectual heritage. It also graphically illustrates situations which demonstrate the need for such protection. In an Australian context:

    i)   "Indigenous Cultural and Intellectual Property Rights" refers to Indigenous Australians rights to their heritage. Such rights are also known as "Indigenous Heritage Rights".

    ii)   Heritage consists of the intangible and tangible aspects of the whole body of cultural practices, resources and knowledge systems that have been developed, nurtured and refined (and continue to be developed, nurtured and refined) by Indigenous people and passed on by Indigenous people as part of expressing their cultural identity, including:

        a. Literary, performing and artistic works (including music, dance, song, ceremonies, symbols and designs, narratives and poetry)

        a) Languages

        b) Scientific, agricultural, technical and ecological knowledge (including cultigens, medicines and sustainable use of flora and fauna)

        c) Spiritual knowledge

        d) All items of movable cultural property including burial artefacts

e) Indigenous ancestral remains

f) Indigenous human genetic material (including DNA and tissues)

g) Cultural environment resources (including minerals and species)

h) Immovable cultural property (including Indigenous sites of significance, sacred sites and burials)

i) Documentation of Indigenous people's heritage in all forms of media (including scientific, ethnographic research reports, papers and books, films, sound recordings.) (Janke, 1998, pp. 11-12)

What then has happened, continues to happen to aspects of Indigenous Knowings that demand such protection including the 'Human Genome Diversity Project' and the 'Appropriation of Indigenous Biodiversity Knowledge: Medicinal Knowledge' (Janke, 1998, pp.24-25, 28-29). The need to include in our discourse the significance of protecting Indigenous Knowings can be no better presented and graphically illustrated as Janke does in these two illustrations. This significantly impacts the cultural interface and insists the requirement to create and establish new terrains for Indigenous Knowings to exist within.

Creating and Establishing New Terrains

It is our challenge as Indigenous peoples and communities to break our silence and create and engage in new terrains of not only resistance and survival but enrichment through the centring and privileging of our own Knowings. One strategy to use could be that of decolonisation. Yes this is one of the bricks in the Western Eurocentric wall. It is one brick which we can remove and choose what elements may be of use to us.

Decolonisation

Where Fanon (Fanon, 2001) 'popularised' the concept of Decolonisation within the realms of qualitative research; more specifically postcolonialism, neo-colonialism and race related emancipatory discourses, Smith engaged Indigenous peoples through the most seminal work involving Indigenous peoples and research (Smith, 1999). Indigenous authors are re-writing and re-righting our spaces and places within research process. Mutua and Swadener (Mutua, 2004) edited a volume of work that 'recognizes the colonizing tendency of the act of research itself as a practice particularly when it is carried out in contexts in which the individuals have been stripped of their power for self-definition and self-expression by being cast in the role of the marginalized Other.' They represent the work of scholars who are attempting to decolonize their work and deconstruct their personal/professional experiences in the context of various framings of cross-cultural research. The authors in this volume engage the reader in the following ideas: forced binaries, opposite poles, the fact that we occupy a multiplicity of the subject positions - emic/etic roles, locating research, reframing, centring/re-centring, notions of allied 'other', the 'unhomely', guidelines for decolonizing research, the notion that decolonising research is messy and collaborative, the concepts of linguicide, auto/ethnography, critical personal narrative and testimonio. They discuss the creation of spaces of liberatory praxis and questions about the dynamics, complexities and contradictory nature of decolonization. They draw on a vast array of cultural experience and reflection from across the globe.

Having said this, what is my rationale for including a section on Decolonisation in this review of literature when I have included discussion on it in Chapter Two? Quite simply I am using the concept of Decolonisation as a process as well as research methodology. Any discussion about Indigenous Knowings is redundant without some insight in to how we as Indigenous peoples 'decolonise our minds' and reclaim and centre our Knowings. I am constantly at battle with myself to 'decolonise' my thinking as illustrated through Story in Chapter One in a discussion about sweet potatoes and below:

> **Story 1:** I attended a seminar with Tony Buzan on Age Proofing The Brain a few weeks ago. He asked his participants to draw a concept that represented old age in the middle of a page so that we could mind map aging and the brain or memory and mental literacy. As with his other seminars around the world over 95% of participants drew an old person hunched, with either a walking stick or wheel chair. I cringed as soon as I did my drawing of the hunched person with a stick and said to myself 'decolonise!' and a few other choice words. Immediately, I redrew my image with Punululu or the Bungle Bungles in Western Australia – the oldest Country in Australia. I was able to reconnect with my own knowing by simply redirecting my thinking to that of my own knowing not the knowledge I gained from being schooled.

Clearly then Decolonisation is a process that we as Indigenous peoples must engage in to revitalise our Knowings our self-determination and our sense of being in the larger world.

Why decolonisation? What really is decolonisation? Fanon defines decolonization in terms of 'two opposing forces meeting as a result of colonization. He believes decolonization transforms and modifies individuals fundamentally, freeing themselves' (Fanon, 2001, pp. 27-28). Smith in contextualising decolonisation and research states : 'it is the corporate institution of research, as well as the epistemological foundations from which it springs that needs to be decolonized' (Smith L. , 2005, p. 88).

Decolonisation is a means for us as individuals to reacquaint with our Knowings, to privilege our Knowings. It is a process within the space identified as colliding trajectories. It will facilitate us to 'cease defining [ourselves] through the categories of the colonizers (Memmi, 1991, p. 152) as language, in particular, can aid in decolonizing the mind (Trask, 1993, p. 43). 'Language as an artistic expression should be left alone to wonder, mutate, and decolonize itself' (Demas, 2004, p. 230).

I believe decolonisation could go further here but the significance of coming to terms with our place within the major Western philosophical and methodological positions by virtue of acknowledging our difference in non-linear constructs goes some way towards a new nourishing and invigorated terrain for us as Indigenous peoples. This is not an easy process of reflection as Mutua (2004, p.256), Hamza (2004, p.130) from Niger and Anzaldua showcase; Anzaldua in her creation of 'mestizaje' is decolonisation in action. Decolonization is about unlearning (Elenas, Gonzalez, Delgado Bernal, and Villenas, 2001, p.598 in Demas & Saavedra, 2004, p.218) and re-envisioning as scholars like Anzaldua has done.

Mutua and Swadener pose some useful questions for us as Indigenous scholars working within The Brick Wall to reflect on; specifically the following:

1. Who has/is colonized/colonizing research?
2. Can it be decolonized?
3. How can it be decolonized? (Mutua, 2004, p. 260).

Ultimately though we must grow our own Knowings as Cavender Wilson (2004) asserts, through a commitment to the notion of praxis as articulated by Freire in his liberatory pedagogy and through a re-articulation and re-languaging of our struggles to fight against our ongoing colonization (Cavender Wilson, 2004, pp. 69-70).

Cree scholar William Wheeler explains that by self-reflection and engagement with decolonisation as a strategy for empowerment, we believe in transformative processes that move us beyond mere survival (Mutua, 2004, p. 12).

Globally, we, as Indigenous peoples, as colonised peoples must find ways, find strategies that are 'distinct to us' (Cavender Wilson, Wilson, 2004, p.71) to decolonise and reinvest and privilege our own Knowings. We must look "inward towards the ancestry to begin the process of decolonizing the mind" (Hamza 2004, p.133). Demas and Saavedra (2004) advocate for a deeper understanding of the Other; the coloniser in the process of decolonisation in order to 'extend positions and dwell in the space of the others' (pp. 153-154).

Many other Indigenous peoples are reflecting and endeavouring to disencrypt contested terrain. Kaomea (Mutua, 2004, p. 27) writes of her dilemma as an Indigenous academic and her "unhomely" feelings of disconnection. Jankie (Mutua, 2004, p. 88) highlights what she refers to as problematizing her positionality; one that pushes her to adopt a self-reflective stance. Matoba Adler draws our attention to the tension between the academic world and the everyday world of participants (Mutua, 2004, p. 108). Morgan has moved away from the terminology of de-colonisation and crafted 'cultural de-contamination'. He identifies 'Cultural decontamination' as being concerned with empowering Indigenous peoples to seek relief from social and political oppression through a process of reclaiming cultural and knowledge authority as a process to rebuild pride and a sense of cultural affirmation in their Aboriginality and identity (personal communication 26/09/2014). This concept appeals to me as it moves the centre and the privilege from colonization to one which speaks to contamination of our Knowings, our Being as Indigenous peoples. I, like Morgan, am playing with this concept at the moment.

This discussion is conceptually much deeper than a discussion about 'insider' /outsider' positioning (Smith, 1999) (Mutua, 2004). It is more than Du Bois's sense of 'double consciousness' (du Bois, 1969) or Fine's notion of 'working the hyphens' (Fine M. , 1994) (Fine M. W.), code-switching as reflected upon by Hamza (Mutua, 2004, p. 130) or even the notion espoused by many of 'the other' (Smith, 1999). The notions of subjectivity and objectivity, the process of identifying participant-observer to accommodate any bias or attachment become void in such circumstance. It goes further than the creation of process and concepts of 'critical theory', 'post colonialism' or even 'decolonisation'. This discussion has embedded within it a sense that goes beyond the notion of semantics. De-emphasising the sole use of colonial languages (wa Thiong'o, 2005) or the 'hegemony of the dominant language; linguicide, (Mutua, 2004, p. 16) is integral to my process but my conceptualisation of the challenges operate from a different layer. If the working and theoretical concept of 'knowledge' is fundamentally different why skirt around the edges with significant but single fringe elements such as those described above? Why not accept fundamental difference and launch process that embodies this?

Survival for Indigenous peoples is more than a question of physical existence; it is an issue of preserving Indigenous knowledge systems in the face of cognitive imperialism (Battiste M. &., 2000, p. 12). Decolonisation or Cultural Decontamination are processes whereby we move closer to such a vision. I have drawn on Mind Mapping® as a tool to do this. I endeavour to support my contention with a demonstration of mind mapping throughout this text with mind maps that I have drawn to herald in each chapter of this book as well as summarise the whole text. The next section explores alternative forms of knowledge and thinking that may or may not reflect on and embody more of the principles of Indigenous Knowings.

MIND MAPPING AND OTHER ALTERNATIVE FORMS OF KNOWING/THINKING

Alternative Pedagogy/Epistemology; Mind Maps, Thinking Maps, Six Different Hats.

In the general discourse about the origins, the concept of knowledge, of Indigenous Knowings, many theoretical options have been presented and debated. These have predominantly been from within the Eurocentric framework. These have predominantly either skirted the edge of difference or dichotomized difference. They have generally been within a context of post colonialism where the 'margins write back' Freire (Freire P. &., 1972), (Freire P. , 1985), (Freire P. , 1998), Memmi (Memmi, 1991), Fanon (Fanon, 2001), Foucault (Foucault, 1972), (Foucault, 1998), and Polanyi (Polanyi, 1962). Even within a Eurocentric frame academics from different disciplines have entered the debate under the guise of emancipatory discourses (Denzin, N. & Lincoln, Y.S. 2005), and Anzaldua (Anzaldua, 1990) to mention a few.

In this book I choose not to elaborate on these theories, philosophies or concepts. I do however acknowledge these contributions as part of the overarching canvas and context for discussion. What I find particularly interesting is how this debate has led to some interesting alternative strategies and practices for the transmission of knowledge. These remain embedded within and emerge from a Eurocentric framework and centre but they have evolved from the margins whether this be discipline based, theoretically based or practitioner based. Some of these alternative strategies have become popularized and find themselves in what many refer to as a 'new age' corner.

Suzuki (Suzuki, 1997) has written about rediscovering our place in nature. Attali (Attali, 1999) and Wolin (Wolin, 1995) use the concept of labyrinths, for the latter, to articulate conflict in social thought, the former to explore what he describes as 'labyrinthine thought'. Popularist authors such as Buzan (Buzan T. , 1997), De Bono (de Bono, 1990) (de Bono, 1999), and Hyerle (Hyerle, 1996), (Hyerle, 2000) have identified and developed different models of 'thinking' that deliberately move beyond the linear frameworks.

Edward De Bono states that 'thinking is the ultimate human resource'. He has developed a concept that 'allows a thinker to do one thing at a time, being able to separate emotion from logic, creativity from information and so on'. His concept is commonly known as the '6 Thinking Hats' (Bono, 1999). I don't find the Six Thinking Hats compatible with Indigenous thinking patterns as it is not holistic and invites conceptual separation of elements of thought in to six categories including; objective facts and figures, emotional response, negative aspects of thought, 'positive thinking', creativity and new ideas, the control and organization of the thinking process (de Bono, 1990, pp. 31-32).

Hyerle (Hyerle, 2000), (Hyerle, 1996) has created the concept of Thinking Maps which he identifies as being based on thorough and well-accepted academic study and research. He separates and categorises eight Thinking Maps to correspond to eight fundamental thinking processes. He believes that Thinking Maps are more than simple graphic organizers, they can be utilized individually or in various combinations to form a common visual language for students and teachers at all grade levels, in all subjects. I find Thinking Maps like Thinking Hats categorise and separate thought and thinking. The point of separation disengages the thinker rendering their thinking fragmented rather than holistic.

A recent small budget film *'What The Bleep Do We Know'* puts forward some provocative questions about 'the way we participate in an unfolding, dynamic reality. It took people by surprise winning many film awards (What The Bleep Do We Know, 2004), (The Institute of Noetic Sciences and Captured Light Industries, 2004). The film draws on quantum physics, philosophy and spirituality to explore the idea that 'there is no solid, static universe, and that reality is mutable – affected by our perception of it' (The Institute of Noetic Sciences and

Captured Light Industries, 2004, p. 2). I mention this here because this film and its ideas are considered marginal by mainstream society yet the film and people's overwhelming responses to it see them searching for a more holistic approach to Knowing.

Mind Maps

Tony Buzan has defined *Mind Maps* as 'an expression of Radiant Thinking, a natural function of the human mind, a powerful graphic technique, which provides a universal key to unlocking the potential of the brain' (Buzan, 1997, p.59). He believes and I know Mind Maps can be applied to every aspect of life where improved learning and clearer thinking will enhance human performance.

The Mind Map has four essential characteristics: the subject of attention is crystallised in a central image, the main themes of the subject radiate from the central image as branches, branches comprise a key image or key word printed on an associated line and finally topics of lesser importance are also represented as branches attached to higher level branches. The branches form a connected nodal structure (Buzan T. , 1997, p. 59).

Buzan's interest in and creation of the concept of Mind Maps sprung from his desire to effectively harness and allow us to "roam the infinite expanse of your brain" harnessing the full range of the cortical skills - word, image, number, logic, rhythm, colour and spatial awareness (Buzan T. , 1997, p. 85).

Although, the Mind Map is drawn on a two-dimensional page it represents a multi-dimensional reality encompassing space, time and colour (Buzan T. , 1997, p. 57). Mind Maps accommodate many more of the characteristics identified as comprising Indigenous Knowings. They accommodate radiant thinking process, they allow for metaphor, they embody pattern, they embody a visual concept of place (through the central nodal structure and branches radiating out from the centre of the Mind Map), a relatedness, a sense of belonging and they indulge and require the use of all of our senses. They indulge holistic process, being.

Cajete's thoughts articulate what I see Mind Maps doing:

> These metaphors – represented in words, images, and symbols – provide food for thought and a way to reflect on how we can use the tools of education in this process of reinventing a contemporary philosophy of Indigenous education. ... As Indigenous people recovering from centuries of colonization, we need a perspective from a higher place to understand where we have come from, where we are, and where we wish

to go. I invite you to use the "Native eye" to look deeply in to the nature
of these relationships (Cajete, 2000, pp. 181-182).

My own journey began with Buzan's *The Mind Map Book*. I share part of this
journey again as. I believe this helps to contextualise the emphasis I place here.

> Prior to working at the University of Newcastle I worked in the Human
> Rights and Equal Opportunity Commission (HREOC). Between 1994
> and 1998 I worked specifically in the Office of the Aboriginal and
> Torres Strait Islander Social Justice Commissioner co-ordinating the
> National Aboriginal and Torres Strait Islander Community Education
> Project (NCEP). The NCEP was a response to Recommendation 211 of
> the Royal Commission into Aboriginal Deaths in Custody.
> Recommendation 211 states;

> That *the Human Rights and Equal Opportunity Commission and State
> and Territory Equal Opportunity Commissions* should be encouraged to
> further pursue their programs designed to inform the Aboriginal
> community regarding anti-discrimination legislation, particularly by way
> of Aboriginal staff members attending at communities and organisations
> to ensure the effective dissemination of information as to the legislation
> and ways and means of taking advantage of it.(Human Rights and Equal
> Opportunity Commission 1995, p.136)

> In essence, the resulting project entitled *Tracking Your Rights* is about us
> as Indigenous peoples crafting local solutions to those instances of
> discrimination, to those breaches of human rights that occur on a daily
> basis. The development of *Tracking Your Rights* involved travelling to
> all states and territories and some islands to talk with as many people as
> possible. The places chosen were representative and diverse. Diverse in
> history, geography, economics, structure, population size and location.
> Over 125 Aboriginal communities were visited, over 300 meetings were
> held and over 1,000 people told us their stories at focus groups, one-on-
> one interviews and community meetings. Four area-based consultant
> groups worked with me as the Co-ordinator of the project. Our
> community visits were not one off visits - all groups were visited twice
> and some three times. Regular newsletters and correspondence kept
> communities in touch with both the process and our progress.

The key question for our first round of consultations was – "What messes up your day?" Human Rights and Social Justice issues that mattered for Indigenous Australians were identified throughout this consultative process.

The dilemma in developing the final product centred around the notion that the information people needed was structured, linear, complex and alien, yet the issues that people wanted to be able to deal with; racism in schools, sub-standard health services, police harassment etc. impinged on every aspect of peoples' lives. The question became how do we in order to achieve the goal of empowering education create a product that people will use; a product that delivered strategies and that allowed people to craft a specific local solution? This was to be done through the facilitation of information and strategies to Aboriginal peoples and Torres Strait Islanders about human rights and anti-discrimination laws; laws that are complex and further complicated by a hierarchy and maze of separate Commonwealth, State and Territory governments and international laws. My first priority was to map the connections between human rights abuses and every aspect of our daily lives. This involved not merely presenting people with a series of facts or referring people to relevant agencies, organisations or departments; their contact numbers and addresses. It was imperative to show people a way they could evolve solutions.

I was introduced to Mind Mapping® through a friend. Mind Mapping empowered me to develop ways to facilitate knowledge of human rights and anti-discrimination laws and strategies to other Indigenous peoples, in a way that respects and responds to their daily life experiences. Mind Mapping in Tracking Your Rights provides a means for people to make connections between human rights abuses in every aspect of their daily lives and the choices available to deal with them. It enables interaction and collaboration of rich and dynamic carefully crafted solutions.

Subsequent training of trainers in the use of Tracking Your Rights and in particular, Mind Mapping has met with an extremely favourable response. I have introduced approximately 200 Indigenous people to the notion of Mind Mapping in the last 4 years and every individual has made verbal comment as well as having commented in evaluation forms about the impact of Mind Mapping. The feeling that their natural thinking processes are freed from decades of restrictive, forced learning and thinking. People wanted to develop the process for other uses. Since having an awareness about Mind Mapping I have met a number of Aboriginal people in community meetings that have watched me Mind Map meeting notes, lecture notes, people who have watched me speak from Mind Maps and who have said 'this is the way I think'. They have gone on to express themselves more freely, more creatively and arguably more often.

Where my journey and intent for this book began with a desire to explore Mind Maps specifically and use them to inform Indigenous Knowings in the process I came to the realisation that I had to start at a different part of the circle. I needed to explore and understand Indigenous Knowings before making connections with Mind Maps. In doing this research I also found the need to connect the notion of Knowing with The Academy; specifically the concept and process of research. It also became apparent that Mind Maps were not my centre; Indigenous Knowings were. My journey therefore took me from Mind Maps to privileging Indigenous Knowings and in so doing, the concept I began with has become an invaluable tool to grow my understanding and to facilitate my decolonisation. I will pursue this in future research. I see Mind Mapping as one of the tools in our tool bag, a tool to empower ourselves, to imbue spirit. Mind Mapping is the printing of the sand painting (Blair, 1998, pp. 38-42).

REFLECTIVE OVERVIEW

This chapter began Storying some of the challenges of conducting a literature review whilst privileging Indigenous Knowings; I 'tried to remain true to my conceptual journey by including illustrations, that is people's Storys in text boxes; keeping Indigenous voices alive and speaking throughout the document'. Thematically the chapter has explored peoples' voices on the following ideas: the concept of 'Country', the concept of 'Knowings', Elders as traditional scholars, Story, the concept of a cultural interface and colliding trajectories. It has looked at how Indigenous Knowings have been used, what happens when The Academy meets Indigenous Knowings and conducts research, as well as The Academy and Knowing as textual thoughts and embodied thoughts. The chapter has looked at how Indigenous Knowings and Self-Determination mesh as does the need to protect Indigenous Knowings. Finally, this chapter has identified the concept and process of decolonisation as a means of engaging in the cultural interface in such a way as to privilege Indigenous Knowings. The concept of Mind Maps® was introduced as a tool to facilitate our decolonisation.

I introduced sliver inserts as sliding thoughts, thoughts that frame the above mentioned themes but which are not headings that assign hierarchy to our thoughts; they are more transient and organic in nature as are the themes, the thoughts that sliver in and out of the thought process.

The majority of scholars including Battiste and Youngblood Henderson (2000, pp.39-41) and Cajete (2006 p.248) acknowledge that Indigenous Knowings and Western Knowledge are two distinct systems of Knowing not a form of 'traditional knowledge' that is made to match or fit in to the existing categories of Eurocentric knowledge; the Brick Wall. Cajete asserts we must 'search for common ground as a basis of dialogue' because Indigenous wisdom might work if only we could stop dismissing it as being "of another time." (Cajete, 2006, p. 248).

Nakata on the other hand believes 'it is not that productive to separate Indigenous Knowledge out and lay claim to a separate domain of knowledge with any authority' (Nakata, 2007, p. 225).

There are two domains of distinct Knowing and there are different systems and structures of Knowing within each domain. The Storys told and voices presented throughout this chapter have clearly articulated elements of Indigenous Knowings whilst not attempting to define it. Elements such as the importance of Country, relationships with and between Country, people, the ecosystem generally, the importance of Story as told by many voices, the role of Elders in the transmission of our Knowing, the concept of space and 'time'; the latter being based on the ecosystem and its dynamic, constant moving nature, a holistic approach to seeing the world and the significance of experiential practice, one that involves all of our senses. Knowing based on patterns rather than triangles; knowing that is non-linear perhaps circular and spiral where there is no one centre. Indigenous peoples see ourselves as carriers not owners of the Knowing.

As has been developed in this chapter there is a cultural interface where Indigenous Knowings and Western Knowledge collide as trajectories. Words like 'contested space', 'cleavage', 'disparate worldviews', diametric trajectories have been used to identify the space between the two domains of Knowing.

Indigenous peoples note how Indigenous Knowings has been identified as 'primitive' with this label and characterisation impacting on our place in the hallowed corridors of Western humanity. The Academy has created and developed this ideal through cognitive and ontolological imperialism. The impact of this has had catastrophic consequences for Indigenous peoples globally with us succumbing to "double consciousness', feeling disembodied as our Knowings become fragmented through the Western need to universalise everything around its centre. The impact has been to fragment, through hierarchic, linear categorisation, through the creation of disciplines which build on and out from Western concepts and elements of Knowledge.

The result? We must 'reclaim our worldviews, knowledge and language to find the path ahead, whilst sustaining our relationship with our environment and following our Elder's advice.' (Youngblood Henderson, 2000, p. 274). As Fanon states 'we do not want to catch up with anyone... we must turn over a new leaf, we must work out new concepts, and try to set afoot a new man (Fanon, 2001, pp. 253-255). In doing this we must ensure that we 'learn to be less complacent and more aggressive when it comes to defining our field' (Swisher, 1998, p. 197).

The Academy as an institution not only speaks and projects from a different epistemological base it is an institution which like other institutions:

> handle complex activities by breaking them up in to smaller tasks and spreading them out among many people. With the organisation to guide them, it is no longer necessary for most people to have an overall understanding of what is being done. As long as they follow instructions the institution will keep working, like a machine with human parts. Institutions can be very powerful, but they can make people dependent on being told what to do. Seeing only a small part of things, people in institutions find it difficult to judge the appropriateness of their tasks. This can cause people to become dispirited, passive, or even self-destructive (Nunavik, February 1992, p. 1)

Indigenous peoples have become dispirited. We see our Knowings, our peoples being fragmented and uprooted. Decolonising research, Cultural Decontamination opens some doors for us if we make the choices about how much we take from Eurocentric Knowledge whilst we privilege our own Knowing.

Anzaldua captures the essence of our challenge:

> Even when our bodies have been battered by life, these artistic "languages," spoken from the body, by the body, are still laden with aspirations, are still coded in hope and "un desarme ensangretado," a bloodied truce. By sending our voices, visuals and visions outward into the world, we alter the walls and make them a framework for new windows and doors. We transform the posos, apertures, barrancas, abismos that we are forced to speak from. Only then can we make a

home out of the cracks....By bringing in our own approaches and methodologies, we transform the theorizing space...(Anzaldua, 1990, p. xxv).

Deloria Jr. challenges those of us in The Academy who have been a 'part of the tradition of Indian scholarship' noting we did not 'consider that the tribal traditions [we] wrote and spoke about represented an alternative philosophy to Western materialism' (Deloria Jr., 2004, p. 16). Cajete reflects on our attempts to be in both worlds and asks us 'to work at it every day, be responsible to ourselves, our communities, our ancestry, and our personal gifts' (Cajete, 2000, p. 189).

As Uncle Paddy states 'You people try and dig little more deep you been diggin only white soil try and find the black soil inside' [Paddy Roe in (Benterrak, 1996, p. back cover)]. I believe we as Indigenous peoples must dig a little deeper too and find our own black soil, our own earth, our core, our essence.

The next chapter weaves together the threads of the book from what my Colleagues voices articulated to me sitting in and being in their Country and what the voices expressed through literature as significant, imperative.

The colonisers came
Constructed walls, fences, boundaries
Walls of bricks
Bricks made from earth's substances; clay, sandstone and more
Walls that stand strong, on top of the earth
Or that stand manually constructed and placed within the earth that is cast out
Walls that cry for their own sense of identity?
Walls that dominate the more organic,
Cutting off the source of water, earth and air; of life
Containing the flow of water, earth and air; the nourishment, the stimulus
Some Waterlilys[3] lay dormant
Revitalised with each new rain
Each new flow of water and ray of sunshine
Replenishing
Nourishing
Waiting for the walls to come down?

---

[3] Waterlily/Waterlilys are spelt this way to embody a re-imaged concept

Searching for,...finding mutual space to co-exist? Perhaps?
Mutual space that embeds Waterlily within the crafted beautiful mosaic
of co-existence
Searching for, space that has no fear to privilege Indigenous Knowings in
the mosaic
The mosaic where Waterlily is embedded not marginalized
The mosaic where Waterlily radiates energy, beauty, connectedness, relatedness
Nourishing identity and Knowings
Nourishing identity and Knowledge

LANGUAGE
BRICOLEUR
DECOLONISATION
INSTITUTIONALISM
OUTCOMES
NOTES
MODELS
MODELS
FABRIC
LISTENING
STILES
CONQUERC
DOLAN
ART
BODY
LANGUAGE
ART
THEATRE
MAPPING
POLICY
UNIS
SPIRIT
STRUCTURE
VOICES
ESSENCE
VOICE
ROLES
COMPETENCE
LINGUISTIC
COMMUNITY
PLACE

CHAPTER 6

Waterlilys and Brick Walls

There is a Story I Know. A Story told by many voices. In fact, a Story that is many different Storys. Storys that do not contradict each other, they simply co-exist as a Story about Indigenous Knowings, decolonisation and Indigenous research. A Story that has presented the spaces around and between the Waterlilys and Brick Wall; between Indigenous Knowings and Western Knowledge in the process and Knowings associated with research. A Story that patterns and connects different Knowings through spider's webs across a zone of colliding trajectories and through sweet potatoes below and above ground; embedded in Country. This Story now brings all the different elements and voices together not with the intent of creating one voice, one Story. But with the intent of growing the Story, engaging in and interacting with the different voices and elements of the Story.

Our entry point in this Story is not at the beginning and not at the end. It is somewhere amidst the voices. It is like a note that holds its own sound, contributes to other sounds surrounding and comprising it. At this point of this Story, the tune or melody, the note that holds its own sound is 'decolonisation'. The surrounding and comprising sounds include concepts impacting on us as Indigenous researchers such as the need for linguistic competence, the impact of colonisation, the ambiguity of our voice and our roles as scholar and community facilitator, and the contested space we play in. In crafting this score we look at Australian experiences of research within the Brick Wall; our participation as scholars, and the Disciplines we have chosen to engage with and how we have done and continue to do this.

REVISITING DECOLONISATION

Decolonisation as evidenced in the last chapter requires that we as Indigenous scholars reclaim and centre our Indigenous Knowings through the challenges associated with decolonising our own minds. The 'decolonization of existing thought and law is already under way in the work of many scholars'. However, the experiences of Indigenous peoples engaging with decolonization are distinct (Battiste M. &., 2000, p. 12). We need to understand the systems of thought that gave rise to the alienation bestowed on us by the Academy; the Brick Wall, through labelling such as savages, boongs, Abos, half-castes, half-breeds just some of the academic descriptors assigned to us. We then need to create a shared language both sides can use to discuss education, science, social sciences, the humanities, and politics and one that leads to Indigenous renaissance and Indigenous self-determination (Battiste M. &., 2000, pp. 12-13).

One of the most important elements of research if it is to be appropriate and effective, is the delivery of tangible outcomes. Indigenous research, as opposed to research done about Indigenous peoples demands emancipatory and liberatory outcomes as well as changes in conditions; economic, social, civil, cultural and political, and the identity, the placement and value of Indigenous peoples and Indigenous Knowings in society generally. Decolonisation is an intertwining thread that weaves its way in and out, over and under, through the various parts of the tune. The tangible outcomes of this research are storyd in Chapter 7.

Is Decolonisation the breve, the note that punctuates the tune or melody? That punctuates and calls for longer silence than other notes in the composition? If Decolonisation is either of these, how is it so? Decolonisation or Cultural Decontamination a term that I am warming to instead of decolonisation asks us as Indigenous scholars to re-imagine, to envision new models that centre and privilege our own Knowing systems as advocated and imagined through Lilyology. This engagement and envisioning requires many layers of linguistic competence.

LINGUISTIC COMPETENCE/SOUND OF THE SONG – THE COMPOSITION

The need for linguistic competence has been identified by my research Colleagues, and various peoples quoted in the review of literature as essential; though it has been stated in different ways, in different contexts and indeed in different languages and/or genres. It introduces a different harmony and rhythm to weave through the main tune or melody. We saw in Chapter Five Battiste and Youngblood Henderson (Battiste M. &., 2000) refer to linguistic competence, Little Bear (Little Bear, 2000) and Youngblood Henderson (Youngblood Henderson, 2000) emphasise the verb-rich aspect of Indigenous languages implying action and process rather than naming in noun-centred languages associated with Eurocentric knowledge, Skutnabb-Kangas (Mutua K. S., 2004, p. 14) using the term 'linguicide' to draw out the impact of colonisation with Mutua & Swadener identifing a 'growing body of scholarship that asserts language is playing an increasingly important role as a means of control and domination (Mutua K. &., 2004, p. 14)'. wa Thiong'o (wa Thiong'o, 2005) illustrated the notion of 'living a translated life' (Youngblood Henderson, 2000, p. 264) and Arrows referred to the colonisers language as a language of deceit (Arrows, 2006, p. 18).

If as Battiste stated language is by far the most significant factor in the survival of Indigenous knowledge (Battiste M. , 2002, p. 17), then we need to listen to the different compositions; the harmonies and rhythms. We need to develop the most appropriate melody and tune for each performance, for each expression of Indigenous Knowings.

There is a Story which illustrates the point I make here; a Story that highlights the use of the colonisers language as a means of linguicide, a means of disharmony, of living a translated life in an Australian context. This Story involves two Balanda[1] people; a male who has lived in Yolngu[2] communities for over three decades and has lived in many different capacities as a community development and capacity building resource, and his sister-in-law sitting on a beach in the community of Nhulunbuy in Gove Peninsula, Northern Territory. They sat watching Yolngu children playing football on the beach just near their family group. The Story as told by Trudgen the Balanda male in the Story goes like this:

> After a while the football came close to us, and one of the Yolngu kids ran to retrieve it. I said hello to him in Yolngu Matha. As soon as he heard me, he called the other children to come and check out this white fella who spoke his language. Three or four children joined us and we started talking about where we came from and that sort of thing. The children were from a homeland centre I had never visited, so they didn't know me.
>
> I chatted to them in Yolngu Matha for some time, trying them out on many subjects. I was interested to determine their level of general knowledge. We talked about a wide range of things, from economics to general niceties. I was surprised at their depth of intellectual language.
>
> The children, in turn, were keen to test out some of the funny stories they had heard about Balanda. They asked to see inside my mouth. They wanted to know if I had any 'toy lirra' (toy teeth).

[1] Balanda : white/non-Indigenous person in Arnhem Land
[2] Yolngu : Indigenous person in Arnhem Land

'No,' I said, 'I don't have toy lirra.'

'Open your mouth so we can see!' the kids insisted.

I opened my mouth, grabbed my teeth with my fingers and pretended to try to move them. I thought they were talking about false teeth. But while my mouth was open they looked inside, and with joy and glee they spotted what they were looking for. The 'toy lirra' were my fillings! I tried to explain what fillings are, but they were not convinced. To them they were 'toy teeth'. Not real.

We had been talking for about three-quarters of an hour, all the time in Yolngu Matha, and the children showed no signs of tiring or becoming bored. Question after question came. We began talking about languages, and I asked the oldest in the group how many languages she spoke. She was twelve years old and said that she spoke five languages, counting them off on her fingers as she recalled them. I tried her on one of the languages that came from north-central Arnhem Land. She was a bit scratchy in that one, but in the other four she was well ahead of me.

I had been translating all this back to my sister-in-law and she now joined the conversation. She asked the girl in English, 'Do you speak English?'

The children were kneeling in front of us in a line. When the girl heard the question, her shoulders drooped and she sank down onto the sand. After a long pause she said in perfect English, 'English makes me tired.'

We talked on for a while but the spell was broken. Before long the children disappeared down the beach, having lost their interest when the switch to English occurred.

… To her, the switch meant having to use a language she did not think or dream in (Trudgen, 2000, pp. 85-86).

English as a language, as the means of composing, constructing, crafting research and Knowledge makes a lot of Indigenous peoples tired. The Brick Wall itself is a construction of English and other Western languages and constructs. We do not dream or think in English when we draw on Garma, Kanyini, Lilyology,

Arlathirnda Ngurkarnda Ityirnda (Arbon, 2008) Quandamoopah (Martin 2008) or Dadirri. In whatever environment we have grown up in and we now live in we may speak English language. We may utter English words as our first language. We may write using English words and constructs. This journey has shown me that there are options even if I don't speak my own Aboriginal language. While I dream or think in English words to engage and research in a linguistically competent way I have had to find a means to translate those dreams, to pay attention to those dreams, those thoughts, to find an alternate language or use one that already exists (that of images) in a more powerful way.

In Coast we spoke in English. In Desert we spoke in English, Amatjere and Walpiri. I do not speak Amatjere and Walpiri. I yarned with my Colleagues in English. Most of the understanding, most of the thinking and visioning came from being in Country, listening and paying attention to Country, responding to and experiencing the doing in Country, seeing and paying attention to body language; not as a study of people's body language in a Western sense, but as an illustration of Knowing, as a process of teaching, facilitating, yarning and learning. In Desert, hunting for and cooking goanna, body painting; storying and dancing with the women, being shown water holes in Country and told Storys through looking, listening and then being told in English words and in being in family space, school spaces, community spaces and sitting together and just doing, just crafting the research fabric were the specific experiences that derived linguistic competence. The webpage takes you the reader of this text to another dimension in which you see and hear some of this shared Knowings; experience with me a different form of linguistic competence.

Other fundamental components of linguistic competence for us as Indigenous peoples involve theatre, performance, art, the embodiment of all of the senses in the doing, the listening and the watching. I would like to share a couple of experiences at this point that illustrate this perspective in the context of my coming to Know for this research journey. In one experience this Knowing came through connections to peoples, their Storys and to Country; Darkinjung Country, the Central Coast of New South Wales. It found voice through performance; a piecing together of a variety of Storys and played and performed as one piece; a specific melody entitled 'Listening'. In another the work of Lin Onus, Aboriginal artist who fashions anew.

Listening

There is a Story I Know ...

In 1999 I was awarded an Aboriginal and Torres Strait Islander Grant (AIATSIS) to investigate 'Darkinjung History: Lands, Waters, Peoples and Culture'. As the chief researcher it was my intent to place Indigenous voices at the centre of Darkinjung Story telling; to breathe life into the local community further enhancing the identity of its peoples. The research process was also to reflect Umulliko's goal at the time 'to increase Indigenous control of research through the development of Indigenous led research initiatives and the development of Indigenous researcher's skills'. This project essentially involved a conventional archival search of material. It was a reconnaissance and scoping of materials available. It was also much more than this, in that it involved a range of people; individuals each playing a role in the hunt for evidence, for voices, for characters, for pieces in the jig saw puzzle. The project laid a solid foundation on which to build future research ideas.

Rather than just spending time in State Libraries and other traditional institutions I formed a Research Working Group. This Group known as the Umulliko Darkinjung Research Working Group (UDRWG) constantly evolved and grew in terms of its membership as information came to light about materials that have been written, and the authors of the material themselves. Members of the group became the sleuths in the process of extricating memories of their own, memories from others and vital bits and pieces of written information.

The UDRWG comprised Indigenous and non-Indigenous members. The Darkinjung Local Aboriginal Land Council (DLALC) was an actively involved partner in this process. The research process was significantly enhanced through the expertise of the members of the DLALC, the sites work being conducted and the general search for knowledge about our local history and sense of place. The process was not a one-way process where Indigenous peoples were used by researchers and treated as the 'other' (Tuhiwai Smith, 1999, p.2, Moreton-Robinson, 2000, pp.138-140). Indigenous peoples were at the center of this process in every way and at every stage. Indigenous peoples controlled the process. Through membership of the group of people from local libraries, historical societies and academics, Indigenous peoples took the opportunity to learn about using local libraries, the State Library and State Archives more effectively.

The UDRWG provided a forum in which dialogue and debate ignited associations and connections, leading to new pieces of information being found to fit the puzzle. This was enhanced by the establishment of an internet e-group, for those members having access to the web. As a result there was an enormous cross-fertilisation of ideas, memories and Storys. There grew a new found energy to question what has until now been represented as fact. This research points to a dichotomy between richness and diversity in the history of the Darkinjung nation and the Central Coast area itself. It reclaims Darkinjung sense of place and Country through the Storys of 'real' people (Blair N. 2001).

Listening: The Performance

> When the moon comes up at night it's like a silvery pathway across the water saying "go on come across"...(McKinnon J. , 2004).

'Listening' as a performance engaged all of the players coming across the contested terrain between traditional research process and Indigenous Knowings. 'Listening' the performance engaged a Non-Indigenous Director, Dr Jocelyn McKinnon and myself to facilitate through different mediums Storys from Darkinjung Country. Each had lines that jumped out about spirituality, Country and the coast as a place of 'belonging'...each with their own Story about why they belonged, each with their own reason for coming across, being drawn to the Central Coast from elsewhere...

Histories evolved from Listening to the Storys, histories never told before, never felt before, never allowed to exist before, be voiced before as the region had already had its written history – one in which all the '[a]boriginal people had died from small pox within the first five weeks of settlement' (Swancott, 1953, p. 9), (Kohen, 1993, p. 54), (Bennett, 1968, p. 3), (Stinson, 1994, pp. 6-12). Darkinjung people, Aboriginal people did not exist...yet we are here, as are the descendants of Darkinjung mob.

The original peoples in the region like many others throughout Australia struggled to place their Story in that of an Australian context, we struggled to find our place and sense of belonging, of taking our Story across, translating as we go not quite capturing the whole Story, the essence, of trying to pick up the pieces after the loss...We were yarning in English as each of the players told their Story in English. We did not dream and think in English as we embarked on the journey that was 'Listening', we Storyd through images, dance, movement envisioning our belonging in this Country, Darkinjung.

Lin Onus: Fashions Anew

The second experience I share involves Lin Onus. Onus reflected 'There is an innate curiosity about different imagery, technology and lifestyle....Artistically, the song lines and trade routes are being rediscovered and fashioned anew (Onus, 2003, pp. 92-93). Is our reclamation and centring of Indigenous Knowings simply different imagery which involves different technology? No, I think not. We are drawing on our cultural core/essence and as Onus claims fashioning anew.

Lin Onus, a Yorta Yorta man, speaking through his art, encapsulated the doer, the seeker of Indigenous Knowings, the presenter of Indigenous Knowings. The painting used here tells his Story. Lin used Western techniques as well as those from Arnhem land in the Northern Territory of Australia. He painted the Arafura Swamp (Fugure 6.1) in 1990 illustrating 'the realist western landscape style punctuated with cutouts through which one could view a traditional bark painting continuing below. The two systems of representing the land each overlaid the other. Archaeologically speaking, the older is below the newer, giving primacy to its more ancient origin' (Neale, 2000, p. 16). This quotation endeavours to explain Onus's art but in reality the painting below has so much to see and to feel if we allow ourselves to do this without translation. The 'Arafura Swamp' painting illustrates the contested space embedding within it Indigenous Knowings as Lin states:

> I kind of hope that history may see me as some sort of bridge between cultures, between technology and ideas.[3]

---

[3] Lin Onus, artist statement, 1990. Jo and Tiriki Onus, see Chronology, Urban Dingo: The Art and Life of Lin Onus (Burrinja), Queensland Art Gallery and Fine Arts Press, Sydney, 2000.

Figure 6.1. Arafura Swamp Lin Onus

Onus makes the point that 'sooner or later, some Aboriginal artists may use lasers and holograms to make their art. Although the materials may change, the imagery and stories will remain strong and everlasting' (Onus, 2003, p. 96). Linguistic competence encapsulates this essence. This painting became a way of modelling my engagement in the Brick Wall; the beauty but tenacity of combined images/imaginings. Onus crafted a new space and representation of Indigenous Knowings.

Narrative, story-telling, oral history and conversation (Josselson, 1997), (Wheatley, 2002), (Brown, 2005), imaging, body movement, use of space as method and theory; elements in the Brick Wall have been identified in both illustrations above; in Listening as the means for gathering, compiling, performing, analysing, evaluating performance and in Onus's art through the paintbrushes, and mediums used on the canvas.

I will return to the notion of linguistic competence in later Storying about operating as Indigenous scholars within a zone of colliding trajectories. Now I introduce another element to the Story; that of our experiences as Indigenous peoples participating as scholars within the Brick Wall; our engagement with Indigenous Knowings and Indigenous Research Methodologies.

AUSTRALIAN EXPERIENCES OF 'BEING' IN THE BRICK WALL

In an Australian context there is a dearth of research on Indigenous Knowings, on Indigenous research methodology; due in part to our experiences of colonisation. Unlike Aoteoroa, Canada, Hawaii and the United States of America Indigenous researchers have primarily focused on issues within independent Disciplines; specifically, history, linguistics/language, anthropology, law, medicine and health, education and art. The lack of Australian literature in Chapter Five is a testimony to this. We have focused on thinking and reacting within the parameters of the Brick Wall, The Academy. The research conducted in the Discipline of education has focused on performance indicators, language of instruction and pedagogy as defined and determined within the parameters of the Brick Wall. An exception to this are the notions of Garma, Dadirri, Kanyini, and Arlathirnda Ngurkarnda Ityirnda (Arbon, 2008) which derive from traditional and semi-traditional contexts and environments. This research as well as Quandamoopah (Martin 2008) gives scope and choice to those of us in urban environments, in fact in any environment to rethink our concept and focus of Indigenous pedagogy and education to one that centers Indigenous Knowings.

As stated earlier, Indigenous pedagogy in Australia evolved and grew as a concept out of political momentum and expediency (Hughes) in the late 1970s, not as a result of traditional research. It grew out of experiential narrative, yarning at conferences, frustration in the educational environments. It has not long been documented. Indigenous researchers have only engaged in research from the 1980s and we have thought and operated from within the fabric of the Brick Wall. Non-Indigenous researchers engaging in Indigenous educational research have operated from within the fabric of the Brick Wall since the 1960s. Our engagement as Indigenous scholars is the result of activism by many. Our engagement has been as scholars who happen to be Indigenous.

The research conducted thus far by Indigenous and non-Indigenous people alike has in the main singularly focused within a Discipline. Interdisciplinary and/or multidisciplinary research which would more closely reflect Indigenous Knowings in terms of holistic patterning, has not occurred very much in an Australian context. This type of research is becoming more popular as we familiarise ourselves with The Academy. As a result we have a situation that showcases Indigenous education and education for and about Indigenous peoples; pedagogy and epistemology, that sit squarely in the center of the Brick Wall. We are yet to familiarise and center ourselves, our own sense of Knowings, to grow our own Waterlilys.

In Australia the concept of decolonisation is trotted out at Indigenous research conferences but we have little dialogue about it. We engage even less in a practice which embodies decolonisation. For example, two courses specifically designed around the notion of decolonisation and Indigenous research methodology at a leading University in NSW, within a Bachelor of Aboriginal Studies were considered redundant in favour of courses about Indigenous peoples in sport. This situation is, I contest, the result of Indigenous staff not wanting to move outside of the Brick Wall, of not seeing the value of decolonising, of Indigenous research methodology. I speak at this point as the instigator, creator, developer and teacher of the above mentioned courses. The student evaluations were extremely positive, though the numbers were small. I comfortably exhibit bias here. I comfortably Know the situation. I respect we as Indigenous scholars make our choices and we play many different songs in many different ways. Some of us are still struggling with the desire to want to 'understand Eurocentric' systems of thought. Some of us are working towards the creation of shared languages. What I am advocating for us as Indigenous scholars is a 'want to understand Eurocentric systems of thought, to create shared languages' (Battiste M. , 2002, p. 4) by centring our own Knowings and not centering the Brick Wall. What I am advocating for is choice. I advocate a place for Indigenous scholars not just scholars who happen to be Indigenous.

In a landscape where 'the enduring impact and influence of deficit thinking, assimilationist ideologies, and race-based assumptions are all built on the legacies associated with dispossession and the ongoing denial of Indigenous sovereignty' [Vass, G p.93] we need choice. If we continue to subject ourselves to the 'different forms of anesthetics being used or applied amongst some of us' we will remain immersed in 'a grogginess that has fogged our hearts, memories and visions' (Martin 2013). Such 'uncritical production, re-production and dissemination of the 'knowledge' that sustains this nexus of domination' cannot continue and 'urgently demands far greater scrutiny' [Vass, G p.93].

It is very difficult to engage in a decolonisation process and the centring of our own Knowings if we are not prepared to create our own models. To create and then hold these up as models. It is difficult if we are 'linguistically incompetent' and not prepared to decolonise our own thinking. We need to go beyond thinking outside the square to reconceptualising our language, our thinking, our projection of ourselves as Indigenous Australians as Lilyology has done for me. Admittedly this can be an isolating and frustrating choice but the more 'Lilys we have and we center, the fewer bricks in the wall, the greater our capacity to survive, thrive and bloom as peoples. To showcase our Knowings and impact on society globally in a way that positions us equally, as just plain different; not more or less.

Participation in Higher Education

The 1960s marked a decade with Aboriginal and Torres Strait Islander participation in the higher education sector by limited research on and about us; what we have come to know as 'The Other', and minimal student participation. The 1970s saw the emergence of National and State Aboriginal and Torres Strait Islander organisations and committees. One such network of organisations included an Aboriginal Education Unit in the NSW Department of Education designed to service schools within its jurisdiction and established in 1973, the New South Wales Aboriginal Education Consultative Group (NSWAECG) designed to advise the State Minister on all matters pertaining to Aboriginal education, in 1977, and the National Aboriginal Education Committee (NAEC) in 1978 designed to advise the Federal Minister of Education on all matters pertaining to education. The creation of Special Programs for Aboriginal and Torres Strait Inslander peoples wishing to enrol in courses in higher education followed. 'Enclaves'; centers designed to provide additional academic and personal support within an area that recognised their identity in a positive way were established. The first being at the South Australian Institute of Technology in Adelaide in 1974. Two such enclaves followed in Western Australia in 1976, James Cook University, Queensland and the South Australian College of Advanced Education, Adelaide in 1978. The first enclaves in NSW were not established until 1982/1983. Special Admission for Aboriginal and Torres Strait Islander students to courses and programs accompanied the establishment of Enclaves as a further Special Program (Blair N. , 1990, pp. 47-55). In 1979 the NAEC developed an additional strategy through the establishment of a target to train 1,000 Aboriginal and Torres Strait Islander teachers by the year 1990.

Watson states that from the outset Aboriginal and Torres Strait Islander participation in higher education was on non-Aboriginal and Torres Strait Islander terms with non-Aboriginal and Torres Strait Islander academics through their research defining using Western concepts, categories and definitions – that is white terms of reference (Watson L. , 1988, pp. 4-6). Such terms of reference became the fodder for Indigenous academics as we found our footing as both students and staff in such Enclaves.

Context is important at this point and presents some contradictions on my part as researcher. My own research for my Master of Arts (Hons in Education) clearly evolved and grew from within and centred the Brick Wall, over a couple of decades ago. How do I respond to this? I acknowledge my growth and essence as an Indigenous person, an Indigenous person with a vision to contribute to academic discourse and to pave some paths for future policy evolution and growth. I acknowledge the importance of getting to know the Brick Wall and all of its components; as many as possible within the time frame of this journey. I acknowledge our need for choice in envisioning our Knowings, conducting research and in contributing to the global discourse of our well being as well as that of this planet and her peoples.

Indigenous scholars such as Bourke (Bourke C. , 1975), (Bourke C. , 1979) Hughes (Hughes P. , 1997), (Hughes P. , 1984), Nakata (Nakata M. , 2007), Moreton-Robinson (Moreton-Robinson A. , 2000), Huggins (Huggins, 2003), (Huggins, 1998), Rigney (Rigney, 1997), Brady (Brady, 1997), Langton (Langton M. , 2006), Behrendt (Behrendt, 1993), Foley (Foley D. , 2002), (Foley D. , 2004) and Maynard (Maynard, 2007), have made choices within the Brick Wall using different pigmentation and vastly different bricks. Indigenous scholars such as Martin (2008) and Arbon (2008) have envisioned their own conceptual frameworks based on their own Indigenous Knowings.

In the Disciplines of history and anthropology Maynard (Maynard, 2007), Langton (Langton M. , 2006) and Huggins (Huggins, 2003) have challenged content but their research framework exists squarely within the Brick Wall. At a time before critical theory emerged as a real possibility for us as Indigenous scholars to frame our research Bourke (Bourke C. , 1975), (Bourke C. , 1979), Hughes (Hughes, First Indigenous Researchers Forum, 1998), (Hughes P. , 1984), (Hughes P. , 1997) and Brady (Brady, 1997) researched within the parameters of Aboriginal Studies, Law and Educational theory. Brady asserts that 'the relationship between Indigenous Knowledge and Western European concepts of Knowledge and Knowing need to placed in a framework of mutual interaction so that not only do Indigenous peoples benefit, but so do non-Indigenous educators and students' (Brady, 1997). I cannot fault this sentiment but I believe that the 'framework of mutual interaction' must evolve from the 'Waterlily' and not the Brick Wall if we are to actively benefit Indigenous and non-Indigenous peoples. To do this we need to engage in The Academy in different ways; ways that privilege our own Knowings.

Rigney and Foley have chosen to work within the frameworks of feminist theory. Moreton-Robinson, Huggins and Behrendt have critiqued feminist theory and our place as Indigenous peoples within this framework but their commentary centers the Brick Wall and the theories associated with feminism and critical theory. Behrendt highlights the tension of working within such frameworks through an illustration of the debate between MacKinnon and Harris where the issue of gender essentialism within the theoretical framework is argued and the notion of a single 'Grand Theory' replace the strategy of telling individual stories. Behrendt asserts that 'the experiences of black women are trivialised when viewed as merely an extension of the experiences of white women' (Behrendt, 1993, pp. 34-40). 'The articulation of theory is a practical and powerful strategy one that consolidates our thoughts and finds for ourselves our own special intellectual terrain' (Behrendt, 1993, p. 41).

I am wanting to take this further and find and center our own terrain before engaging with any of the bricks in the wall. The degree and type of engagement is then determined from a powerful core and emanates out with beauty, diversity and spirit. We are no longer groggy though we will be challenged at every opportunity available to those within the Academy. Some of us have engaged with Indigenous Standpoint Theory as a means to strengthen our voice: a theory that places us as entangled in a very contested knowledge space at the Cultural Interface (Nakata M. , 2007, p. 215). Moreton-Robinson 'represents an Indigenous standpoint within Australian feminism'. She further engages and critiques some important issues including the significance of 'whiteness', the 'new theories of difference', and the use of 'life writings' by Indigenous women to describe certain aspects of the social construction of Indigenous women's subjectivity (Moreton-Robinson, 2000, pp. 3, 33). She asserts that 'whiteness remains centred and is masked in pedagogy' and that until this challenge is addressed, Indigenous women will continue to resist this dominance by talkin' up, because the invisibility of unspeakable things requires them to be spoken' (Moreton-Robinson A. , 2000, p. 186).

I am talkin' up as an Indigenous researcher endeavouring to re-present Indigenous sites of dominance, sites in their own right, not as sites embedded within or made to fit in to Western Knowledge theories and practices.

Nakata (Nakata, 2007) and Foley (Foley D. , 2002) as seen in Chapter Three engage in Indigenous Standpoint Theory. This theory asserts Nakata advocates working, theorising within the Brick Wall because

> It is not that productive to separate it out and lay claim to a separate domain of knowledge with any authority....We need to scrutinise it for

how it discursively and textually produces a position for us and Others to read ourselves in this world (Nakata M. , 2007, p. 228) .

I agree with Nakata that we must open up 'theoretical discussions for more complicated discussions so that the dynamics of the Cultural Interface are not sutured over in favour of the Western order of things and its constitution of what an 'Indigenous opposition' should be' (Nakata M. , 2007, p. 221). By way of engaging in such discussion I believe that we should do this privileging our own Knowings which gives us greater strength and positioning to understand 'Others and read ourselves in this world'.

Indigenous scholars such as Hanlen (Hanlen, 2007), Collins-Gearing (Collins-Gearing, 2008), (Collins-Gearing, 2006) and Watson (Watson, 1988) have engaged in decolonisation as a tool but they have not published widely in mainstream.

Our landscape is one of recent engagement in higher education with less than 400 Indigenous peoples in Australia having research PhD's; forming 0.04% of completed PhD's in Australia (Department of Education 2013). Our overall population is less than 2% of the total population in Australia. We must grow scholars and engage new ones through 'intellectual self-determination developing new analyses and methodologies to decolonise ourselves, our communities and our institutions (Battiste M. , 2002, p. 4)'.

Colleagues from Coast and Desert both spoke about the importance of decolonisation even though they used different terminology. They felt they must center their cultural Knowings, learn about their cultural Knowings before being able to truly participate and engage in mainstream society, in mainstream theorising and practise.

> Yeah. What you've seen and what you know yourself. That what keeps you going, our culture....Yeah, it was mainly just um, like I said, it was mainly just remembering things. You never really think about it you just live it. You just go through it. Yeah (Leucopogan).

> A lot of people don't know their culture today and our people, and they go off track. It's important to know your culture, where you come from, and who your relations are. It's very important now to keep your culture, especially your identity (Hibbertia).

Finding space and ways to decolonise ourselves and create new methodologies is a massive challenge. Sometimes we need to reach to the Brick Wall for tools to disencrypt. Mind Mapping has been one such tool for me.

Zone Of Colliding Trajectories

The wave within the zone of colliding trajectories sounds like a cacophony of instruments tuned in to different songs/tunes. It is as Garma implies a space that is murky, muddied, unclear. In this space we find like-minded theories and frameworks which this next section will Story. It will also Story some of the challenges associated with engagement in these frameworks; including the challenge of "double-consciousness" (DuBois, 1982,pp.45-46) and the challenge of feeling the need to 'fit in'.

Denzin and Lincoln's commentary on bricoleur is engaging as a point of reference in this space (Denzin, N. & Lincoln, Y.S. 2005, pp.4-6). It is engaging through notions such as the 'bricoleur researcher' who invents, pieces together new tools or techniques as required and the bricoleur theorist who works between competing and overlapping perspectives and paradigms. They explore the different bricoleur's understanding, their nature and in some instances their products; specifically the interpretive bricoleur, the critical, the political, the gendered narrative bricoleur. They identify the product as:

> A complex, quiltlike bricolage, a reflexive collage or montage – a set of fluid, interconnected images and representations. This interpretive structure is like a quilt, a performance text, a sequence of representations connecting the parts to the whole (Denzin, N. & Lincoln, Y.S. 2005, p.6).

It is easy to be seduced by this idea, this metaphor and means of thinking, doing, engaging in research as practitioner and theorist. However, quilts have boundaries, structured and crafted boundaries. Quilts too exist centering the Brick Wall .

Australian artist Lin Onus's work has been described as a bricolage within a postmodernist frame in a space that Onus himself could not locate within any existing schools of art, becoming a bricoleur (McLean (p.43). Onus 'agonised over the loss of his language' but realised in order to survive he had to pick things up – like a Bower Bird – picking up bits and pieces, here and there, with no particular plan or formula.' Onus existed and practised within the zone of colliding trajectories. He found the space and he created the naming to locate and grow as a person and as an artist. He clearly demonstrates in his work the need to centre his Knowings and to grow beyond this and strengthen this with the incorporation of Western Knowledge. Onus was a Master of linguistic competence in a Zone of colliding trajectories.

In this context what I find interesting is the way non-Indigenous people find the need to locate Onus within a Western School of Knowledge; for example postmodernism. They try to 'fit him in' as they did my father and I (as evidenced in the Prologue), into a framework that they could understand rather than unequivocally accept the difference and grow from Knowing this difference. (McLean, pp. 41-46). For Onus, like so many others where the impact of such gaze, such labelling could have led to a sense of 'double consciousness', where he found himself 'looking at one's self through the eyes of others, of measuring one's soul by the tape of a world that looks on in amused contempt and pity'(DuBois, 1982, pp. 45-46). Onus clearly conquered such contempt and assimilative ideals.

Taussig offers a contemporary view of 'double-consciousness'. He reflects on "second contact" where the radically different border between West and the rest, between civilization and its Others has been punctured porous by the global market and multinational corporations. He explores the inscribing of oneself against the Alter, the Other, one where 'borders are like membranes and constantly shifting'(Conquergood, 2002, p.145) and where 'mimesis turns on itself, on its colonial endowment, on each other as never before' (Taussig 1993, pp.251-252).

In Knowing our Knowings, in centring our Knowings we strengthen our position as Indigenous peoples to pick and choose the elements from the Brick Wall, the elements of Western Knowledge we consider appropriate in our journey to secure a rightful position of equality. We do this within a zone of colliding trajectories where waves overlap, where waves and still water meet and converse and where we can choose to privilege either essence of Knowing or Knowledge.

Like-Minded Disciplines and Associated Theories: A Search for Belonging?

Performance-Based Theory, Feminism, Critical Race Theory, Rhizomatics are theories that many Indigenous scholars have gravitated towards, have made use of in different ways. The Disciplines of Anthropology and Geography have been the source of identity for many of us on our research journeys.

Performance-Based Theory

Performance based theory and studies offer an interesting discussion about identity within The Academy (Dolan, 1997), and the boundaries drawn between them and other Disciplines within The Academy (Conquergood, 2002). This is the battle of the bricks! Dolan (Dolan, 1997, p. 2), advocates for the dismantling of borders 'too often drawn in our field, in order to proactively represent ourselves to The Academy...as teachers and writers in a postmodern context...recasting our engagements over disciplinary knowledge'. In order to work together I see our task as Indigenous peoples differently. We need to do more than 'recast', we don't have the Disciplines as identified in the Brick Wall. Where Theatre Studies recognise the inconsistency and complexity in the creation and the existence of Disciplines we do not have the same and do not necessarily want the same parameters set by such Disciplines. The Disciplines serve merely as culturally inappropriate signposts and parameters. I endorse Theatre Studies recognition of inconsistency and a complexity of creation working within the existence of Disciplines. Where Dolan (Dolan, 2001) asserts that the 'theatre department is seen as a service unit with no inherent historical or critical discourse of its own and it does this in a way that acknowledges that creative and performance arts are political' I draw strength. Aboriginal Studies Departments in Australia have been seen as service and support units with no critical discourse of their own.

In my assertion of difference I am not advocating apartheid. I, like Dolan am advocating to:

> Create a space for dissent and debate, disagreement and critical refinement and a forum through which to think about values and in which to install new visions of self, community and nation (Dolan, 2001, p. 3).

Through Lilyology from the position of a centred Waterlily I reach to the Brick Wall and explore theatre and cultural performance studies further. There is much similarity through a sense of being branded by many of the bricks in the Wall as 'other', or as having little of meaning to say, to contribute to society. I feel a philosophical befriending within the zone of colliding trajectories in both theory and practice; the'space of exile, objects bought and sold, of not being assimilable where advocacy means political currency to be heard, seen, encountered as someone who has something to say in our cultural systems of power and representation' (Dolan, 2001, pp. 7-9).

Denzin (2005) asserts that 'performance-based human disciplines can contribute to radical social change' and further a 'change that envisions democracy founded in social justice,…to be part of a larger conversation, a global decolonizing discourse' (p.933). I too advocate such change but from a different vantage that is not made to 'fit into' the fabric and structure of the Brick Wall by extending 'localized critical race theory and the principles of radical democracy' (Denzin, N. & Lincoln, Y.S. 2005, p.933).

There are these similarities and I emphasise that these clearly exist. Performance Studies and theorists engage their struggle centering the Brick Wall, based on a Western frame of Knowledge. I draw on some of the sandstone constructing the brick that is performance theory and find a space to voice our dilemma 'more safely and comfortably'. This is where and how Performance Studies and theorists exist for me within the Contested Space. Indigenous Knowings emanate from the Waterlily, the earth and surrounding relationships. Indigenous Knowings in a contemporary environment are 'a tool for participating in democracy'; one that if centred equips us and engages us as we remain rooted in our Country, our relationships. Performance in Indigenous Knowings is much more however than an expressive mode of 'being heard, seen, encountered, contended with as someone, an artist, scholar and citizen, who has something to say in our cultural systems of power and representation'. Performance is an integrated component of Indigenous Knowings, of our individual and collective place in Country, in family. Performance embodies the petals of the Waterlilys.

I return to the performance that was 'Listening' to illustrate the synergies with performance based theories and Indigenous Knowings, Indigenous Research Methodologies. Synergies of the use of space, place, dance, use of body, community engagement and partnering and the delivery of life-changing moments.

> … 'Listening' the performance, engaged and centered Indigenous community people telling their stories. It contextualises this in country, environment and place. An interdisciplinary approach to the research ensures that Indigenous ways of learning and communicating stories remain whole, organic and reflective of diversity. 'Listening' was fuelled by the ethos of community theatre and performance ultimately leading to the creating of a socio-political voice for marginalised social groups via the medium of performance (cultural).

> The research process itself has engendered new ways of creating partnerships between Indigenous communities and the University. It has

also constructed a sense of belonging and identity for the Central Coast community, in Darkinjung country.

> This production was not performance for performance sake, it was a life journey for every individual involved. It was a creative means for community capacity building for both Indigenous and non-Indigenous peoples in the community. It is research that has delivered tangible results to the community, research that made a difference in the lives of those involved and those 'viewing' it (McKinnon J. , 2004).

'Listening' and the UDRWG sourced place and space for Indigenous peoples to re-create our sense of belonging as lost, displaced peoples; lost and displaced in terms of being able to center our Indigenous Knowings. These events and practices did not draw on Indigenous Knowings as a center from the beginning as I was still evolving the concept, the model. However the model appeared in practice in different ways. It 'became' and contributed to this research as a component, as a petal on the lily as it drew on mediums beyond the English spoken word and constructs. The process integrated community theatre and performance-based theory and practice which is one of the bricks that is easy to use elements from and harness their energy through the Lily. The process for the UDRWG may be seen as an example of radical pedagogy. Different bricks or components of the bricks are emerging as significant and useful in the telling of this Story. They don't however frame the journey or serve as the foundation for it.

… Storys, many Storys coming across the zone of colliding trajectories to the creation of something vibrant, energetic and sensory.

Is this what we as Indigenous peoples need to do more of; to invite non-Indigenous peoples to come across the water to our Lilys, our concepts, our dreams and our thoughts? Not simply to be pulled across to the Brick Wall as if caught in a rip; being tussled, drawn, sucked in to the Brick Wall of Eurocentric knowledge and research process.

Performance-based theory offers linguistic competence based on more than English words strung together in linear sentences which are branded on lined pieces of paper. It offers greater choice in terms of voice, play, use of the human body, silence, sound, art, imagery, space to mention a few elements. I draw on the use of the body as in Image Theatre and the work of Boal (Boal, 1985), (Boal, 1995) where the use of the body lessens the need or the use of words. In Desert the use of the body as a medium of linguistic competence was integral, it laid the foundations for conversation, yarning for the research journey of the PhD thesis in ways I had not envisaged. The accompanying webpage illustrates this through video; a teaching and learning engaging the body initially through body painting; identifying your place in the story through imagery on the body, dance and gesture. Many of my Desert Colleagues referred to body painting as a means of learning, coming to Know. In Coast the body had meaning in terms of gesture when speaking and through its placement in Country especially on special Country sites.

This research journey has needed competency in listening, being in silence, sitting in silence, hearing, an ability to be non-judgemental, imagery, visualisation, the ability to see aerially, seeing, being able to see and identify the whole picture, smell, taste, touch, having a sense of timeliness, identifying and being comfortable in space and with this place within Country and community, and being comfortable with my body. These elements had more to do with my linguistic competence than my grasp of English or Amatjere in the case of Desert.

Boal (Boal, 1985) recognises the need to 'free the body', see it as the centre piece for solving problems, moving bodies through the problem, in transition. 'Listening' highlights this use of the body as well as other elements and signifiers that illustrate the physicality of the piece (it was all choreographed) the use of multi-media (especially screen images used as 'backdrop' but also as a further component of Story through images, the importance of the visual) soundscape, song, lighting, a set using natural elements (for example sand covered the ground and formed shapes and patterns as the light changed as the movement took place; it evolved the space). In the production of 'Listening' the non-verbal signifiers of performance were more conducive to Indigenous culture and holistic expression (McKinnon J. , 2004).

Many of us as Indigenous peoples today, need to decolonise not only our minds but our bodies to become free and connect more with Country, culture and identity before we can communicate and express through the body; freeing ourselves from social constraints, conditioning to move in certain ways. We need to find emancipation and reconnection through the body as a fundamental component of Indigenous Knowings. Callistemon from Coast best illustrated this through the importance of breathing correctly, using our bodies, our breath to be one with Country, the environment;

> … Yeah, I was just saying that when, when you're deep when you're breathing like ahhhhhhhh, (Callistemon inhaled for a while loudly and exhaled) it's just, it's just something that you're um, that you're only speaking but the whole environment, the land it's just giving to you and

it's helping you get out of it if you, you know you say it you know –
Darrrramahhhhhhhhh, (x breathes explicity as she says the word) you
know, so. And Darramah means Great Spirit. It means Creator in our
language (C#3,p.33).

Anzaldua eloquently asserts the significance of linguistic competence residing in
the body and our need to engage this in order to 'transform the theorizing space',
to engage the essence of our challenge:

> Even when our bodies have been battered by life, these artistic
> "languages," spoken from the body, by the body, are still laden with
> aspirations, are still coded in hope and "un desarme ensangretado," a
> bloodied truce. By sending our voices, visuals and visions outward into
> the world, we alter the walls and make them a framework for new
> windows and doors. We transform the posos, apertures, barrancas,
> abismos that we are forced to speak from. Only then can we make a
> home out of the cracks....By bringing in our own approaches and
> methodologies, we transform the theorizing space. ... (Anzaldua, 1990,
> p. xxv).

We could focus less on the western appreciation of linguistic competence and
more on the elements associated with Indigenous Knowings illustrated above at
the same time drawing on the Western theories and practices that grow our
centred Knowings.

Textocentrism and scriptocentrism (Conquergood, 2002, p. 147) appear as
part of the debate in the Brick Wall; the battle between the bricks. As people with
oral traditions our Knowings are subjected to the contest between linear text and
other ways of Knowing. Conquergood uses the work of de Certeau, Jackson,
Geertz, Gramsci, Fabian, Hurston and Williams, R. to highlight his notion of text-
performance hybridity (Conquergood, 2002, pp. 146-152). His discussion is
embedded in 'two different domains of knowledge; specifically that of the map
and that of the story'. In essence this is a discussion about the binary opposition
between theory and practice, analysis and action.

> Marching under the banner of science and reason, academic knowing has
> been pre-eminent and has disqualified and repressed other ways of
> knowing that are rooted in experience, orality and local contingencies.
> Between objective knowledge which is consolidated in texts, and local
> know-how that circulates on the ground within a community of memory

and practice there is no contest. It is a choice between science and "old wives tales" (Conquergood, 2002, p. 146).

Burke, K. in Conquergood critiques the limitations of literacy leading to print-based scholarship with built-in blind spots and conditional deafness. De Certeau (1984, p.161) in Conquergood alerts the reader and thinker to the fact that scholarship is so skewed toward texts that even when researchers do attend the extralinguistic human action and embodied events they construe them as texts to be read (Conquergood, 2002, p. 147). Jackson (2000, p.20 in Conquergood)) states that the root metaphor of the text underpins the supremacy of Western knowledge systems by erasing the vast realm of human knowledge and meaning action that is unlettered (Conquergood, 2002, p. 147). Jackson speaks of the Garifuna peoples whose notion that the pencil is not a neutral instrument has led to translations of words people with pencil and people without pencils. Hurston (in Conquergood) in his discussion of textocentrism asserts that 'the white man researcher is a fool not because he values literacy but because he valorized it to the exclusion of other media, other modes of knowing (Conquergood, 2002, p. 151). De Certeau in Conquergood states that Performance Studies struggles to open the space between analysis and action and to pull the pin on the binary opposition between theory and practice. It cuts to the root of how Knowledge is organised in The Academy (Conquergood D. , 2002, pp. 145-146). Conquergood asserts that 'Performance Studies is uniquely suited for the challenge of braiding together disparate and stratified ways of knowing' (Conquergood, 2002, p. 152).

Indigenous peoples in Australia, I believe, would agree with all of the assertions identified in Conquergood (Conquergood, 2002). However the discussion is again played out centering Brick Wall. I see Indigenous peoples and Indigenous Knowings gravitating towards performance-based theory and action because of its reliance on alternate mediums, its play between and relationship between all of the senses. Indigenous Knowings are not one of the braids able to be braided as part of the challenge for Performance Studies. The braids are themselves based on Western Knowledge. The links, the notes played could easily form part of the same tune but only at our choosing, both in terms of the timing, placement and rhythm of the tune. Perhaps as a chord, rather than as a harmony within the tune.

Conquergood's emphasis on the experiential, the action, the doing; 'the nourishing ground of participatory experience' (Conquergood, 2002, p. 154) is one fundamental to Indigenous Knowings as evidenced earlier throughout this text. Again this is some of the organic material from the brick that we can use to nourish the Waterlily.

Feminisim

Feminism is another theory or brick in the wall where some Indigenous researchers have sought friends, like mindedness. Moreton-Robinson asserts that the challenge for feminists remains one of the relinquishment of power and the deconstruction and acceptance of whiteness (Moreton-Robinson A. , 2000, p. 129). Rigney, Foley and Behrendt were identified earlier in this chapter as people seeking friendships with Feminist theory in the telling of their Storys.

Critical Theories

Critical Theories also derive from and for change and transformation; those of critical race theory, critical pedagogy, postcolonialism, anti-racial education, critical multiculturalism, liberal multiculturalism, engaged pedagogy, essentialism, and culturally relevant pedagogy. With each tide, each ebb and flow new ideas emerge, new elements swirl and gurgitate. This is a space where Indigenous scholars have begun to play the most and gravitate towards. Grande with Red Pedagogy, (Grande,S., 2008), Brayboy with Trib Crit (Brayboy, 2005), Wilson with 'Research as Ceremony' (Wilson, 2008) and Smith with Kaupapa Maori (Smith, G. cited in Bishop, R. 2010). The space I choose to write in 'wilfully blurs' (Grande, 2008, p.198) these boundaries but attempts to privilege one form of Australian Aboriginal Knowing in the form of Lilyology (Blair,2015, in press).

Heurmeneutics and Phenomenology

Arbon with Arlathirnda Ngurkarnda Ityirnda (2008, p.22), and Martin with Quandamoopah (Martin, 2008) have engaged with heurmeneutics. Arbon (2008) draws on phenomenology and hermeneutics as an alternative to the fragmentary, dominating and legitimising features held within most western philosophies (p.99). Martin (2008) refers to this relationship as 'heuristic indwelling' (pp.98-99). Both centre their own Knowings but visit and use elements of such theoretical frameworks to grow their ideas; thus working within the contested zone differently to most other Indigenous Australian researchers.

Rhizomatics

Rhizomatics describes theory and research that allows for multiple, non-hierarchical entry and exit points in data representation and interpretation. The principle characteristics of rhizome according to Deleuze and Guattari include the following;

i)   The rhizome is an acentred, non-hierarchical, non-signifying system without a General and without an organizing memory or central automation.

ii) In a rhizome any point connects to another point and the traits are not necessarily linked to traits of the same nature. They cannot be reducible to one or to multiples as they are composed of dimensions; directions in motion where there is no beginning and no end – only a middle from which it overspills.

iii) A rhizome constitutes linear multiplicities with many dimensions and has neither a subject or object that can be laid out on a plane of consistency.

iv) The rhizome operates by variation, expansion, conquest, capture, offshoots.

v)   Rhizomes pertain to a map that must be constructed, produced; something that is detachable, connectable, reversible and modifiable with multiple entryways and exits.

vi) A rhizome is made of plateaus, a plateau is always in the middle and can be read starting anywhere and can be related to any other plateau (Deleuze, 1987, pp. 21-22).

vii) It has ruptures and is not holistic (Deleuze G. &., 1987, p. 7).

Rhizomatics as a paradigm is conceptually one that as an Indigenous person I find myself drawn to. The sweet potato and bush potato are rhizomes which symbolically embody for me Indigenous Knowings; at least an expression of it.

Rhizomatics unlike other Western paradigms has not yet been popularised amongst Indigenous researchers. I do believe however that rhizomatics offers us as Indigenous peoples a concept that does more than 'fit' a pigmented brick in the wall. It is however, still a western concept which does not privilege Indigenous values, Knowledges, languages, frames of reference.

The rhizome 'ceaselessly establishes connections between semiotic chains, organizations of power, and circumstances relative to the arts, sciences and social struggles (Deleuze G. &., 1987, p. 7)', it therefore potentially connects Disciplines of knowledge in an interdisciplinary/multidisciplinary way.

Rhizomatics is however more linear than as an Indigenous person I connect to as a researcher. I do however acknowledge the fact that rhizomes conceptually do not limit their expression to linear words;

> A rhizome ceaselessly establishes connections between semiotic chains ... (which is) 'like a tuber agglomerating very diverse acts, not only linguistic, but also perceptive, mimetic, gestural and cognitive ...' (Deleuze G. &., 1987, p. 7).

Rhizomes allow for inspirational and environmental literacies embodied in Indigenous Knowings (Hanlen, 2007), as discussed in Chapter Three. Deleuze and Guittari (Deleuze, 1987, pp. 7-8) through rhizomatics identify language within the principles of connection and heterogeneity as only being able to be analysed by de-centering it on other dimensions and other registers. They assert that 'there is no language in itself, nor are there any linguistic universals, only a throng of dialects, patois, slangs and specialised languages. There is no ideal speaker-listener, any more than there is a homogenous linguistic community.' Linguistic competence in the context of Indigenous Knowings can draw on rhizomatics as an element to grow our own understanding in the zone of colliding trajectories. It does this as the need for us to de-center language grows, to decolonise language grows.

Deleuze and Guattari (Deleuze G. &., 1987, pp. 12-14) explore the difference between maps and tracing in rhizomes and tree/roots respectively. Of interest here is the notion that 'it is not the essence of the map to be traceable it reproduces itself injecting and propogating redundancies; impasses, blockages' (Deleuze G. &., 1987, p. 13). Colonisation itself follows this pattern; this tracing where Indigenous Knowings, Indigenous peoples and cultures have been 'stabilized and neutralized' according to the 'axes of significance and subjectification'. Colonisation has injected redundancies in the form of Western Knowledge and propagated this at the expense of Indigenous peoples, cultures and Knowings.

I find comfort and a point of reference in the notion that 'thought is not arborescent, and the brain is not rooted or ramified matter (Deleuze G. &., 1987, p. 13). The notion of rhizomes complements my concept of Waterlily; itself a rhizome, and sweet potatoes or mind mapping and decolonisation. Another point of reference is the notion that there are no end points and the notion of plateaus (Deleuze G. &., 1987, pp. 22-23).

The structure of my thesis and ultimately this book and my thought processes identify with this notion rather than any of the other philosophical underpinnings that form the Brick Wall; at least the ones I have encountered at this point of my ongoing scholarship. Again, the plateau does not serve the Waterlily particularly well. The Waterlily is just different and exists in this difference.

Disciplines: Anthropology and Sociology

The study of Indigenous peoples has been the staple of the Eurocentric discipline of anthropology and the related discipline of ethnography (Battiste & Henderson, 2000, pp. 30-31). Butler-McIllwraith began her PhD journey in the Discipline of Anthropology but shifted to Sociology (Butler-McIlwraith, 2006, p.369. Her story is presented here to illustrate the quandary we face as Indigenous researchers when we are trying to 'fit into' the Brick Wall. Her words follow in a large quote, a story in context.

> While anthropology is steeped in a self-identified colonial past (Cowlishaw, 1992), I reasoned that transformative action from within might facilitate Indigenous empowerment in a number of domains (Butler-McIlwraith, 2006, p. 370)....I realized, that in my eagerness to do anthropology 'properly', I had been teaching anthropology in a manner that was merely reproducing Western patriarchal hegemony (Cowlishaw, 1992). I had fallen into the trap of co-option. …. [In sociology] because there were no entrenched pedagogical frameworks on contemporary Aboriginality I was able to blend sociology and anthropology into a paradigm reflecting my understanding of the urban Indigenous cultures … (Butler-McIlwraith, 2006, p. 371).

> It is only very recently that literature has begun to comment on the Indigenous absence from Australian sociology (Butler-McIlwraith, 2006, p. 370). Examining the urban experience through the lens of sociology created insights, not only in to scholarship, but also of personal epiphany – I *lived* in the field (Butler-McIlwraith, 2006, p. 371)....[f]eminist sociology, coupled with Indigenous epistemology, provided a valuable key for me to create a new professional persona (Butler-McIlwraith, 2006, p. 373).

> My own response is that the task is not confusing, but necessarily requires deliberation, because the terrain, both cultural and political, that we are negotiating is constantly shifting. When I engage with sociology I do not want to replicate its elements of Whiteness. Yet at the same time my sociological work has meant, if not an adoption, at least an accommodation with 'dominant cultural values and practices' (Lynes,

2002; 1046). Even, as I attempt to temper these, I recognize that the act of critique itself means that Western knowledge is engaged (Butler-McIlwraith, 2006, p. 374).

In this way, I would like to think that my scholarship is modelled on Habermas's intellectual marauding, in that it provides an exploration across disciplines, incorporating those elements that are relevant to the aims of this work. There is no essentialized demarcation of an externally determined 'appropriate' literature based on the author's racial positioning, although this may be a factor in framing my analysis. I therefore do not make a claim for the universal inclusion of Western knowledge but caution that rejecting a discipline does not advance the cause of critical thinking. Rather, it simply inverts the binary by privileging the marginal and dismissing the mainstream (Butler-McIlwraith, 2006, p. 375).

Disciplines: Geography

The Discipline of Geography has been hailed as a friend by some because of its relationship to Country and environment. I engage the words of Yi- Fu Tuan (Tuan, 1977), and Massey (Massey, 2005) on 'space' and 'place' within the field of Geography. Yi-Fu Tuan proposed that "space" is more abstract than "place" (Tuan, 1977, p. 6). Philosopher Edward Casey asserts that to 'live locally, and to know is first of all to know the place one is in (Casey, 1996, p.18) and social theorists not infrequently aver that 'Place is space to which meaning has been ascribed' (Carter et al, 1993, p.xii) [in (Massey, 2005, p. 183)]. In Chapters Three and Five I discussed the notion of 'place' as inscribed (Langton M. , 2000, p. 263) in relation to the concept of Country; within Indigenous Knowings. The Discipline of geography is engaging in discussion which Indigenous peoples have Known for centuries. Coast and Desert Colleagues referred to Indigenous Knowings existing by 'Knowing the place one is in'.

Buttimer explores this when he asserts that 'each civilization has a story to tell. The unfolding patterns of the earth around us invite a sharing of these stories as one essential step toward discovering mutually acceptable bases for rational discourse and wiser ways of dwelling' (Buttimer, 1993, p. 3). Within the Discipline of Geography, Buttimer speaks about the integration of different Knowledges; scientific versus humanist approaches, the desire for emancipation and a desire for a wider picture; one which integrates scientific and humanist points of view (Buttimer, 1993, pp.211-225).

This discussion occurring within the fabric, the sediment of the Brick Wall is like the discourse occurring in Performance Studies and Practice much like an oyster enduring and being nourished in the converging waters within the contested zone. This discussion is being had across all facets of both quantitative and qualitative research theorisation.

MIND MAPPING

Mind Mapping is a tool, an instrument being played in the arena of colliding trajectories. It is a rhythm within the silence of the breve note that is decolonisation. It is the moment that an essence of the whole of Knowing is gathered and reflected upon. Mind Mapping is the spiders and the sweet potatoes in Lilyology; the connectors across a contested zone.

My Colleagues in Coast and Desert used the essence of 'mind mapping' in some of their journey with me:

> They take us out, we walk along the bush, they show us that hills men's business, women's business or us...well that hills a, something Dreaming, Snake Dreaming or Kangaroo Dreaming. Yeah. Then,...they show us, like sit down with us on the ground and they show just...show where all the place are like they draw a little map on the ground in sand and show us where we are and where all this other stuff and...waterholes and ...(Cactus).

and

> And kids learn through listening to old people, yeah, yeah and showing, um, designs in the ground and going to, different places, yeah (Yam).

These quotes illustrate how people sit in Country and imagise places, people and their relationships with each other. This sitting down, being told and shown on the sand in the landscape was a regular part of my experience with Colleagues from both locations. The Story would be wiped as we moved to other Storys as we physically moved location. The accompanying webpage illustrates some of this in the hyperlinks on page four entitled Tellin' Me and Showin' Me.

Mind Mapping created by Tony Buzan in the 1960's as a tool for the facilitation of mental literacy has found favour as a tool to organise thoughts, to take notes and to engage our memories specifically in the fields of business and education. Virtually all Fortune 500 Companies use Mind Mapping including

IBM, Boeing Aircraft, Microsoft and the BBC. Recently Al Gore, former Vice President of the United States of America and more recently Nobel Peace Prize recipient was pictured in Time Magazine at his desk with a Mind Map on the wall in front of him. The article points out that he used Mind Mapping to help him keep control of his thoughts and that he used Mind Mapping software when working on his recent book (Time Magazine, 2007). Bill Gates (2006), the Chairman of Microsoft, proclaimed in a Newsweek Article that Mind Mappers and Mind Mapping software were the "Road Ahead" and are "leading the way in to the next stage of our new information democracy".

Educators and trainers use and are now writing about mind mapping (Mueller, 2002) as a tool to enhance critical thinking and view the world holistically. Text books such as 'Mind Maps in Medicine' use mind maps to 'provide an overview of the subjects and are designed to 'prime' the brain to remember the information in the textbook' (McDermott, 1998). The advent of mind mapping software has led to ontology engineering to enable the semantic web (Sure, 2002).

Mind Maps are an effective tool that some countries, some companies/corporations, education institutions and students, some governments are using to assist with different elements of learning and teaching. To date the uses are fragmented and broken in to bits, just like all other forms of Western Knowledge. I trained as a Licensed Buzan Instructor with Tony Buzan and Vanda North in 1998. In renewing my License I discovered a new raft of people showing interest in using the technique, the tool and using it for a greater variety of reasons, within a greater diversity of sectors. [The accompanying webpage provides a link to the Buzan Centre and Mindwerx International for further information].

What then of Mind Maps? They emerge from the Brick Wall. They are a tool and have their birth in a philosophy drawn from within the Brick Wall. People could argue there are many such tools. I mentioned Thinking Maps and De Bono's Six Thinking Hats in Chapter Five. The experience I described in Chapter Three with Indigenous peoples in Australia, my own personal experience and that of people I have trained through special adult education programs and in community groups has led me to experience, has led me to Know that Mind Maps are much more than a note-taking tool, a tool to organise thoughts and a tool to switch our memories in to gear. Mind Maps offer a multi-dimensional holistic frame of reference for us to engage and embody our Knowing as Indigenous peoples. Mind Maps can act as translator from traditional Knowing to and from Western Knowledge. Mind Maps inhabit the contested zone and offer a form of liberation and decolonisation which assists us to privilege Indigenous Knowings. Mind Maps can be a way to engage our linguistic competence, to Know in ways that embody the essence of Indigenous Knowings more effectively.

INDIGENOUS KNOWINGS EXISTING IN THEIR OWN RIGHT

The challenge emerges for us as Indigenous peoples when we ourselves imbue double-consciousness or mimesis and alterity in the construction of our Knowing, our research frameworks and process. Our challenge goes beyond developing strategies to contend with the differences. Our challenge goes beyond struggling with the ambiguity of our voices and roles as researcher, facilitator. Our challenge must be to grow ourselves from the inside out not centering Western theories or superficially masking, suturing over the 'gaping bits', but to create our own distinct models of Knowing, value, privilege and grow with them.

Battiste explores a 'respectful way to compare Eurocentric and Indigenous ways of Knowing and include both in to contemporary modern education' (Battiste M. , 2002, p. 4). The notions of 'binary' and 'essentialism' cannot be avoided and should not be in the course of the global conversation. I have tried not to compare but to set up a dialogue and negotiation between different systems where one is not judged as superior, both co-exist in their own right; it is quite normal that the different Storys which contradict each other, do not conflict, but simply co-exist (Hokari, 2000, p. 8)'. Like Wilson (2008) it is not my intent to 'judge any one paradigm as being better or worse than another' (p.35) but to Story each in their own right.

Indigenous research is not 'just another brick in the wall' (Floyd, 1979). Indigenous research is conceptually different. As Swisher (1998) states we have to 'learn how to become more aggressive when defining our field' (p.197). We must respond to the calls from Mihesuah (1998) to re-set the standards for writing about [us] (pp.5-6), whether this is done through Garma, Dadirri, Kanyini, Quandamoopah, Arlathirnda Ngurkarnda Ityirnda, Red Pedagogy, Research as Ceremony, Kaupapa Maory, Trib Crit., Lilyology or another imaging of Indigenous Knowing. The task ahead for us as Indigenous scholars in an Australian context is to:

i)   Privilege/Centre Indigenous Knowings;
ii) Recognise the oldest continuing intellectual tradition inscribed in the Countrys within Australia;
iii) Draw on our Knowings, our Story, our imagery, our sensuality to develop models outside of the Brick Wall.

As an individual Indigenous researcher (who never really stands alone), my journey has evolved Lilyology. It may be obscure for some. It may not resonate for some but at the very least Lilyology is an articulation of my Indigenous Knowing.

There are those who will want to operate within the parameters of the Brick Wall. There are those who will want to work by drawing on the bricks metamorphosing and/or tinting the existing bricks. Others will evolve Indigenous Knowing models that engage some of the bricks, some of the elements of the bricks and Indigenous Knowing and Indigenous concepts and metaphors.

I have journeyed from a place of ambiguity, tenuousness and complete misfit using the bricks from within the Brick Wall to a place of Garma. My resting and reflecting place at this point in time is simply embedded in the concept, essence and image of Lilyology. I am in no way alone in this reflection as evidenced in this book and the growing numbers of publications by Indigenous scholars. When we create our own models of Knowing and practise research that embodies our essence we will no longer be dominated:

> (Colonialism's) most important area of domination was the mental universe of the colonised, the control, through culture, of how people perceived themselves and their relationship to the world (wa Thiong'o, 2005).

There are some reflections that I believe can take us beyond the cynicism to the creation of our own models. These include our need to engage in Imaging/Imagining, Storying as 'Intellectual Traditions', Silence, Reflexivity, Listening, Envisioning, Performance, Theorising our own, Relationships, Connections, Spirit, Community of Scholars, Dynamic, and Country in whatever ways we can to decolonise our minds, our practice.

What follows next is traditionally known as a conclusion. This Story, this journey has no conclusion. It cannot if I truly privilege Indigenous Knowings. I offer instead an overview, a repetition and re-telling of the Story to date so that it can be grown and so that it may add to the 'transformation of the theorizing space (Anzaldua, 1990, p. xxv)'. A demonstration of Indigenous intellectual self-determination (Battiste M. , 2002, p. 4)

CHAPTER 7

Not a Conclusion!

> Through this act of intellectual self-determination, Indigenous academics
> are developing new analyses and methodologies to decolonize
> themselves, their communities, and their institutions (Battiste, 2002, p.
> 4).

A Story, parts of a Story have been told and shared in the pages beyond. A Story
that involves an act of intellectual self-determination as I have thought, spoken
and imaged new analyses and an Indigenous research methodology framed within
my local context. This Story has been a profoundly emotional and personal
journey in an effort to honestly source, capture, reflect and decolonise all that my
involvement in The Academy and in my communities have 'put out there' to
engage and in some cases not engage in.

So, what of the Story...what is its essence? I spoke in Chapter One about this
Story being like 'waves along the shore in a constant sea...waves that roll forward
and mingle with others. That retreat into others. That feed the rivers, the lakes and
in turn is fed....is constant, always returning.' The essence is in the voices of
Indigenous peoples, constantly rolling in and out of experiences, reflections and
Knowings. As the researcher, I have been a facilitator, the footsteps (on the
fabric) constantly moving physically, intellectually and spiritually from one site
to the other. The waves of Knowing have embodied voices and imaging of the
notion of Western research and the impact of Western research on Indigenous
peoples. This Story has listened to and seen how Indigenous peoples have and
continue to engage in Indigenous Research or Research involving or about
Indigenous peoples. The waters themselves are contaminated by and therefore
contextualise the Story through people's encounters with and experiences of
Colonialism, Imperialism and Eurocentrism. Such contamination challenges
Indigenous peoples Knowings of ourselves. It challenges our means, our energies
and our desires to engage in The Academy; the Brick Wall. Globally, Indigenous
peoples have crafted alternate concepts, metaphors and models. My dilemma is
that we craft from within the Brick Wall; the space that is Western Knowledge.
The theories, philosophies and paradigms that have constructed 'our being', 'our

identity' and have been rolled out as 'truths'; in reality mis-truths told from behind Eurocentric, colonial, imperial lenses.

Tjukurrpa and Kanyini, Garma, Indigenist Research, Indigenous Standpoint Theory and Dadirri swirl amidst Australian waters with The Knowledge Dreaming Model. Globally the waters merge as do other Indigenous models, metaphors and explanations including; Hampton's Six Directions from Canada, Pagtattanong-tanong from the Phillipines, the Rubber Sheet from Ghana, the Spiral from the South Pacific, Kaupapa Maori and the Model of Maoritanga and Maori Worldview from Aoeteorora (New Zealand).

This zone of colliding trajectories is like Garma itself and it has the potential to grow some extraordinary, some powerful and some sensory theories that will sustain us as Indigenous peoples, that will nourish us and the wider world around us. To do this we must privilege Indigenous Knowings; what I have termed Lilyology,

When waves dance naturally, unharnessed by Brick Walls their voices verbatim emit power, beauty and Knowing that exist in their own right, in their own locale. This research listened to the voices. As the researcher I have been shown (and share with my readers) by my Colleagues from Desert and Coast, Indigenous Knowings are not something to translate, to categorise, to thematically misconstrue but to listen verbatim encapsulating their rhythms.

Some of the waves are laden with textocentrism and impart concepts worthy of reflection. Reflection in terms of a review of the text, the literature, an oxymoron perhaps but we must engage with, in the challenge of 'Knowing', if we are to reclaim and re-position our worldviews and find the pathways ahead. Conversing about 'Country', Indigenous Knowings, Story and the role of our Elders as traditional and contemporary scholars form the sediment of our yarns, our conversations. Conversations about The Academy, its use of and engagement of Indigenous research and peoples add a further dimension to the wash taking us to new terrain where we craft new tools and use old tools to decolonise our approaches to research, to our contributions to Knowledge production.

I have been led to spiders, sweet potatoes and waterlilys as a means to engage in the The Academy: the Brick Wall, to make sense of a discourse that alienated me. To decolonise my concept of research and Knowledge. To find alternate paths to engage in research in ways that privilege and centre Indigenous Knowings, that delivers tangible results and ultimately reclaims and re-positions our world views. This re-positioning recognises the oldest continuing intellectual traditions, inscribed in Country, inscribed in Countrys throughout Australia.

Our journeys, our imaging, our crafting of new theories and new paradigms enable us to re-engage in the conversation, the discourse occurring within The

Academy in ways never before imagined. In ways that enrich and nourish The Academy as much as our sense of being and Knowing as Indigenous peoples. This engagement will breathe life in to the creation and delivery of policy. It will through the use of our own languages, our own languages of Knowing stop making us tired through conversations in English. If we find the patterns from our own worlds, our own environment we strengthen and give spirit to our souls.

This book endeavoured to harness the energies and Storys from Indigenous peoples within Australia and around the globe to converse, link, reflect, listen to, practice, experience and create relationships, create webs of connections between the Brick Wall and the Waterlilys; where the Waterlily is centred through Lilyology not the Brick Wall.

The PhD thesis was a journey of conceptualisation. Post PhD has thus far been a journey of reflection, doing and being. A number of events helped to take the original idea, the imagery and metaphor into the concept and framework of Lilyology; a mosaic of performative knowledge and Story based on Aboriginal ontology and epistemology.

In the phase that was conceptualisation the tangible outcomes centred around the process of working an academic thesis, of developing my model and engaging with others about it has been liberatory, emancipatory and tangible for me as an individual researcher. One could argue that such philosophical change is not tangible. I advocate that it has given me a platform for my voice, a platform to be a facilitator for other voices, and a concept that I can truly engage with and privilege; Indigenous Knowings not Western Knowledge. The more we are able to privilege Indigenous Knowings the more valuable the discourse in The Academy and government policy development at all levels for Indigenous and non-Indigenous Australians. The greater value and greater sense of identity for this country; Australia. Different voices woven together playing different songs with different melodies, different notation and different scores.

I was also drawn to the potential for delivering tangible outcome/s which impacted on government policy, during the PhD dissertation phase. I used the concepts I had been developing and the tools of mind mapping in many different contexts including as a strategy embedded within a national Training Manual and Program on human rights and social justice for Indigenous Australians, accredited training programs on Indigenous leadership and more recently training strategies with and for Indigenous media broadcasters especially staff employed at remote radio stations and other associated networks. Though limited as examples these are significant in terms of the impact of such thinking, concepts and practices on individuals and communities involved. They offer us as Indigenous peoples alternatives for the creation, development, implementation, presentation, practice and evaluation of policy and programs at all levels; individual, community, local, regional, state, national and international.

Post PhD a number of events allowed me to enhance the learnings, grow the metaphor and to engage more fully in Lilyology itself. These events include a Research Forum at which I presented a paper, Curriculum development at an Aboriginal and Torres Strait Islander College of Dance in the Vocational Education Sector, a Conversation with an Aboriginal colleague working within the Brickwall, Higher Degree Research supervision and membership and engagement with Brick Wall Ethics Committees.

RESEARCH FORUM

The University of Newcastle conducted a Research Forum for Indigenous researchers at which I was invited to present on 'Privileging Indigenous Knowings'. I diligently prepared my presentation and spoke about Lilyology though I had not named it this, at this point. The audience included Indigenous peoples from Australia, New Zealand and Canada; people I mostly knew and had worked with in different ways for decades. At the end of the presentation I was inundated with people remarking how the presentation, the concept made sense to them, touched them, engaged them in ways they had not thought before. This is the first time I felt my ideas were affirmed by and related to amongst my Colleagues, my Indigenous Colleagues; it was the first such forum in which I had presented though I had been using it in my curriculum development content and process and in presentations to forums like AARE (Australasian Association of Research and Education) and others associated with initial teacher education. A validation was unfolding.

CURRICULUM DEVELOPMENT

Curriculum makes space like nothing else I know in education (Kovach p.6)

Recent curriculum work at NAISDA (National Aboriginal and Islander Skills Development Association) has embraced Lilyology to assist staff in navigating the relational nature of writings, curriculum structures and formats that appear in linear structure but have relational links which are important to acknowledge. The mosaic engages metaphors and images that perform a meta-story against a grand narrative. They provide a map where the parts of something may seem important but so is the world/grand view.

The curriculum development to ready NAISDA for re-accreditation afforded an opportunity to reconceptualise how we[1] as an organisation centred, engaged and did Indigenous Knowings. NAISDA is a college that teaches Certificate, II, III, IV, and a Diploma in Careers in Dance to Aboriginal and Torres Strait Islander students from all over Australia. Previously the curriculum was responsive to accreditation authority rules and regulations, frameworks. The content obviously had Indigenous contexts but this was limited to 'fit within' what was expected by the western regulatory authorities. Lilyology gave staff, Board of Studies members and the Curriculum/Accreditation consultants the chance to re-envision their curriculum content and process because it centers Indigenous Knowings not western regulatory frameworks, and goes beyond simply grafting on the acceptable stories without the depth of context through an understanding of Indigenous Knowings. Anything less simply exoticises Indigenous content and experiences. Lilyology in practice gave access and understanding to differences as well as the map for the flow of cultural units as the core allowing other activities to be linked in to this core rather than linked in to western frameworks, boxes or bricks from the Brickwall. It gave the Aboriginal staff member a safe place to voice his Knowings to the point that he said : it comes from the roots , the roots of the Lily when speaking about the map before us as a Board of Studies. He said "when you start to feel it you carry it with you" It gave the Vocational Educational Training consultant; the 'authority' on the sector regulations and standards to make compliance as a registered training authority rigorous, the space to converse, listen, dialogue, reflect on the centred Lily rather than the VET standards.

The Dialogue was circular not determined by western concept of agenda, spiralling back on the Lily with the staff member stating 'I came in this morning with a list of things to do and a plan and sequence for how this meeting would go, and it isn't going this way and I feel great about it'. We centred our Storying around the Lily, spoke of the Brick Wall...and then breathed a relatedness to feeling what we were doing not responding to Brick Wall requirements – remembering his earlier comment: "when you start to feel it you carry it with you". The Storying has seen a rich and deep interconnected web emerge that places Indigenous Knowings more at the centre of what we do; more at the centre than western regulations that we try to 'fit into'.

Non-Aboriginal students often ask me 'why do we have to do more on the Stolen Generation, Aboriginal history', in effect the gloom and doom of

---

[1] I currently Chair the Board of Studies for NAISDA and as such facilitate the curriculum conceptualisation and re-development.

disadvantage? If we don't embed our own Knowings, our own understanding of 'Country' then our students; Aboriginal and non-Aboriginal students have no foundation, no portal to contextualise and fully understand the histories that are their histories too. The fact that we are only now engaging in curriculum discussions which center Indigenous Knowings reflects the educational understanding or lack of understanding of the place of Indigenous Knowings in Australia. This is the place I most see Lilyology contributing to new knowledge. It does this by imaging how we can delve into the contested spaces and emerge with pathways that extend Indigenous Knowings rather than restrict them to "fitting into" western knowledge frameworks, concepts and processes.

I WORK WITHIN THE BRICK WALL

Recent conversations with a colleague; Dr Brooke Collins-Gearing, an Indigenous academic in the Faculty of Social Sciences and Arts, University of Newcastle showcase how Lilyology can be used to frame our understanding. The words below are Brooke's words; they are her words because in our conversation we both realized that I was too immersed in conceptualisation and the doing of the concept was organic but not centre of my thinking. Brooke had begun to engage with Lilyology in her reflections and reactions to meetings with the Brick Wall; meetings where she is portrayed as 'not fitting in'.

Knowing and growing within Lilyology.

- It is alive and breathing
- Pulsating and rhythmic with life/energy/consciousness
- It is a metaphor and a model
- It is a story of growing survival in western academia
- It is nourished by Country and nourishes Country
- It nourishes me and in doing so, I grow my understanding of it more
- It is not hierarchical, inflexible, immovable and hard (like a brick wall)
- the brick wall also grows from sources that have been nourished by earth and water, minerals and atoms. It has been carved, shaped and constructed by the hands of humans: the epistemological centre it represents privileges notions of evolution, progress, measurement, compartmentalisation, empiricism and hierarchies. You can only grow/build the brick wall if you conform to the built structure, materials, brick sizes and stableness. The edges, walls, surfaces, boundaries are hard, cemented and disconnected (from other bricks which they are mortared to and from the earth which originally birthed it)

-   Lilyology breathes, it moves, it repeats patterns that have rippled from the original source, the seed, the initial act of consciousness when the seed opens, reaches out and grows until it returns again to its moment of birth.
-   For me, Lilyology – tangible in its manifested form of a real plant that intangibly links to knowledge and energy which I cannot see or every really know – teaches me patience and listening. Patterns are revealed, slowly, and at the appropriate time and space. Wrapped within the physicality of the Lily that can be seen, touched, smelled, tasted, is life, energy, consciousness. The Brick Walls can be seen, touched, smelled, climbed, knocked into, maybe even knocked over, but it does not grow on its own, it is shaped, constructed, controlled by Western minds and hands, it can even be pulled apart brick by brick.
-   Potentiality
-   A performativity (transmutation from unborn to growing and living)
-   A thirsty reaching out (life and light)
-   A vital force
-   Pedagogically Lilyology allows me to draw knowledge from the western wall, sit with it, breathe it in, feel its energy and then situate it in a way that nourishes me. I work within the bricks of the wall, I have been indoctrinated into an ontology that was shaped, crafted, blocked by the bricks within the wall. Lilyology allows me to grasp onto something real and tangible that pulls me out of the wall. As I climbed the wall throughout my western education, scaling it from Kindergarten to a PhD, I hurt myself more and more. Grazes, cuts, bruises, headaches, heartaches, falls , caused by climbing up it, even when I didn't want to, even when I had nothing to hold onto, to pull myself along or lower myself down, stranded, dangling, grasping for a hold on something in the wall that would sustain me.
-   Lilyology as a model reminds me to seek the feeling of all life-energy around me, to suck in the moment, breathe in the air. In the classroom, literally within the brick walls of the academy but also figuratively confined within its imperial, colonial, Eurocentric paradigms, it encourages me to rhizomatically explore ways of stepping away from the wall. It nourishes my learning, my slow growth, rather than forcing me to present myself a certain way – as a teacher, a lecturer, an "expert", an "authority", forcing acknowledgement and perpetuation of the very disciplines of knowledge (and all the isms within it – postmodernism, poststructuralism, feminism, cosmopolitanism) that only brick up my

ability to reach out discursively, non-hierarchically, patiently. (Collins-Gearing conversation. 2015)

SUPERVISION OF POSTGRADUATE STUDENTS

The Authentic Dissertation is a road map for students who want to make their dissertation more than a series of hoop-jumping machinations that cause them to lose the vitality and meaningfulness of their research (Four Arrows , 2008.)

One of the most challenging areas for those of us working in the Brick Wall: The Academy is the supervision of Higher Degree students; students doing dissertations within the Brick Wall. A space where we are busy 'hoop-jumping' and losing or not even finding, coming to Know the vitality and meaningfulness of the research by centering their/our own Indigenous Knowings.

A current experience engaged the concept of Lilyology. The result has been the development of a Performative Dialogue and presentation of it at the 2015 Annual Qualitative Methods Conference, held in Melbourne, Australia. An Aboriginal and Torres Strait Islander PhD student has a non-Indigenous supervisor in the discipline of Health; this is where the dissertation is methodologically and theoretically located within The Brick Wall. I co-supervise. Our student is using images, poems; many different expressions to convey the journey of her research participants; Aboriginal women and her own journey. At one point we had a challenge with our 3 different voices contributing to the dissertation in different ways (clearly the central voice is that of the students and her research participants) specifically, regarding the theories and the methodologies used and the form of presentation. None of the supervisors wanted this to be an exercise of 'hoop-jumping machinations' but the power of the Brick Wall to ensure conformity within a discipline was at times overwhelming for each of us.

Lilyology was used to talk through Indigenous Research Methods and different forms of thesis presentations. It was used to map and facilitate the differences between the student's lived reality as well as those of her participants and the lived experiences of both supervisors. The Performative Dialogue will be reproduced in journal article engaging all three players.

BRICK WALL HUMAN RESEARCH ETHICS COMMITTEE: MY 'DOING' ON THE COMMITTEE

Sitting on Ethics Committees I see many applications concerning 'researching our mob'. Some of this is done by Non-indigenous people and some by Indigenous people. When Indigenous people do research and claim it to have cultural context I worry when I don't see reference to Indigenous Research Methodologies, Indigenous Ontologies and Epistemologies. It is the most common experience. I have used Lilyology with members of my current HREC and this has given them the space to understand Indigenous Knowings – not as something in competition, not as something 'out-privileging' something else. As something that is different, and unique; valid in its own right.

These experiences are all ongoing and I sure there will be many more but this snap shot gives you the reader a chance to connect to 'the doing' of Lilyology.

HOW CAN WHAT I LEARNT FROM THE MANY VOICES STORYD BE SHARED, TAKEN AWAY AND BECOME A PART OF OTHER PEOPLES LIVED EXPERIENCES?

We can have knowledge about something, we can believe in something, we can experience and do it but when we Know it, it is our Knowing. It becomes embodied within us, through us and around us being connected to and related to everything we feel, hear, see, touch, smell. We cannot have this Knowing, these Knowings if we do not holistically contextualise all of these.

As Indigenous scholars and educators, we must use whatever it takes for us to connect to our/your own sense of Knowing and it will propel us to honour those that we have sought counsel from, shared Storys with whilst grounding us in the essence of our being. We need to find the bridge, between the Brickwall and Waterlilys and remember to centre your own Knowings for this is what I believe will authenticate Indigenous research and Indigenous education not just research and education that happen to have the word 'Indigenous' at the front of the phrase.

Are there any recommendations from the PhD thesis? Are there any findings? Is there any conclusion? Not really. We are at a point at which we take breath, reflect, listen to what is around us and then embark further on a journey to enrich the one just taken, just experienced. Self-reflection garnishes connectedness and relatedness, to our 'new old knowledge', to each other, to our Elders and to Country.

Like Irene Watson, an Indigenous woman whom I am indebted to for her courage and wisdom I believe the 'horizon can be changed' so that we shift from a 'right way of knowing' to one where we are free to Know in the way of the grandmothers, where we can sit and see the horizon from an Indigenous place and space Knowing the mother beneath our feet (Watson I. , 1998, p. 31).

Epilogue

> If research doesn't change you as a person, then you haven't done it right (Wilson, p.135)

The day began full of expectation. It was a crisp Autumn morning with a slight breeze blowing and the scent of eucalyptus, and wet palms clearly in the air. Amidst reading, reflection, note-taking and writing...amdist feelings of fear, stress, anxiety and confusion an event was about to unfold. An event that would provide the portal to new learning, new old learning and the impetus to embody what had been learnt so far to the point of producing text for publication. But, first let me take you back about 10 years; a time when a PhD was in the final stages of being written – the due deadline for submission was not far off and the field research had been 'concluded'.

The research journey as you now know took me to Country in the Northern Territory, that did not become the site for yarning about 'research' and 'Indigenous Knowing'. It was here that Trakka a Queensland blue heeler dog had installed himself in the research journey that at this point...wasn't. Trakka's owner's said "do you want to take him back home with you". Of course I said but I live in an apartment and will have to buy a house. Mmmm, much thinking but knowing it had to be. A pole home at the foot of Mt Kincumba in Darkinjung Country, NSW was bought. This house was 'right' from the moment I walked in to it; it felt culturally safe, it felt the Knowings attached to this Country. The house was prepared for Trakka but like the 'field research' in Trakka's Country it didn't eventuate. Trakka was embedded in the wildness of his Country. The shift to regional suburban Country where a home surrounded by casuarina and eucalyptus trees was made ready for him was too disorienting; the dislocation, the move from Country and all that was familiar would be too much for Trakka.

A few years passed and another 4-legged boy Jaambe[1] arrived at this home; a few years of writing, thinking, reading, reflecting and of feelings of panic, fear and anxious moments about the authenticity of my thinking, of my approach to the research journey especially when my approach was not meeting the requirements of the Academy within which the process was occurring. The PhD writing had stalled. My head was in a quagmire, the writing paralysis had truly set in; the fear of failure, the insecurities of 'novel' thoughts led to a deep depression within me – my spirit was sad. The experiences; the doing of the research in Countrys kept me going but the writing – the how to became claustrophobic.

---

[1] Jaambe is a Gunditjmara word from south-eastern Victoria meaning special friend

Jaambe arrived nourishing my spirit, my story in ways never imagined. Those of you who have a dog know you can't stand still and own a dog; you have to get up and walk them, you have to feed them and pay attention to them just as they feed you with unconditional love. Movement whether it is physical, spiritual or emotional is a powerful thing. The movement saw the successful completion of the PhD but then something else happened; the demand of the Academy to publish became debilitating.

My PhD journey to this point left me exhilarated but exhausted. The learnt new knowledge was profound. Voices, ideas, images churned inside my head and body like a stormy sea in summer – waves of these slashing in and out. The doing, the experiences in different Country, in different head spaces were without comparison in my life. The Academy had given a big tick to the PhD but there were those who mocked about my 'left of centre, out there thinking' and it really didn't fit within the Academy. Self-doubt creeps in...and leads to new jobs one outside of the Academy but like a homing pigeon back into the Academy; but to an institution far more conservative and less ready than the previous institution I had worked for my constructs and my 'truths' about Indigenous Knowing. Life continues ...

One unforgettable long weekend in October my world it felt, was shattered, as overnight a seemingly perfectly happy and healthy dog was diagnosed with the most aggressive form of lymphatic cancer. 11 months of life ensued on this earth for my soul mate Jaambe. The day came to put him down though even this day was tainted with words from the veterinary specialists versus the words from the naturopaths. Who do you believe I asked myself over and over. Ultimately, you can only believe in your own Knowing. It is like the journey of an Indigenous academic doing a PhD functioning in two opposing worlds; weighing up science and Eurocentric frameworks and structures versus our own Knowing.

Months have passed and the pole home needed smoking, cleansing; a practice important in our cultures after the passing of people, animals, plays – any living things.

So, on this crisp Autumn morning an Aboriginal man arrives with eucalyptus leaves, clap sticks, didgeridoo and ochre. He reflects before smoking on the Country we are in, the place the home is in. To the south-east, a short distance away is Mt Kincumba; a women's site, a special place. Living in this place, so close and so culturally disconnected from the depth of Knowing around me inspired the steps needed to walk through the portal from a space of contradiction, confusion and disbelief to a space of clarity, connectedness and relatedness of self to Country and Knowing...to the steps forward in producing the text for the publication of what was a PhD.

This Story tells of the long journey between PhD submission and publication. It explores the fears associated with doing research as an Indigenous person, the fear of letting the mob down, of getting their voices out there in the most authentic way, at the right time; of honouring them. It connects Country to the way the research process and ongoing journey occur. Like Kovach (2008, p.11) I identify the new tensions associated with publishing the text when it is deep within and associated with Western systems of research.

Kovach speaks of what she got from her research journey and acknowledges 'stories will wait for us until we are ready. They will reveal themselves in purposeful and powerful ways and when this happens we are in the midst of the sacred' (Kovach, p.184).

Like Kovach I Know what I Know from where I stand. I have a responsibility to help create entry points for Indigenous Knowings to come through (Kovack p.6). Lilyology is one such entry point.

WHY DID I DO THIS RESEARCH?

I did this research because 'best fit' is not enough. I like Kovach and Smith (Kovach, p.88) believe that there must be room for choice, the 'buffet table of methodological options' must be expanded (Kovach, p.79). The expansion cannot be at the expense of our own Indigenous ontologies and epistemologies. Landscapes and geographys constantly change and the way we connect to them must change accordingly if transformation is an outcome of Indigenous research: one which privileges Indigenous Knowings – Knowings embedded and conceptualised in Country, embedded in constant change.

A FINAL REFLECTION

A final reflection which did not connect with me when I identified the Waterlily as my Metaphor for Indigenous Knowings but was the Story told and performed at an 'Aboriginal Moomba: Out of the Dark', the first Moomba festival in Melbourne, 1951. The Story from which I was named.

> The initial stage of knowing concerns the very young child who is given a name, which captures or responds to an aspect of his or her individual character. The name begins a process of affirming identity in the world. This name is used for all one's life. (Arbon, V. 2008. p.44)

Nerida: Storyd

Nerida and Berwain are two young lovers, from the wrong clans for marriage. They would rendezvous each afternoon at the nearby billabong. Wahwee, the spirit of thunder who lives in the billabong, develops an overpowering desire for Nerida. One afternoon Nerida arrives and Berwain is not with her. Wahwee sees his chance because Nerida would not give herself to him. Berwain arrives later and looks everywhere for Nerida. He looks in to the billabong and sees a waterlily; the waterlily is smiling at him. Berwain knows that Wahwee has used his powers to turn Nerida into a waterlily. Berwain dives in to the water to be with Nerida. Wahwee transforms him into bulrushes. This is why you always find waterlilys and bulrushes together in fresh water.

There is no Berwain and no Wahwee in the Story this book traverses; though one could ponder Wahwee as the Western Academy and Berwain as those of you reading and engaging with this book in ways that see us together in a zone of colliding trajectories; a zone in which we simply co-exist as different. The Waterlily is very much a part of the journey: it is as Arbon identifies 'the initial stage of knowing capturing, responding to an aspect of my individual character, beginning a process of affirming identity in the world'.

Remember Wilson's words; 'Storys allow listeners to draw their own conclusions and to gain life lessons from a more personal perspective. By getting away from abstractions and rules Storys allow us to see other's life experiences through our own eyes' (2008, p.17). Throughout this book we have all shared Storys, we have engaged in 'Tellin' me and 'Showin' me...where ultimately Country calls me home...for more tellin' and showin'! I hope that Australians will connect with Country, diverse Countrys, and come to Know their Storys as Australian; Storys that give us all identity that is connected and related to hundreds of thousands of years of living, Knowing and doing

.

There is a story I Know …
Waterlily flowers visibly float listlessly, serenely atop fresh water
Emerging out of a subterranean world
A subterranean world busy with rhizomes
Rhizomes patterning, weaving, threading and connecting
Rhizomes reaching out to others, creating relationships, webs of connections
Storing starches, proteins, nutrients
To propogate, to reproduce
To grow and strike newness that reaches from below
Grounded in Country

Grounded in water
Grounded in the dynamics of air, water and soil,
Dynamics that are Country
Dynamics and space that are Indigenous Knowings
Rhizomes reaching from subterranean worlds to worlds above
Worlds where sunlight and air take over
Re-cast from rhizomes to a stem, slender and strong
A stem reaching upward transplanting the food, the nourishment from below
To leaves which offer breath and oxygen, down
Cyclically reinvigorating the rhizomatic world below
A stem reaching upward transplanting the food, the nourishment from below
To flowers with petals, delicate, elegant, vibrant and colourful
Varying sizes, shapes and shades
Curving and reaching up to the sun, the light, the warmth
Layering
Overlapping petals, not homogenous
Joined by a stamen centred and strong
Petals held together
Blooming daily at times, only for a few days at a time
Several every day when the conditions are right
A cyclic, holistic patterning of life
Patterning of Indigenous Knowings; of connectedness
Cast in the story that is the waterlily

Spiders weave webs, woven webs
Weaving fine, strong, transparent
Gossamer
Sticky
Vibrations felt from one end to the other
Sensory, connecting, patterning
Connecting across colliding trajectories
Trajectories from Brick Walls, from waterlilys

Sweet potatoes
Rhizomes radiating out from a nourishing, rich core
A core of starch, of carbohydrate
Sustaining, energising, foundation for growing, for life, for living
Rhizomes radiating above and below the earth

Inwards and outwards from the centre,
The periphery.
Sweet potatoes grounded
Grounded in Country
Grounded in Indigenous Knowings
Sweet Potatoes
Patterning, connecting, radiating
Like
Spiders and
Waterlilys.

The colonisers came
Constructed walls, fences, boundaries
Walls of bricks
Bricks made from earth's substances; clay, sandstone and more
Walls that stand strong, on top of the earth
Or that stand manually constructed and placed within the earth that is cast out
Walls that cry for their own sense of identity?
Walls that dominate the more organic
Cutting off the source of water, earth and air; of life
Containing the flow of water, earth and air; the nourishment, the stimulus
Some waterlilys lay dormant
Revitalised with each new rain
Each new flow of water and ray of sunshine
Replenishing
Nourishing
Waiting for the walls to come down?
Searching for,...finding mutual space to co-exist? Perhaps?
Mutual space that embeds waterlily within the crafted beautiful mosaic of co-existence
Searching for, space that has no fear to privilege Indigenous Knowings in the mosaic
The mosaic where waterlily is embedded not marginalized
The mosaic where waterlily radiates energy, beauty, connectedness, relatedness
Nourishing identity and Knowings
Nourishing identity and Knowledge

References

Adler, S. (2004). Multiple Layers of a Researcher's Identity : Uncovering Asian American Voices. In K.Mutua and B.B. Swadener (Eds.), *Decolonizing Research in Cross-Cultural Contexts. Critical Personal Narratives* (pp. 107-122). Albany, New York, U.S.A: State University of New York Press.

Anzaldua, G. (1999). *Borderlands. La Frontera. The New Mestiza* (2nd ed.). San Francisco, California, U.S.A.: Aunt Lute Books.

Anzaldua, G. (1990). *Making Face, Making Soul.* San Francisco: Aunt Lute Books.

Arbon, V. (2008). *Arlathirnda Ngurkarnda Ityirnda. Being-Knowing-Doing. De-Colonising Indigenous Tertiary Education.*Teneriffe, Queensland: Post Pressed

Arrows, F. (2006). Introduction. In F. Arrows, & F. Arrows (Ed.), *UnLearning the Language of Conquest. Scholars Expose Anti-Indianism in America* (pp. 18-28). Austin, Texas, USA: University of Texas Press.

Atkinson, J. (2002). *Trauma Trails, Recreating Song Lines: The Transgenerational Effects of Trauma in Indigenous Australia.* North Melbourne, Victoria, Australia: Spinifex Press.

Attali, J. (1999). *The Labyrinth in Culture and Society. Pathways to Wisdom.* Berkeley, California, USA: North Atlantic Books.

Battiste, M. &. Youngblood Henderson, S. (2000). *Protecting Indigenous Knowledge and Heritage. A Global Challenge.* Saskatoon, Saskatchewan, Canada: Purich.

Battiste, M. (2002). *Indigenous knowledge and pedagogy in First Nations Education : A Literature Review with recommendations.* Ottawa: National Working Group on Education and the Minister of Indian Affairs Indian and Northern Affairs Canada (INAC).

Battiste, M. (1996). Indigenous Knowledge and Research. *unpublished* (pp. 223-238). Sydney: Jumbunna Caiser Conference.

Beckett, C. &. Proud, D. (2004). Fall from Grace? Reflecting on Early Childhood Education While Decolonizing Intercultural Friendships from Kindergarten to University and Prison. In K.Mutua and B.B. Swadener (Eds.), *Decolonizing Research in Cross-Cultural Contexts. Critical*

Personal Narratives (pp. 147-158). Albany, U.S.A.: State University of New York Press.

Behar, R. & Gordon, A. (1995). *Women Writing Culture.* Berkeley: University of California Press.

Behrendt, L. (1993). Aboriginal women and the white lies of the feminist movement:implications for Aboriginal women in rights discourse. *The Australian feminist Law Journal , 1*, 27-44.

Bell, D. (1998). *Ngarrindjeri Wurruwarrin. A World That Is, Was, And Will Be.* North Melbourne, Victoria, Australia: Spinifex Press.

Bell, D. (2001). The word of a woman: Ngarrindjeri stories and a bridge to Hindmarsh Island. In P. Brock (Ed.), *Words and Silences. Aboriginal women, politics and land* (pp. 117-138). Crows Nest, NSW, Australia: Allen & Unwin.

Bennett, F. (Ed.). (1968). The story of the Aboriginal people of the central coast of New South Wales. *Historical Monograph , 1* . Wyong, New South Wales, Australia: Brisbane Water Historical Society.

Benterrak, K. M. (1996). *Reading the Country.* South Fremantle, WA, Australia: Fremantle Arts Centre Press.

Bhabha, H. (1994). *The location of culture.* London: Routledge.

Binet, A. S. (1980). *The Development of Intelligence in Children.* Originally published: Baltimore : Williams & Wilkins, 1916 (Publications of the Training School at Vineland, New Jersey, Dept. of Research ; no. 11).

Bird Rose, D. (1996). *Nourishing Terrains. Australian Aboriginal Views of Landscape and Wilderness.* Canberra, ACT, Australia: Australian Heritage Commission.

Bishop, R. & Glynn T.(1999). Culture counts: Changing power relations in education. Palmerston North, New Zealand: Dunmore Press.

Bishop, R. (2005). Freeing Ourselves from Neocolonial Domination in Research : A Kaupapa Maori Approach to Creating Knowledge. In N. Denzin & Y. Lincoln (Eds.), *The Sage Handbook of Qualitative Research* (3rd ed., pp. 109-138). Thousand Oaks, California, U.S.A.: Sage Publications Inc.

Blair, N. (1990). A Descriptive Analysis of Aboriginal Participation and Equity Issues in New South Wales Higher Education - A Participant's Observer's View. *Master of Arts (Honours) Thesis* , 48-55. University of Wollongong, NSW.

Blair, N. (2001). Darkinjung - Our People and the NSW Supreme Court 1820's - 1840's. In W. R. Havemann (Ed.), *Prospects and Retrospects: Law in History.* Hamilton: The Australia and New Zealand Law and History Society.

Blair, N. (1998, Spring/Summer). Tracking Your Rights. *Synapsia* , pp. 38-43.

Boal, A. (1995). *The rainbow of desire: The Boal Method theatre and therapy* . London: Routledge.

Boal, A. (1985). *Theatre of the Oppressed.* New York: C.A.McBride & M.-O.Leal McBride, Trans. Theatre Communication Group.

Bourke, C. (1975). Aboriginal Culture and Schools. *Polycom* .

Bourke, C. (1979). Aboriginal Education. *Unicorn* .

Brady, W. (1992). Beam Me Up Scotty! Communicating Across World Views on Knowledge Principles and Procedures for the Conduct of Aboriginal and Torres Strait Islander Research. *National Higher Education Conference Aboriginal and Torres Strait Islander.* Hervey Bay.

Brady, W. (1997). Indigenous Australian Education and Globalisation. *International Review of Education , 43* (5-6).

Brown, J. (2005). *The World Cafe : Shaping our futures through conversations that matter.* San Francisco, California, USA: Berrett-Koehler Publishers, Inc.

Buchanan, A. (2007). Hands of Moments. *Reflexology World.* September, Issue 45, Sydney, Australia.

Bunge, R. (1984). *An American Philosophy BP (Before Pragmatism).* Lanham: University Press of America.

Butler-McIlwraith, K. (2006). (Re)presenting Indigeneity. The possibilities of Australian sociology. (A. S. Association, Ed.) *Journal of Sociology , 42* (4), 369-381.

Buttimer, A. (1993). *Geography and The Human Spirit.* Baltimore, Maryland, U.S.A.: The John Hopkins University Press.

Buzan, T. & Keene, R. (1996). *The Age Heresy.* London: Ebury Press.

Buzan, T. (1997). *The Mind Map Book.* London: BBC Books.

Cajete, G. (2000). Indigenous Knowledge: The Pueblo Metaphor of Indigenous Education. In M. Battiste (Ed.), *Reclaiming Indigenous Voice and Vision* (pp. 181-191). Vancouver, British Colombia, Canada: UBC Press.

Cajete, G. (2004). *Look To The Mountain. An Ecology of Indigenous Education.* Skyland, NC, USA: Kivaki Press.

Cajete, G. (2006). Western Science And The Loss Of Natural Creativity. In F. Arrows, & F. Arrows (Ed.), *UnLearning the Language of Conquest. Scholars Expose Anti-Indianism in America* (pp. 247-259). Austin, Texas, USA: University of Texas Press.

Canete, L. (2004). Education Research with Philippine Communities in Greece : Intricacies and Possibilities. In K.Mutua and B.B. Swadener (Eds.), *Decolonizing Research in Cross-Cultural Contexts. Critical Personal Narratives* (pp. 135-144). Albany, New York, U.S.A.: State University of New York Press.

Cannella, G. (1997). *Deconstructing early childhood education: Social justice and revolution.* New York: Peter Lang Publishing.

Cardinal, D. &. Armstrong, J.(1991). *The Native Creative Process.* Penticton, British Colombia, Canada: Theytus Books.

Cary, L. (2004). Always Already Colonizer/Colonized: White Australian Wanderings. In K. &. Mutua (Ed.), *Decolonizing Research in Cross-Cultural Contexts. Critical Personal Narratives* (pp. 69-83). Albany, New York, U.S.A.: State University of New York Press.

Cavender Wilson, A. (2004). Reclaiming Our Humanity. Decolonization and the Recovery of Indigenous Knowledge. In D. &. Mihesuah (Ed.), *Indigenizing the Academy. Transforming Scholarship and Empowering Communities* (pp. 69-87). Nebraska, USA: University of Nebraska Press.

Chamberlin, E. (2000). From Hand to Mouth: The Postcolonial Politics of Oral and Written Traditions. In M. Battiste (Ed.), *Reclaiming Indigenous Voice and Vision* (pp. 124-141). Vancouver, BC, Canada: UBC Press.

Chamberlin, E. (2004). *If This Is Your Land, Where Are Your Stories* (2nd ed.). Cleveland, Ohio, USA: Pilgrim Press.

Christensen, P. & Lilley, I. (1997/1998). The Road Forward? Alternative Assessment for Aboriginal and Torres Strait Islander Students at Tertiary Level. (U. o. Aboriginal and Torres Strait Islander Studies Unit, Compiler) Queensland, Australia.

Christie, M. (1985). *Aboriginal perspectives on experience and learning the role of language in Aboriginal education.* Geelong, Victoria, Australia: Deakin University Press.

Churchill, W. (1996). *From A Native Son. Selected Essays on Indigenism 1985-1995.* Cambridge, MA, USA: South End press.

Collins-Gearing, B. (2008). Not All Sorrys Are Created Equal, Some Are More Equal than 'Others'. *Journal of Media and Culture, 11* (2).

Collins-Gearing, B. (2006). Re-Reading Representations of Indigenality in Australian Children's Literature: A History. *The Australian Journal of Indigenous Education, 35*, 61-67.

Conquergood, D. (2002). Performance Studies Interventions and Radical Research. *The Drama Review*, 145-156.

de Bono, E. (1999). *New Thinking for the New Millennium.* Ringwood, Victoria, Australia: Viking. Penguin Books.

de Bono, E. (1990). *Six Thinking Hats.* Ringwood, Victoria, Austrlia: Penguin Books.

De La Torre, J. (2004). In The Trenches. In D. A. Wilson (Ed.), *Indigenizing The Academy. Transforming Scholarship and Empowering Communities* (pp. 174-190). Nebraska, USA: University of Nebraska Press.

Deleuze, G. & Guittari, F. (1987). *A Thousand Plateaus. Capitalism and Schizophrenia.* (B. Massumi, Trans.) Minneapolis, Minnesota, U.S.A.: University of Minnesota Press.

Deloria Jr., V. (2004). Marginal and Submarginal. In D. M. Wilson (Ed.), *Indigenizing The Academy. Transforming Scholarship and Empowering Communities* (pp. 16-30). Nebraska, USA: Nebraska University Press.

Deloria, V. J. (1999). *Spirit and Reason.* Golden, Colorado: Fulcrum Publishing.

Demas, E. & Saavedra, C. (2004). (Re)conceptualizing Language Advocacy: Weaving a Postmodern Mestizaje Image of Language. In K. &. Mutua (Ed.), *Decolonizing Research* (pp. 215-233).

Denzin, N. & Lincoln, Y.S. (2005). The Discipline and Practice of Qualitaive Research. In N. Denzin & Y. Lincoln (Eds.), *The Sage Handbook of Qualitative Research* (3rd ed., pp. 1-32). Thousand Oaks, California, U.S.A: Sage Publications.

Denzin, N. & Y. Lincoln, Y. (Eds.). (2005). *The Sage Handbook of Qualitative Research* (3 ed.). Thousand Oaks, California, U.S.A.: Sage Publishing Inc.

Denzin, N. (2005). Emancipatory Discourses and the Ethics and Politics of Interpretation. In N. Denzin & Y. Lincoln, (Eds.) *The Sage Handbook of Qualitative Research* (3rd ed., pp. 933-958). Thousand Oaks, California, USA: Sage Publications Inc.

Dodson, M. (1993). *Aboriginal and Torres Strait Islander Social Justice Commission First Report.* Canberra: Australian Government Publishing Service.

Dodson, M. (1997, October). Tracking Your Rights - ATC, Tasmania, Victoria and New South Wales. Sydney, NSW, Australia: Human Rights and Equal Opportunity Commission.

Dolan, J. (1997). Advocacy and Activism: Identity, Curriculum and Theatre Studies. *Theatre Topics* , 1-10.

Dolan, J. (2001). Rehearsing Democracy: Advocacy, Public Intellectuals, and Civic Engagement in Theatre and Performance Studies. *Theatre Topics* , 1-17.

du Bois, W. (1969). *The Souls of Black Folk.* New York: New American Library.

Eades, D. (1988). They Don't Speak an Aboriginal Langugae or Do They? In *Being Black.* Canberra: Aboriginal Studies Press.

Elkin, A. (1977). *Aboriginal Men of High Degree.* University of Queensland Press.

Ermine, W. (1998). Aboriginal Epistemology. In M. B. Barman (Ed.), *First Nations Education In Canada. The Circle Unfolds* (pp. 101-112). Vancouver, BC, Canada: UBC Press.

Evans, Saunders & Cronin (1993). *Race Relations in Colonial Queensland : a history of exclusion, exploitation and extermination.* Brisbane : University of Queensland Press.

Fanon, F. (2001). *The Wretched of the Earth.* London: Penguin Classics.

Fine, M. W. (2005). Compositional Studies, In Two Parts. Critical Theorizing and Analysis on Social (In) Justice. In N. Denzin & Y. Lincoln, (Eds.), *The Sage Handbook of Qualitative Research* (3rd ed., pp. 65-84). Thousand Oaks, California, USA: Sage Publications Inc.

Fine, M. (1994). Working the hyphens: Reinventing the Self and Other in qualitative research. In N. Denzin & Y. Lincoln, (Eds.), *The Sage Handbook of Qualitative Research* (3rd ed., pp. 70-82). Thousand Oaks, California, USA: Sage Publications Inc.

Fixico, D. (1998). Ethics and Responsibilities in Writing American Indian History. In D. Mihesuah (Ed.), *Natives and Academics. Researching and Writing about American Indians* (pp. 84-99). Nebraska, USA: University of Nebraska Press.

Fixico, D. (2003). *The American Indian Mind. In a Linear World.* New York: Routledge.

Floyd, P. (Composer). (1979). [P. Floyd, Performer]

Foley, D. (2002). An Indigenous Standpoint Theory. *Journal of Australian Indigenous Issues , 5* (3), 3-13.

Foley, D. (2004). Indigenous Standpoint Theory. Why? When and Who For? *AIATSIS Conference.* Canberra: unpublished.

Foucault, M. (1998). *Aesthetics, the essential works. Method and Epistemology* (Vol. 2). (J. D. Faubion, Ed., & R. H. others, Trans.) Allen Lane,The Penguin Press.

Foucault, M. (1972). *The Archaeology of Knowledge.*

Freire, P. & Freire, Myra Bergman Ramos. (1972). *Pedagogy of the Oppressed.* Ringwood: Penguin.

Freire, P. (1998). *Pedagogy of Hope. Reliving Pedagogy of the Oppressed.* (R. R. Barr, Trans.) New York, USA: The Continuum Publishing Company.

Freire, P. (1985). *The Politics of Education. Culture, Power and Liberation.* South Hadley, Massachusetts, USA: Bergin & Garvey Publishers Inc.

Gates, B. (2006, January 25). *Bill Gates on the Future of Information Democracy.* Retrieved July 2008, from MSNBC.com Newsweek: http://www.msnbc.msn.com/id/11020787/site/newsweek/

Gore, J. (1993). *The Struggle for Pedagogies.Critical and Feminist Discourses as Regimes of Truth.* New York, New York, U.S.A.: Routledge.

Greville. (2000). *Chapter Three : Defining Moments - Transforming Curriculum.* Retrieved from library.uws.edu.au/adt-NUWS/uploads/approved/adt-NUWS20050714.135530/public/04Chapter3.pdf view as HTML

Hampton, E. (1998). Towards a Redefinition of Indian Education. In M. B. Battiste (Ed.), *First Nations Education in Canada : The Circle Unfolds* (pp. 5-46). Vancouver, British Colombia, Canada: UBC Press.

Hamza, H. (2004). Decolonizing Research on Gender Disparity in Education in Niger: Complexities of Language, Culture and Homecoming. In K. &. Mutua (Ed.), *Decolonizing Research in Cross-Cultural Contexts. Critical Personal Narratives* (pp. 123-134). Albany, New York, USA: State University of New York.

Hanlen, W. (2002, March). Emerging Literacy In New South Wales Rural And Urban Indigenous Families. *Thesis for Doctor of Philosophy .* N.S.W., Australia.

Hanlen, W. (2007). Indigenous literacies: Moving from Social Construction. In L. D. Makin (Ed.), *Literacies in Childhood: Changing Views, Challenging Practice* (2nd ed., pp. 233-234). Sydney: Elsevier Australia.

Harkins, J. (1994). *Bridging Two Worlds: Aboriginal English and Cross-Cultural Understanding.* Brisbane: Queensland University Press.

Harris, S. (1982). Traditional Aboriginal Education Strategies and their Possible Place in a Modern Bicultural School. (J. Sherwood, Ed.) *Aboriginal Education: Issues and Innovations* .

Harris, S. (1990). *Two-way Aboriginal Schooling: Education and Cultural Survival.* Canberra: Australian Institute of Aboriginal Studies Press.

Higgins, R. (2004). He tanga ngutu, he Tuhoetanga te mana motuhake o te ta moko wahine: The identity politics of moko kauae. . *PhD thesis, University of Otago.* New Zealand: u.p.

Hokari, M. (2000). History Happening in/between Body and Place: Journey to the Aboriginal Way of Historical Practice. *Habitus: A Sense of Place*, (p. 2). Perth.

Howard, J. (1996, October 30th). Different Perspectives on Black Armband History. *5, 1997-1998* . Canberra, ACT, Australia: Commonwealth Government.

Howard, J. (1996, November 18th). Sir Robert Menzies Lecture. 9. Australia.

Huggins, J. (2003). Always Was Always Will Be. In I. A. Grossman (Ed.), *Blacklines: Contemporary Critical Writing by Indigenous Australians* (pp. 60-65). Australia: Melbourne Universiy Press.

Huggins, J. (1998). *Sister Girl.* St Lucia, Queensland, Australia: University of Queensland Press.

Hughes, P. (1984, August). A Call for an Aboriginal Pedagogy. *The Australian Teacher* .

Hughes, P. (1997). Aboriginal Ways of Learning and Learning Styles. *Australian Association for Research in Education.* Brisbane.

Hughes, P. (1998). First Indigenous Researchers Forum. Newcastle, NSW, Australia.

Hyerle, D. (2000). *A Field Guide to Using Visual Tools.* Association for Supervision and Curriculum, USA.

Hyerle, D. (1996). *Visual Tools for Constructing Knowledge.* Association for Supervision and Curriculum USA.

Institute for Aboriginal Development. (2006). 2006 ukurrpa diary. Alice Springs, N.T., Australia.

Isaacs, J. (1990). *Arts of the Dreaming. Australia's Living Heritage.* Weldon Publishing.

Janke, T. (1998). *Our Culture: Our Future. Report on Australian Indigenous Cultural and Intellectual Property Rights.* Canberra: Australian Institute of Aboriginal and Torres Strait Islander Studies and Aboriginal and Torres Straait Islander Commission.

Jankie, D. (2004). "Tell Me Who You Are". In K. Mutua & B Swadener (Eds.), *Decolonizing Research in Cross-Cultural Contexts. Critical Personal Narratives.* (pp. 87-106). Albany, New York, Australia: State University of New York.

Josselson, R. L. (1997). *Conversation as Method. Analyzing the Relational Worldof People Who Were Raised Communally.* Thousand Oaks, California, USA: SAGE Publications.

Kelly, R. (2006). Personal Communication. Newcastle, N.S.W, Australia.

Kemmis, S. (1997). Rethinking Equity and Justice in the University. *Research papers , 4/1997 .* Centre for Aboriginal Studies, Curtin University.

King, T. (2003). *The Truth About Stories. A Native Narrative.* Minneapolis: University of Minnesota Press.

Kohen, J. (1993). *The Darug and Their Neighbours. The Traditional Aboriginal Owners of the Sydney Region.* New South Wales: Darug Link in association with the Blacktown and District Historical Society.

Kovach, M. (2009). Indigenous Methodologies. Charateristics, Conversations and Contexts. Toronto:University of Toronto Press.

Kwaymullina, A. (2014). *Walking Many Worlds: Storytelling and Writing for the Young.* Retrieved http://www.wheelercentre.com/notes/e221876968a8/ J une 30 in Diversity. Melbourne, Australia : Wheeler Centre

Langton, M. (2006). Out from the Shadows. *Meanjin. Blak Times: Indigenous Australia , 65* (1).

Langton, M. (2000). Sacred Geography Western Desert traditions of landscape art. In *Papunya Tula Genesis and Genius.* Sydney: Art Gallery of New South Wales.

Lincoln, Y. & Denzin, N. (2005). Epilogue : The Eighth and Ninth Moments - Qualitative Research in/and the Fractured Future. In N. Denzin & Y. Lincoln (Eds.), *The Sage Handbook of Qualitative Research* (3rd ed., pp. 1115-1126). Thousand Oaks, California, U.S.A.: Sage Publications Inc.

Little Bear, L. (2000). Jagged Worldviews Colliding. In M. Battiste, *Reclaiming Indigenous Voice and Vision* (pp. 77-85). Vancouver: UBC Press.

Lomawaima, K. (2000). Tribal sovereigns : Reframing research in American Indian Education. *Harvard Educational Review , 70* (1), 1-21.

Manuelito, K. (2004). An Indigenous Perspective on Self-Determination. In K. Mutua & B Swadener (Eds.), *Decolonizing Research in Cross-Cultural Contexts. Critical Personal Narratives.* (pp. 235-253). Albany, New York, USA: State University of New York Press.

Marika, R. (1999). The 1998 Wentworth Lecture. *Australian Aboriginal Studies , 1.*

Martin, K. (2008). *Please Knock Before You Enter. Aboriginal regulation of Outsiders and the implications for researchers.* Teneriffe, Queensland: Post Pressed.

Mason, J. (1995). *Bush Practice at Northern Territory University: An Educational, Financial and Political Tale.* Retrieved July 2008, from nrha.ruralhealth.org.au/conferences/docs/PAPERS/3_JANMAS.pdf view as HTML

Massey, D. (2005). *for space.* London: SAGE Publications.

Maynard, J. (2007). *Fight for Liberty and Freedom. The origins of Australian Aboriginal activism.* Canberra, A.C.T., Australia: Aboriginal Studies Press.

McCarthy, C. (1998). *The uses of culture: Education and the limits of ethnic affiliation.* New York: Routledge.

McConchie, M. (2003). *Elders. Wisdom from Australia's Indigenous Leaders.* Cambridge, UK: Cambridge University Press.

McDermott, P. &Clarke, D.N. (1998). *Mind Maps in Medicine.* Retrieved from books.google.com.

McKinnon, J. (2004, July). Growing Australian History : Listening to Indigenous Knowledges. NSW, Ourimbah.

McKinnon, J. (Director). (2004, June). *Listening.* NSW, Australia.

McLean, I. One mob, one voice, one land. Lin Onus and Indigenous postmodernism. In M. Neale (Ed.), *Urban Dingo the art and life of lin onus 1948-1996.* Queensland, Australia: Queensland Art Gallery.

Memmi, A. (1991). *The Colonizer and The Colonized.* Boston, Massachusetts, USA: Beacon Press.

Meyer, M. A. (2001). Our own liberation:Reflections on Hawaiian Epistemology. *The Contemporary Pacific ,* 124-148.

Mignolo, W. (2000). *Local histories/global designs: Coloniality, subaltern knowledges, and border thinking.* Princeton: Princeton University Press.

Mihesuah, D. (1998). Introduction. In D. Mihesuah (Ed.), *Natives and Academics. Researching and Writing about American Indians* (pp. 1-22). U.S.A.: University of Nebraska Press.

Moreton-Robinson, A. (2000). *Talkin' Up To The White Woman. Indigenous Women and Feminism.* St Lucia: University of Queensland Press.

Moreton-Robinson, A. (1998). When the Object Speaks, A Postcolonial Encounter: anthropological representations and Aboriginal women's self-presentations. *Discourse: studies in the cultural politics of education , 19* (3), 275-289.

Morgan, R. (2014). Personal communication; 26/09/2014.

Morgan, S. (National Indigenous Researchers Foruum, Canberra, Australia.

Mueller, A. M. (2002, January). Joining Mind Mapping and Care Planning to Enhance Student Critical Thinking and Achieve Holistic Nursing Care. *International Journal of Nursing Terminologies and Classifications , 13 , 1*, 24-27.

Mutua, K. & Swadener, B.. (2004). *Decolonizing Research in Cross-Cultural Contexts.* Albany: State University of New York Press.

Mutua, K. S. (2004). Introduction. In K. Mutua & B Swadener (Eds.), *Decolonizing Research in Cross-Cultural Contexts. Critical Personal Narratives* (pp. 1-23). Albany, U.S.A.: State University of New York Press.

Nakata, M. (2007). *Disciplining the Savages, Savaging the Disciplines.* Canberra, Australia: Aboriginal Studies Press.

Nakata, M. (2004). Indigenous Australian Studies and Higher Education. *The Wentworth Lectures - 2004* . Canberra, A.C.T.: Australian Institute of Aboriginal and Torres Strait Islander Studies.

Nakata, M. (2001). Multiliteracies and Indigenous Standpoints. In M. Kalantzis & B. Cope (Eds.), *Transformations in Language and Learning: Perspectives on Multiliteracies* (pp. 113-120). Melbourne: Common Ground.

Neale, M. (2000). Urban Dingo. In M. Neale (Ed.), *Urban Dingo the art and life of lin onus 1948-1996.* Queensland: Queensland Art Gallery.

Neidjie, B. (1998). *Story About Feeling.* (K. Taylor, Ed.) Broome, Western Australia, Australia: Magabala Books.

Nunavik, Educational Taskforce. (February 1992). *Silatunirmut. The Pathway to Wisdom.* Lachine, Quebec: Makivik Corporation.

Onus, L. (2003). Language and Lasers. In M. Grossman (Ed.), *Blacklines. Contemporary Critical Writing by Indigenous Australians* (pp. 92-96). Carlton, Victoria, Australia: Melbourne University Press.

Pearson, R. & Eysenck, H.J. (1991). *Race, Intelligence, and Bias in Academe.* Scott-Townsend Publishers.

Polanyi, M. (1962). *Personal Knowledge.* Chicago: University of Chicago Press.

Pryor, J. & Ghartey Ampiah J. (2004). Listening to Voices in the Village : Collaborating through Data Chains. In K. Mutua & B. Swadener (Eds.), *Decolonizing Research in Cross-Cultural Contexts. Critical Personal Narratives* (pp. 159-178). Albany, New York, U.S.A.: State University of New York Press.

Rains, F. A., Archibald, J. & Deyhle, D. (2000). Introduction: Through our eyes and in our own words. *Qualitative Studies in Education , 13*, 337-342.

Randall, B. (2003). *songman the story of an aboriginal elder.* Sydney, NSW, Australia: ABC Books.

Raw, L. (n.d.). Retrieved from Human Health in Relation to Pets in Urban and Indigenous Communities, Dogs and indigenous health.: http://www.alice.id.au/anangu_dogs.htm

Reynolds, H.(2007).*The Other Side of the Frontier: Aboriginal Resistance to the European Invasion of Australia.* Sydney: New South Publishing.

Rigney, L. (1997). Internationalisation of an Anti-Colonial Critique of Research Methodologies : A Guide to Indigenist Research Methodology and its Principles. *HERDSA Annual International Conference.* Adelaide.

Rueben, K. (1984). Dungati elder. *Personal Communication .*

Russell, L. (2005). Indigenour knowledge and the archives: Accessing hidden history and understandings. *Australian Indigenous knowlege and libraries* (Vol. 36). Kingston, A.C.T., Australia: Australian Academic & Research Libraries, Australia Library and Information Association.

Sandoval, C. (2000). *Methodology of the oppressed.* Minneapolis: University of Minnesota Press.

Smith, L. (1999). *Decolonizing research methodologies.* Dunedin, NZ: University of Otago Press.

Smith, L. (2005). On Tricky Ground. Researching the Native Maori. In N. Denzin & Y. Lincoln (Eds.), *The Sage Handbook of Qualitative Research. Third Edition* (3 ed., pp. 85-107). Thousand Oaks, California, U.S.A.: Sage Publications Inc.

South Australian Department of Education. (1991). Students and Schools, Aboriginal Education R-12 Resource Papers. Adelaide, South Australia, Australia.

Spearman, C. (1927). *The abilities of man.* London: Macmillan.

Spearman, C. (1923). *The nature of 'intelligence' and the principles of cognition* (2nd ed.). London: Macmillan.

Spencer, W. & Horn, W.A. (1896). *Report of the work of of the Horn Scientific Expedition to Central Australia* . Dulau and University of Michigan (original).

Spivak, G. (2003). *A Critique of Postcolonial Reason. Toward A History of the Vanishing Present.* Cambridge, Massachusetts, U.S.A.: Harvard University Press.

Stinson, E. (1994). *A Pictorial History of the Wyong Shire* (Vol. i). Wyong, New South Wales, Australia: Wyong Shire Council.

Stockton, E. (1995). *The Aboriginal Gift. Spirituality for a Nation.* Alexandria, NSW, Australia: Millenium Books.

Sullivan, R. (2005). The English moko : Exploring a spiral. In H. &. McNaughton (Ed.), *Figuring the Pacific: Aotearoa and Pacific Cultural Studies* (pp. 12-28). Christchurch, New Zealand: Canterbury University Press.

Sure, Y. E., Erdmann, M. Angele, J., Staab S., Studer, R. & Wenke . D. (2002). OntoEdit: Collaborative Ontology Development for the Semantic Web. *The Semantic Web — ISWC 2002 , 2342/2002* , 221-235. Germany: Springer Berlin / Heidelberg.

Suzuki, D. (1997). *The Sacred Balance. Rediscovering Our Place in Nature.* St Leonards, NSW, Australia: Allen & Unwin.

Swancott, C. (1953). The Brisbane Water Story, Part 1 Gosford. Gosford: Brisbane Water Historical Society.

Swisher, K. (1998). Why Indian People Should Be The Ones To Write About Indian Education. In D. A. Mihesuah (Ed.), *Natives and Academics. Researching and Writing about American Indians* (pp. 190-199). USA: University of Nebraska Press.

Taussig, M. (1993). *Mimesis and Alterity. A Particular History of the Senses.* New York, NY, USA: Routledge.

The Institute of Noetic Sciences and Captured Light Industries. (2004). *What the Bleep Do we Know? Study Guide and Manual for Navigating Rabbit Holes.* Retrieved from http://www.whatthebleep.com/guide/

Threlkeld, L. & Gunson, N. (1974). *Australian Reminiscences & Papers of L.E. Threlkeld, Missionary to the Aborigines 1824-1859.* Canberra: Australian Institute of Aboriginal Studies.

Time Magazine. (2007, May 17). Retrieved July 2008, from Al Gore's American Life: http://www.time.com/time/photogallery/0,29307,1622338,00.html

Tindale, N. &. (1974). *Aboriginal Tribes of Australia : Their Terrain, Environmental Controls, Distribution, Limits and Proper Names.* Canberra: Australian National University Press.

Trask, H. (1993). *From A Native Daughter.* Honolulu: University of Hawaii Press.

Trudgen, R. (2000). *Djambatj Mala. Why Warriors lie down and die.* Darwin, NT, Australia: Aboriginal Resource and Development Services Inc.

Tuan, Y.-F. (1977). *Space and Place. The Perspective of Experience.* Minneapolis, Minnesota, U.S.A.: University of Minnesota Press.

Ungunmerr-Baumann, M. R. (n.d.). *Dadirri.* Retrieved from http://www.liturgyplanning.com.au/documents/main.php?g2_view=core.D ownloadItem&g2_itemId=4832&g2_GALLERYSID=95770b3ca936d505 dea3d4fcfb658955

Verran, H. (2005). Retrieved 2007, from cdu.edu.au/centres/ik/pdf/knowledgeanddatabasing.pdf

Viruru, R. & Cannella, G.G. (2004). *Childhood and Postcolonization. Power, Education and Contemporary Practice.* Routledge.

wa Thiong'o, N. (2005). *Decolonising the Mind. The Politics of Language in African Literature.* Oxford, England: James Curry.

Watson, H.& Chambers, D. (1989). *Singing the Land, Signing the Land.* Geelong, Victoria, Australia: Deakin University Press.

Watson, I. (1998). Power of the Muldarbi, The Road to its Demise. *The Australian Feminist Law Journal, 11*, 28-45.

Watson, I. (1992). Surviving as a People. In J. Scutt, *Breaking Through: Women, Work and Careers* (pp. 177-186). Melbourne: J Artemis Publishing.

Watson, L. (1988, December 11). Aboriginal Studies in Tertiary Education - An Aboriginal Perspective. Brisbane, Queensland: Trans Aboriginal and Islander Studies Unit, University of Queensland.

Watson, L. (1988). The Meting of Two Traditions: Aboriginal Studies in the University - A Murri Perspective. Armidale, NSW: The University of New England.

West, E. (1998, April). Speaking Towards an Aboriginal Philosophy. *u.p.* (L. L. Conference, Compiler)

What The Bleep Do We Know (2004). [Motion Picture].

What the people had to say. (2008, February 27th). *The Koori Mail* . Lismore, New South Wales, Australia.

Wheatley, M. (2002). *Turning to One Another: Simple Conversations to Restore Hope to the Future.* San Francisco, California, U.S.A.: Berrett-Koehler Publishers, Inc.

Willmot, E. (1986, September 16). Future Pathways : Equity or Isolation. *The Frank Archibald Memorial Lecture Series, University of New England* . Armidale, NSW, Australia.

Wilshire, B. (2006). On The Very Idea Of "A Worldview" And Of Alternative Worldviews". In F. A. Jacobs (Ed.), *Unlearning the Language of Conquest. Scholars Expose Anti-Indianism in America* (pp. 160-272). Austin, Texas, USA: University of Texas Press.

Wilson, S. (2001). Self-as-relationship in Indigenous Research. *Canadian Journal of Native Education.* 25(2):

Wilson, S. (2008).Research Is Ceremony. Indigenous Research Methods, Halifax: Fernwood Publishing.

Windschuttle, K. (2002). *The Fabrication of Aboriginal History* (Vol. 1). Sydney: Macleay Press.

Wolin, R. (1995). *Labyrinths. Explorations in the Critcal History of Ideas.* Amherst, Massachusetts, USA: University of Massachusetts Press.

Youngblood Henderson, J. (2000). Ayukpachi: Empowering Aboriginal Thought. In M. Battiste (Ed.), *Reclaiming Indigenous Voice and Vision* (pp. 248-278). Vancouver, BC, Canada: UBC Press.

Yunupingu, M. et al. (1994). *Voices from the Land.* Sydney: ABC Books.